NO CURE FOR THE FUTURE

Recent Titles in Contributions to the
Study of Science Fiction and Fantasy

Transrealist Fiction: Writing in the Slipstream of Science
Damien Broderick

Science Fiction, Children's Literature, and Popular Culture: Coming of Age in
Fantasyland
Gary Westfahl

Kurt Vonnegut: Images and Representations
Marc Leeds and Peter J. Reed, editors

Science and Destabilization in the Modern American Gothic: Lovecraft, Matheson, and
King
David A. Oakes

J.R.R. Tolkien and His Literary Resonances: Views of Middle-earth
George Clark and Daniel Timmons, editors

Rewriting the Women of Camelot: Arthurian Popular Fiction and Feminism
Ann F. Howey

Monsters, Mushroom Clouds, and the Cold War
M. Keith Booker

Science Fiction, Canonization, Marginalization, and the Academy
Gary Westfahl and George Slusser, editors

The Supernatural in Short Fiction of the Americas: The Other World in the New World
Dana Del George

The Fantastic Vampire: Studies in the Children of the Night
James Craig Holte, editor

Unearthly Visions: Approaches to Science Fiction and Fantasy Art
Gary Westfahl, George Slusser, and Kathleen Church Plummer, editors

Worlds Enough and Time: Explorations of Time in Science Fiction and Fantasy
Gary Westfahl, George Slusser, and David Leiby, editors

NO CURE FOR THE FUTURE

Disease and Medicine in
Science Fiction and Fantasy

Edited by
Gary Westfahl and George Slusser

Contributions to the Study of Science Fiction and Fantasy, Number 102
Donald Palumbo, Series Adviser

GREENWOOD PRESS
Westport, Connecticut • London

Library of Congress Cataloging-in-Publication Data

No cure for the future : disease and medicine in science fiction and fantasy / edited by
Gary Westfahl and George Slusser.
     p.   cm.—(Contributions to the study of science fiction and fantasy, ISSN 0193–6875 ;
no. 102)
     Includes bibliographical references and index.
     ISBN 0–313–31707–0 (alk. paper)
     1. Science fiction, English—History and criticism.   2. Science fiction,
American—History and criticism.   3. Fantasy fiction, American—History and criticism.
4. Fantasy fiction, English—History and criticism.   5. Medical fiction—History and criticism
6. Diseases in literature.   7. Medicine in literature.   I. Westfahl, Gary.   II. Slusser, George
Edgar.   III. Series.
PR830.S35N6   2002
823'.087609356—dc21   2002067917

British Library Cataloguing in Publication Data is available.

Library of Congress Catalog Card Number: 2002067917
ISBN: 0–313–31707–0
ISSN: 0193–6875

First published in 2002

Greenwood Press, 88 Post Road West, Westport, CT 06881
An imprint of Greenwood Publishing Group, Inc.
www.greenwood.com

Printed in the United States of America

Copyright Acknowledgment

The editors and publisher gratefully acknowledge permission for use of the following:

A transcript of Greg Bear's speech, "Doctors of the Mind: Effective Mental Therapy and Its Implications," originally presented at the 1996 J. Lloyd Eaton Conference on Science Fiction and Fantasy
Literature in Riverside, California.

Contents

Acknowledgments

We must first thank the many people who contributed to the long process of assembling this volume, including Darian Daries, David G. Hartwell, Susan Korn, Sheryl Lewis, Gladys Murphy, David Pringle, and Eric S. Rabkin; Sara Fitzpatrick merits special mention for her help in tracking down texts and resources. For guidance and assistance during the preparation of the manuscript, we thank Donald A. Palumbo, George F. Butler, Terri M. Jennings, and other colleagues at Greenwood Press. We finally thank friends, family members, and colleagues too numerous to name who have provided encouragement and support while we worked on completing this project.

Introduction: Of Plagues, Predictions, and Physicians

Gary Westfahl

By most accounts, science fiction is a literature that began with a novel, Mary Shelley's *Frankenstein, or, The Modern Prometheus* (1818), describing a projected medical breakthrough, the creation of an artificial human being. Other nineteenth-century authors celebrated as science fiction pioneers contributed visions of doctors engaged in fantastic work: a dead man is kept alive by hypnosis in Edgar Allan Poe's "The Facts in the Case of M. Valdemar" (1845); a doctor transforms the people of a Flemish town with a mysterious gas in Jules Verne's "Doctor Ox's Experiment" (1874); the evil memories of patients are scientifically removed in Edward Bellamy's *Dr. Heidenhoff's Process* (1880); and secret operations turn beasts into men in H. G. Wells's *The Island of Dr. Moreau* (1896).

While such portrayals of isolated, individual researchers have lingered on in twentieth-century film portrayals of "mad doctors," the actual field of medicine has evolved into a collective, bureaucratic, and scientifically sophisticated system, so that now, for most individuals, the nearest equivalent to traveling through time into the distant future is becoming a patient at a modern hospital. Suddenly, one is whisked away from her familiar environment into a stark, sterile room, where she is attached to various pieces of machinery that mysteriously flicker and hum while intravenous sedative drugs dull her mind and alter her perceptions as she overhears people whispering in incomprehensible jargon. It is little wonder that, as I once opined,[1] popular images of hospitals, and popular images of the future, seem inextricably intertwined.

Due to both distinguished literary ancestry and contemporary experience, then, one would expect science fiction to deal with disease and medicine frequently and conspicuously, making medical science fiction one of the field's most important subgenres. Yet as contributors to this volume have discovered, this is manifestly not the case. In contrast to the numbers of stories dealing with topics like the colonization of space, contact with alien life, travel through time, and futuristic cities, stories focusing on physicians or improvements in medical care are fewer in number. There exists, as H. Bruce Franklin will remind us, a long tradition of stories about devastating global plagues, ranging from Mary Shelley's *The Last Man* (1826) to Norman Spinrad's *Journals of the Plague Years* (1988), but the medical profession is usually characterized as helpless in the face of the epidemics. We also observe on a regular basis the *effects* of some super-scientific medical treatment, at levels of complexity ranging from the fascinating hermaphrodites of Ursula K. Le Guin's *The Left Hand of Darkness* to the comic-book heroes of television's *The Six Million Dollar Man* and *The Bionic Woman*; yet how these transformations were accomplished, and the motives and activities of the pioneers who accomplished them, are largely left unexamined.

As to why this might be the case, the chapters in this volume will suggest a number of answers, but one might begin by examining the history of medicine in the last two centuries. Throughout the nineteenth century, humanity seemed poised to make tremendous progress in this area: Luigi Galvani's experiments in getting the legs of dead frogs to twitch suggested that the secret of life itself might soon emerge from scientific research, and innovations in medical treatment such as vaccines and antiseptic surgery saved many lives and indicated that many more lives might be saved by further developments. However, by the early twentieth century, the field of medicine seemed to be stagnating, especially in contrast to the revolutionary developments in physics and astronomy that were garnering headlines and the innumerable new inventions, such as telephones, radios, airplanes, and automobiles, that were transforming everyday life. In the popular imagination, the achievements of Louis Pasteur were forgotten, as people now idolized figures like Albert Einstein and Thomas Alva Edison. Even as other scientific fields appeared to be advancing at breakneck speed, Lewis Thomas reminds us in *The Youngest Science* that the medicine of that era was still not a true science; the primary job of the physician, Thomas learned from observing his father, remained largely to diagnose patients and to comfort them while hoping that their bodies would heal themselves.

Thus, at the very time when science fiction was emerging as a distinctive genre in the pages of Hugo Gernsback's pioneering magazine *Amazing Stories* during the 1920s, none of the era's most exciting scientific frontiers involved medicine. Early issues of the magazine did feature a number of stories about doctors in hospitals and laboratories engaged in experiments—some written by two noted physicians turned authors, David H. Keller and Miles J. Breuer—but readers were not interested; they wanted to discuss, and read stories about, the exciting possibilities of rocketships, time travel, robots, and other dimensions.

Other aspects of the genre's evolution during the magazine era also shifted the attention of science fiction away from medicine. Gernsback had reached out to readers of all ages, but by the 1930s, it had become evident that most science fiction readers were adolescent males. And with some unfortunate exceptions, young people are typically very healthy; they spend little time with doctors and pay little attention to medical issues, which they associate primarily with the elderly. Further, young men crave action and excitement, and stories featuring doctors, usually taking place in cramped offices and featuring lots of expository conversation, could seem dull and confining; far more attractive to these adolescents were the dynamic interplanetary adventures of the emerging subgenre of space opera. (To this day, the only way to achieve a successful series of medical stories in science fiction, it seems, is to combine medicine with space travel, as occurs in Murray Leinster's Med Service stories, James White's Sector General stories, and S. L. Viehl's StarDoc novels.)

All of this might serve to explain why medical science fiction, so prominent in the nineteenth century, tended to fade from view during the decades when the genre was largely associated with colorful pulp magazines; but by the 1960s, the situation should have changed. The development of antibiotics during World War II, and Jonas Salk's spectacular conquest of polio in the 1950s, signaled that medicine had indeed finally become a true science, deploying new technology and effective therapies developed in state-of-the-art laboratories sponsored by universities, private companies, and the federal government; so, doctors of Lewis Thomas's generation were expected to cure their patients, not merely to counsel them. The readership of science fiction had matured somewhat, as shown by the more introspective and experimental literature of the New Wave, which should have created a receptive atmosphere for stories about posited new medical treatments. Further, as medicine evolved into a vast bureaucratic enterprise largely under the control of government, pharmaceutical companies, and HMOs, one might imagine that the field would be a perfect target for science fiction satires along the lines of Frederik Pohl and C. M. Kornbluth's famed assault on the advertising industry, *The Space Merchants* (1954).

Still, even during the past four decades, medical science fiction has failed to emerge as a major aspect of the genre. Doctors have appeared as supporting characters in televised space adventures, like the various *Star Trek* series and *Babylon 5*, but the only program exclusively devoted to space medicine in the future, *Mercy Point*, was quickly canceled. The new field of cyberpunk science fiction in the 1980s displayed great interest in possible ways to change and enhance the human body—identified by spokesperson Bruce Sterling as "The theme of body invasion: prosthetic limbs, implanted circuitry, cosmetic surgery, genetic alteration"[2]—yet as in Sterling's own novel *Schismatrix*, readers still tended to observe the product more than the process, and these transformations were motivated more by vanity and a quest for novelty than a desire to heal or improve one's health. And while science fiction has occasionally offered probing looks at the contemporary medical establishment, as in Spinrad's *Bug Jack Barron* (1969) or Andrew J. Offutt's "For Value Received" (1972), this important new facet of our society has been examined more frequently outside of the genre, in the "medical thrillers" of Robin Cook and a number of medical horror novels written by Michael Crichton, John Saul, Dean Koontz, and others.

The curious situation makes the figure of the physician an intriguing focus for critical inquiry. Why has science fiction been so willing to address the problems facing medicine, and the effects of medicine, but not to address the profession of medicine? Is there something about the figure of the medical doctor that is especially disquieting or inharmonious within the context of science fiction? Several chapters in this volume will search for answers, in particularly advancing the theory that science fiction is a literature devoting to overcoming the body, not improving the body, so that a character dedicated to preserving the health of the body appears to be working at cross purposes to the deeper impetus driving the genre.

If the relationship between medicine and science fiction has remained problematic, one might look for a better relationship between medicine and fantasy, a form of imaginative literature that has grown increasingly popular in recent decades. However, despite an announced intention to address this genre as well, potential contributors to this volume found it difficult to discuss this subject at any length. As one indication of the problem, it might be noted that John Clute and Peter Nicholls's *The Encyclopedia of Science Fiction* includes a lengthy entry on "Medicine," citing over 60 authors and texts, whereas Clute and John Grant's *The Encyclopedia of Fantasy* includes only a short general paragraph on the comparable topic of "Healing" in the sense of curing diseases.

On one hand, to be sure, there are indeed any number of healers in fantasy, employing magic or special craft to cure various ailments, such as Paksenarrion in Elizabeth Moon's *Sheepherder's Daughter, Divided Allegiance*, and *Oath of Gold* and Alvin Maker in Orson Scott Card's *Seventh Son* and its four sequels; one also thinks of Croaker in Glen Cook's Black Company novels, who treats his fellow warriors' bloody injuries. The figure of the miraculous healer is also ubiquitous in fantasy role-playing games or video games, since the ability to revive injured cohorts can be essential in achieving final victory. And in that playful but deeply earnest form of the fantastic that has come to be known as magic realism, pervasive images of disease and degeneration may be tellingly deployed, as David K. Danow will demonstrate.

However, the genre of fantasy as a whole seems hesitant to confront the larger issue of avoiding death. On rare occasions, characters will die and return to life, like Gandalf in J. R. R. Tolkien's *The Lord of the Rings* (1954–1955) or Aslan in C. S. Lewis's *The Lion, the Witch, and the Wardrobe* (1950), but the process of revival is deliberately left unseen and, we are told, should be understood as a singular event, allowed only in certain extraordinary circumstances. Otherwise, fantasy seems prepared to accept the inevitability of death and fundamental limitations on the powers of healers. At the end of the final volume of *The Lord of the Rings, The Return of the King*, Frodo tells Sam that he "has been too deeply hurt" and that "it will never really heal" before he departs on a voyage that we recognize as a voyage to his death.[3] All the magic of Middle-Earth cannot save Frodo, and Tolkien further makes it clear that Frodo *should not* be saved; after all, fantasy is a literature that accepts the past, embraces the old and familiar, and hence allows for certain acts of healing but otherwise continues to insist upon the ancient pattern of birth, life, and death. In such a context, medicine must always be consigned to a secondary role.

Marginalized by fantasy because of that genre's insistence upon respecting the status quo, marginalized by science fiction because of that genre's insistence upon changing the status quo, the field of medicine does emerge from the literary perspective as both a significant and rather forlorn discipline, explaining the rather bleak title for this volume (for which we thank Kirk Hampton and Carol MacKay). For, if humanity is simultaneously determined to maintain the current realities of the human body, as suggested by fantasy, and to transcend those realities, as suggested by science fiction, then there are indeed no cures for humanity's future.

The contributors to this volume will address the topic of disease and medicine in science fiction and fantasy from a variety of perspectives. In Part I, "Population Studies," noted scholars H. Bruce Franklin and Frank McConnell attempt to define the relationship between medicine and science fiction in the broadest possible terms, Kirk Hampton and Carol MacKay offer an insightful survey of science fiction physicians focusing on the literature, and Joseph D. Miller provides a comprehensive overview of doctors and scientists in science fiction films and television programs. In Part II, "Case Histories," other commentators explore disease and medicine in particular texts or areas. George Slusser examines the two versions of Guy de Maupassant's "Horla" to explicate the functioning of the "medical frame" in science fiction; David Hinckley considers *Frankenstein* and *The Island of Dr. Moreau* as links between science fiction and horror; David K. Danow analyzes Joseph Conrad's *Heart of Darkness* (1902) and Louis-Ferdinand Celine's *Journey to the End of the Night* (1932) as fantastic journeys into sickness-ridden environments; and Robert Van Cleave explores George Orwell's *Nineteen Eighty-Four* as a story about disease and medical treatment. Moving to more recent texts, I take a look at one of the most popular series of medical adventures in science fiction, James White's Sector General stories, while Greg Bear discusses his own novels as extrapolations of current developments in effective therapy for mental problems. The volume concludes with three chapters involving science fiction films: Susan A. George ponders the varying roles of doctors in the films of the 1950s, Mary Pharr studies the four *Alien* films as commentaries on human versus synthetic life, and Howard V. Hendrix describes several films of the 1980s and 1990s as responses to our era's "Military Industrial Medical Establishment complex." To aid future researchers of this important topic, we also include a bibliography of 687 novels, stories, films, television programs, and nonfictional works involving disease and medicine in science fiction and fantasy.

A volume of this sort by its very nature cannot be comprehensive, but we believe that we have identified some major concerns and important texts to provide a solid foundation for ongoing scholarship and commentary. Physicist and science fiction author Gregory Benford is fond of observing that while the twentieth century was the century of physics, the twenty-first century will be the century of biology. Since the anticipated breakthroughs in this discipline will invariably have a significant impact on human health and medical care, it will become more and more important to examine and learn from the literature that predicts and assesses future medical developments. And there is much to gain from pondering both science fiction's provocative statements about medicine and its equally provocative silences.

Notes

1. Gary Westfahl, "For Tomorrow We Dine: The Sad Gourmet in the Scienticafé," in Westfahl, George Slusser, and Eric S. Rabkin, editors, *Foods of the Gods: Eating and the Eaten in Fantasy and Science Fiction* (Athens: University of Georgia Press, 1996), 213–223.

2. Bruce Sterling, "Preface," in Sterling, editor, *Mirrorshades: The Cyberpunk Anthology* (1986; New York: Ace Books, 1998), xiii.

3. J. R. R. Tolkien, *The Return of the King* (1955; New York: Ballantine Books, 1965), 382, 378.

Part I

Population Studies

2

The Science Fiction
of Medicine

H. Bruce Franklin

What is called "modern medicine" or "Western medicine" emerged in the nineteenth century as part of the same historical process that generated another characteristically "modern" or "Western" phenomenon: science fiction. The Industrial Revolution of the late eighteenth century led, as we all know, to the ever-accelerating development of science and technology, which have continually transformed both the material and cultural environments that we inhabit. We beings of the early twenty-first century can hardly imagine a world that is *not* being changed by technology, and our conceptions of time, space, matter, mind, and human destiny are all products of this environment. This consciousness is of course the very heart of science fiction.

Meanwhile, nothing enters our daily life more dramatically than disease and medicine. So it is no surprise that for almost two centuries, science fiction has been exploring the terms "disease" and "medicine"—with all their problematics. After the gloomy twilight of the fading years of the twentieth century, the period that many have called "postmodern," this exploration seems to be ever more relevant. For we are now also seeing our own bodily existence in the ambiguous dawning light of a new century that may make the most grandiose scientific fantasies of the past and present seem primitive—and innocent.

We are all aware of the contradictions. On one hand we know about the marvels of medical technology—genetic engineering, magnetic resonance imaging, organ transplants, arthroscopic surgery, *in vitro* fertilization, cyborg fantasies materializing as we mechanize the body and vitalize machinery, boundless promises of health and life. On the other hand we see all around us a disintegrating health delivery system, closed and understaffed hospitals, medical dollars and time gobbled up by endless bureaucratic paper pushing; the resurgence of supposedly archaic diseases like tuberculosis and lurking ones like ebola; epidemics of AIDS, drug addiction, and cancer; and of course the headlong plunge into the vortex of what we should properly call *mis*managed care, which blatantly makes profits, not health, the goal of medicine. And if the individual's life *is* extended, where does it end? In the abyss of a nursing home? As an appendage to life-support machinery? Or with the mercies of a Dr. Kevorkian? Our ability to arrest the processes of death, without necessarily restoring health, gives a new and biting relevance to Edgar Allan Poe's 1845 story "The Facts in the Case of M. Valdemar," in which a man dying of tuberculosis is kept in a state of mesmeric suspension until he rots into "a nearly liquid mass of loathsome—of detestable putridity."[1]

To use a fashionable slogan of the day, let's go back to basics. In fact, let's begin with the most basic fact of life: death. We human beings are "*mortals.*" Our essential dialectic is that of life and death. As soon as we attain life we begin the inexorable process of moving toward death. So is death—that essential part of humanity—a disease? And can it be cured?

Four celebrated works of science fiction—Mary Shelley's *Frankenstein, Or, The Modern Prometheus*, Olaf Stapledon's *Star Maker*, Greg Bear's *Blood Music*, and Octavia E. Butler's *Parable of the Sower*—offer a continuum from the early nineteenth century to the late twentieth century, displaying the shifting problematics of "disease" and "medicine."

The most famous doctor in science fiction (who of course was not a doctor at all but a college dropout—we seem to have some sort of cultural imperative that makes us call him doctor) begins his quest by seeking to "banish disease from the human frame, and render man invulnerable to any but a violent death." Possessed by this ambition, Victor Frankenstein becomes "capable of bestowing animation upon lifeless matter."[2] But, one asks, would lifeless matter find animation to be a state of health? Or, from its presumably deathless point of view, would life appear as a disease?

In his 1937 masterpiece *Star Maker*, Olaf Stapledon describes an attempt by our future cosmos, trapped in the late stages of the heat death of the universe but now possessed of a cosmic consciousness, to reach back through time to establish contact with the vast primeval nebulae from which the first stars are being formed. But the gigantic nebulae, whom Stapledon endows with a kind of preconscious meditative consciousness, can only experience what is happening to them as "a strange sickness": "The outer fringes of their tenuous flesh began to concentrate into little knots. These became in time grains of intense, congested fire. In the void between, there was nothing left but a few stray atoms. At first the complaint was no more serious than some trivial rash on a man's skin; but later it spread into the deeper tissues of the nebula." The awakened cosmos of the far future attempts to explain to the nebulae that what seems their disintegration and death is in reality the birth of a far richer and more complex universe, but this proves futile, as Stapledon explains in one of his most spectacular metaphors: "As well might a man seek to comfort the disintegrating germ-cell from which he himself sprang by telling it about his own successful career in human society."[3]

Half a century after *Star Maker*, Greg Bear's 1985 novel *Blood Music* projects a cosmic transformation that originates as a disease introduced into his own body by another modern Prometheus, a failed doctor now working as researcher developing "Medically Applicable Biochips" for a corporation in La Jolla,

California. When he turns the cells of his own body into a hyperintelligent entity, this late-twentieth-century doctor begins to transmute the human species into the progenitor of "an intelligent plague" with a transcendent "purpose"—which is to reshape some of the fundamental principles of the universe.[4]

Octavia E. Butler's 1993 novel *Parable of the Sower* envisions a more mundane and much bleaker future. Both the environment and the social infrastructure have collapsed, unleashing the most virulent physical and psychological diseases. A drug originally developed to help victims of Alzheimer's disease has been converted into a designer drug named pyro, that creates mobs of pyromaniacs.[5] For most people, no medical services at all are available, and the only doctor we meet is a 57-year-old former family physician who can no longer practice medicine amid society's ruins.

But we must first look more intently at the book that looms over science fiction, and indeed over modern society, the book that Brian W. Aldiss has incisively labeled the "first great myth of the industrial age,"[6] with its gigantic twin shape of Victor Frankenstein and his monstrous alter ego. Whether or not we consider *Frankenstein* as the fountainhead of modern science fiction, we must recognize that no literary work has penetrated our culture more deeply. Of course *Frankenstein* is everywhere in medical science fiction. Some characters, like the professor in C. L. Moore's 1944 story "No Woman Born" who resurrects a beautiful entertainer from a fire that has almost devoured her body and transforms her into one of the first female cyborgs, actually wonder whether or not "I am Frankenstein."[7] In Greg Bear's *Blood Music* not only does a scientist come to consider himself both "Frankenstein and the monster" but the nurses in an ordinary hospital refer to the high-tech diagnostic area as the "Frankenstein wing" (58).

Why should *Frankenstein, or, The Modern Prometheus*, a novel written by a teenager and published back in 1818, have such sustained relevance? If we view the book through the lens of disease and medicine, its relevance comes into sharp focus. And we can also understand why Mary Shelley, just eight years later, was to publish another wildly innovative novel, *The Last Man*, one of the first science fiction visions of the end of the world.

Mary Shelley was looking forward into the century in which modern Western medicine was created, the century of Semmelweis, William T. G. Morton, Pasteur, Theodor Billroth, Joseph Lister, and Robert Koch. Frankenstein was to have a long line of science fiction successors, including Drs. Rappaccini, Chillingworth, Heidenhoff, Jekyll, and Moreau, while science fiction itself was being recreated by such famous doctors as Oliver Wendell Holmes, Silas Weir Mitchell, and Arthur Conan Doyle.

To comprehend the relevance of Shelley's achievement to our medical environment today, we need to look at the medical environment of her day, including both its history and its direct effects on her own life.

The swift rise of Western medicine over the past two centuries or so looks especially spectacular because it was starting from such an abysmal level. Throughout the middle ages, European medicine, like that in most societies then in

Asia, Africa, and what we now call the Americas, was based mainly on empirical methodology, passed on orally from generation to generation. Because the exceptionally large skull of human babies often necessitates assistance in the birth process, all peoples have had to learn the basic principles of obstetrics. In Europe, as elsewhere around the world, the particular people who provided obstetric care were of course almost all women. Because Europe was largely agricultural, other medical tasks also fell largely to village healers, who were usually women. These healers developed techniques for resetting broken bones and performing other operations. They learned to diagnose a variety of diseases. They provided contraceptives and performed abortions. They assembled a massive pharmacology of herbal remedies, many of which are still in use today. For example, they used ergot derivatives to relieve pain and to induce uterine contractions to eject the placenta after birth, just as ergot derivatives are used today. They used belladonna to inhibit uterine contractions when miscarriage threatened. They used foxglove (that is, digitalis) to treat heart disease (not until 1785 did a practitioner of "modern" medicine, William Withering, research this important drug, and his discovery came from observation of its successful use in folk medicine). The healers had a wide assortment of herbal pain-killers, digestive aids, and anti-inflammatory agents.[8] These healers, like their contemporaries around the world— as well as most medical practitioners today—also used incantations and rituals to promote the psychological component of their healing arts.

Because these healers were mainly women, and because they excluded men from the scenes of birth, they always posed something of a threat to male prerogatives. They also posed a threat to the Church, which of course excluded them entirely from the rival profession of priest, who was supposed to be able to cure diseases through divine intervention. But their most direct threat was to the *profession* of medicine, which was to be reserved for a handful of men who studied at universities. In 1221, Holy Roman Emperor Frederick II decreed that no one could practice medicine until he had been publicly approved by the masters of the University of Salerno. This was the century when the witch hunts began.

From the thirteenth through the seventeenth centuries, just as the all-male, university-trained medical profession was becoming hegemonic, the women village healers found themselves labeled as witches. Tortured until they confessed that their powers derived from Satan, they were then hanged or burned alive. The European witch hunts killed at least hundreds of thousands and perhaps as many as two million people, mostly women. By the time it was over, the infrastructure of the traditional European health care system had been shattered. In its place was a system that largely disdained empirical methods, basing itself on theory inherited from classical texts and using a variety of medical instruments derived from developing technology. What we call "modern" or "Western" or "scientific" medicine—as if these were interchangeable terms—arose from the ruins of a medicine that was probably more scientific than the early forms of its successor.

The relative backwardness of European medicine by the eighteenth century can be glimpsed from the fact that one of the exceedingly few successes in disease prevention, inoculation against smallpox, came from a practice long in use in the Arab world, brought back to England by an English woman who had herself been a victim of smallpox before her stay in Turkey. An early work of American science fiction, Mary Griffith's 1836 utopia entitled *Three Hundred Years Hence*, used this example to show how men tend to ignore women's contributions to medicine and science. For, as Griffith pointed out, it was Lady Mary Wortley Montagu who introduced "into England the practice of inoculation for the small-pox," thus saving "thousands of lives" and preventing "hideous deformity, deeply scarred faces, from being universal."[9]

By the eighteenth century,

it was possible for male practitioners to make serious inroads into that last preserve of female healing—midwivery. Nonprofessional male practitioners—"barber-surgeons"—led the assault in England, claiming technical superiority on the basis of their use of the obstetrical forceps. (The forceps were legally classified as a surgical instrument, and women were legally barred from surgical practice).[10]

By the early nineteenth century, university-trained professional doctors—all male— had become the main deliverers of health care in Europe, England, and America for the upper and middle classes, especially in urban settings. Most had been taught to rely on what were called "heroic" measures: massive bleeding, huge doses of laxatives and cathartics—including calomel, a form of mercury (mercury chloride)—emetics, and, somewhat later, opium. Dr. Oliver Wendell Holmes, the distinguished American physician and author of psychological science fiction, expressed his contempt for the medicine being practiced by his professional contemporaries when he said that if all the medicines they used were thrown into the ocean it would be so much the better for mankind and so much the worse for the fishes.[11]

A striking example of how the achievements of modern Western medicine can look overblown is the case of puerperal fever, also known as childbed fever—a disease poignantly relevant to Mary Shelley and her science fiction. Until the middle of the nineteenth century, the mortality rate among women giving birth in European hospitals was between 25 and 30 percent. It was not until 1847 that any European physician did anything constructive about puerperal fever. Ignaz Semmelweis, now regarded as one of the great innovative geniuses of modern medicine, then an assistant at the famed obstetric clinic of the University of Vienna, noticed that women who gave birth at home and who had not undergone internal examination during labor—that is, women tended by traditional midwives rather than modern doctors—had a far lower mortality rate. He also observed that among women in the division of the clinic where medical students and physicians attended the delivery, the death rate from puerperal fever was up to three times as great as the death rate from puerperal fever in the division where only midwives attended. He conjectured that the medical students were bringing some kind of contagion from the dissecting room. In 1847, he ordered the students to wash their hands in chlorinated lime before conducting internal obstetrical examinations or assisting delivery. The death rate from puerperal fever immediately dropped from nearly 20 percent to 1.3 percent. Semmelweis might have reached the same conclusion if he had known of the 1843 book *The Contagiousness of Puerperal Fever* by none other than Dr. Oliver Wendell Holmes.

Mary Shelley was born in 1797, exactly half a century before Semmelweis figured out how to reduce the disastrous mortality rate from puerperal fever caused by the most up-to-date medical practice. Eleven days later, as a consequence of Mary's birth, her mother, Mary Wollstonecraft, one of the towering figures in the history of women's liberation, died from puerperal fever. What effect could this horrible event have had on young Mary's psyche and, eventually, her creative consciousness?

Mary's own experience with birth and death in the medical environment of the early nineteenth century no doubt was also a shaping influence on her imagination. Only one of her four children lived past the age of three. Her first child, born in 1815, died after twelve days. A few days later, seventeen-year-old Mary wrote in her journal: "Dream that my little baby came to life again; that it had only been cold, and that we had rubbed it before the fire, and it had lived."[12] Nine months after this journal entry, Mary gave birth to her son William, who became the namesake for Victor Frankenstein's young brother, the monster's first victim. Within months of William's birth, Mary began writing *Frankenstein*, which she completed in May 1817 while pregnant with her second daughter, Clara. *Frankenstein* was published in January, 1818. Clara died that September at the age of one. William died the following June at the age of three. This experience with European medicine evidently influenced revisions Mary Shelley made to the 1831 edition of *Frankenstein*, which she referred to in her "Introduction" as "my hideous progeny."

Victor Frankenstein grows up with Elizabeth, a beautiful little girl whom he calls "my more than sister." In the 1831 edition, Elizabeth's mother, like Mary Shelley's, "had died on giving her birth," leading to her adoption by Victor's parents.[13] Just as Victor is about to set off to begin his studies at the university of Ingolstadt, comes the first fatal event in his life. Elizabeth contracts scarlet fever and is "in the greatest danger." Victor's mother insists on attending "her sick bed,— her watchful attentions triumphed over the malignity of the distemper,—Elizabeth was saved, but the consequences of this imprudence were fatal to her preserver." She catches the disease and dies within three days as "her medical attendants" look on helplessly.[14] On her deathbed, she joins the hands of Victor and Elizabeth, and pledges them to marry each other. Elizabeth, thanks to the impotent medical care of her environment, has now caused the death of both her natural and her adoptive mother.

It is prior to his mother's death and his study at Ingolstadt that Frankenstein, his imagination possessed by reading medieval alchemists, aspires to "banish disease from the human frame, and render man invulnerable to any but a violent death." But when he "becomes capable of bestowing animation upon lifeless matter," his goal shifts. Frankenstein no longer seems concerned with either the prevention or the treatment of disease. What he now dedicates his own life to is "the creation of a human being" (54–55).

At this point, we need to recognize the gender issues at the heart of Mary Shelley's prevision of modern science and technology, especially as manifest in this ultimate quest of her medical practitioner. If Frankenstein simply wants to create a human being, there would be a relatively easy way to go about it. But this would involve having sex with Elizabeth or some other woman. But what he wants to do is create a human being all by himself, without any contact with a woman, substituting for sexual and human intercourse what he construes to be science. To make his creature, he has already cut himself off entirely from all communication with Elizabeth, whom he claims to love so passionately. Later, when his father suggests that he marry Elizabeth, this is his response: "to me the idea of an immediate union with my Elizabeth was one of horror and dismay" (130). This is *before* the monster, a creature that has emerged from Frankenstein's mind and body, threatens, "I shall be with you on your wedding-night" (142). On the wedding night, Victor has this to say to his bride: "Oh! peace, peace, my love . . . this night and all will be safe: but this night is dreadful, very dreadful" (163). Then despite the obvious fact that the creature plans to kill Elizabeth, Victor sends her alone to their bridal bed while he, armed with sword and pistol, waits for the monster to attack *him*. The psychological significance of Victor's obsession had come out clearly in the dream he had the night he created his monster:

I thought I saw Elizabeth, in the bloom of health, walking in the streets of Ingolstadt. Delighted and surprised, I embraced her; but as I imprinted the first kiss on her lips, they became livid with the hue of death; her features appeared to change, and I thought that I held the corpse of my dead mother in my arms; a shroud enveloped her form, and I saw the graveworms crawling in the folds of the flannel. (58)

We do not need Freud's *The Interpretation of Dreams*, published more than eight decades later, to recognize that Frankenstein's monster is in fact what that wonderful 1956 science fiction movie *Forbidden Planet* called a "Monster from the Id."

Disease, death, and the impotence of European medicine continued to haunt the imagination that had conceived *Frankenstein*. Between the 1818 and 1831 editions, Mary Shelley brought forth one of the bleakest books in modern literature, *The Last Man*, perhaps the first novel to imagine a disease that brings about the extinction of the human species.

Published in 1826, *The Last Man* is told by its title character, who now wanders in total loneliness over the planet, sampling the futile achievements of all human society. Mary Shelley sets this scene in the year 2100. It is war that introduces the plague into the action. An insatiable pestilence sweeps through Constantinople during a remorseless siege by a Greek army. The remaining two-thirds of this quite lengthy novel are devoted to the plague's unstoppable advances, as it marches around the globe, besieges England, and finally cuts down all the narrator's companions and loved ones.

All efforts at prevention or treatment prove futile. Nobody even understands how it spreads:

> That the plague was not what is commonly called contagious, like the scarlet fever, or extinct small-pox, was proved. It was called an epidemic. But the grand question was still unsettled of how this epidemic was generated and increased. . . . individuals may escape ninety-nine times, and receive the death-blow at the hundredth; because bodies are sometimes in a state to reject the infection of malady, and at others, to imbibe it.
>
> The air is empoisoned, and each human being inhales death, even while in youth and health. . . .

Convinced that the plague is "immedicable," people give up trying to understand, prevent, or treat it.[15] It is perceived as some kind of attack from "Nature." Some people form religious cults. Most just flee. The boundless faith in science that Victor Frankenstein had acquired at the modern university never even appears in *The Last Man*. Medicine and science in fact have no presence whatsoever in the novel, even though this plague is taking place in the last decade of the twenty-first century.

Science fiction that projects the possibility of a global plague has had a rich history since *The Last Man*. Jack London's *The Scarlet Plague*, which appeared in 1915, less than ninety years after Shelley's novel, suggests the immense transformation that had taken place in medical knowledge and practice while also offering some intriguing similarities in outlook.

Set, like *The Last Man*, in the twenty-first century, the story is narrated in the year 2073 by old man Granser to his savage grandsons in a world populated by a handful of barbarians, all that remains of the human species after the Scarlet Death that broke out in 2013. Granser had been a professor at the University of California in Berkeley, a member of what he calls "the ruling classes" who "owned all the land, all the machines, everything" in an America governed by a cabal of the ultra-rich.[16] Medical science had conquered not only the great diseases of the past—cholera, bubonic plague, tuberculosis, and so on—but many new ones that had emerged in the overpopulated world of the late twentieth century. Granser tries futilely to explain the invisible world of microorganisms, antibiotics, and inoculations to his primitive offspring. But all the twenty-first-century wonders of bacteriology were impotent against the Scarlet Death, which was so virulent and swift that it killed the bacteriologists in their laboratories.

The rich, fleeing in their private airships, had spread the plague throughout the world. Civilization had collapsed. The barbarism that replaced it sprung partly from the viciousness of this early twenty-first-century capitalist dictatorship: "down in our slums and labor-ghettos, we had bred a race of barbarians, of savages" (379). Among the handful of those people with natural immunity, it is these civilization-bred savages who attain power. At the end, Granser warns his grandsons against the newly arisen "medicine-men" who "call themselves *doctors*, travestying what was once a noble profession." These false "doctors must be destroyed," Granser declares, "and all that was lost must be discovered over again" (448). Although *The*

Scarlet Plague ultimately projects a cyclical view of human history, Granser, like London himself, still believes in the wonders of science and technology.

Let me pass over many other twentieth-century stories of global plague, including George R. Stewart's 1949 *Earth Abides*, which is actually a kinder, gentler rewrite of *The Scarlet Plague*, in order to contrast London's vision with that of a work that returns to the gender issues underlying *Frankenstein*.

Teaching Vonda N. McIntyre's 1973 story "Of Mist, and Sand, and Grass" can be an especially revealing experience about contemporary attitudes toward medicine. A woman healer named Snake arrives at a tiny matriarchal, polyandrous, and xenophobic community, precariously clinging to life amid a vast desert. She has with her three snakes, which she uses to cure a young boy's malignant tumor. The setting is evidently after a nuclear holocaust. Snake has received her medical training in a "station," beyond which lies a city inside a mountain. She has been immunized against a wide spectrum of snake poisons, and she uses her snakes to synthesize and deliver potent biochemical concoctions to cure cancer. I ask students in my course, which is entitled "Science Fiction, Technology, and Society," when is this story set? And what is the level of technology? A few recognize that this seems to be a post-nuclear world. Most describe this as a nontechnological world or one with a backward technology. Why? Evidently because McIntyre has returned to the female healer and because this healer's medical instruments are snakes, most students fail to recognize her practice as scientifically or technologically advanced. To drive the point home, either I or some student has to ask, "What cures for cancer do *we* have that are more advanced?"

With this in mind, let us return to fiction about the threat of global disease. Perhaps the most widely known twentieth-century work in this genre is Michael Crichton's 1969 best-seller *The Andromeda Strain*. In *The Last Man*, the plague turned into a global menace during, and evidently because of, human warfare. But nobody intended to use disease as a weapon. The basic premise of *The Andromeda Strain*, which appeared just as many Americans were becoming aware of our nation's fiendish use of chemical warfare in Vietnam, is that the Pentagon may be orbiting satellites to collect microorganisms even more virulent than those being developed by the biological warfare facilities at Fort Detrick, Maryland, and Harley, Indiana. Operation Scoop succeeds in capturing from space the Andromeda strain, a microscopic life form that is airborne and almost instantly fatal to almost all humans and other mammals. Most of the novel is devoted to the efforts of an all-male team of four medical and scientific geniuses, working deep underground in a supersecret ultratechnological military facility, to comprehend the Andromeda strain and thus prevent global catastrophe. (Robert Wise's 1970 movie version makes what seems a concession to the consciousness of the day by casting a woman as one of the four genius scientists; but she is a harridan whose failure to reveal her own disease comes close to dooming the world.) Crichton, himself a graduate of Harvard Medical School and a former doctor, lures us into the mindset of this elitist technocracy, obsessed with technology and possessed by the military, in order to display its Frankenstein-like impotence to control the menaces it unleashes upon the world.

The subtext for *The Andromeda Strain* is that by the late 1960s the human species, through its stupendous development of science and technology, had in fact finally developed the means of its own extinction. This is precisely the destiny imagined by Victor Frankenstein when he decides not to complete the mate that his monster had demanded: "I shuddered to think that future ages might curse me as their pest, whose selfishness had not hesitated to buy its own peace at the price, perhaps, of the existence of the whole human race" (141). The Vietnam War was demonstrating the willingness of one nation to buy its own definition of peace by indiscriminately spraying chemical agents containing dioxin, the substance with the most extreme rate of teratogenicity in laboratory animals, one already known by then to have caused large numbers of mutated births in Vietnam. People back then were also becoming aware that the official government policy about nuclear weapons was Mutual Assured Destruction, the guarantee that if either side launched a nuclear attack both sides would be utterly destroyed. And in this situation, as Crichton explicitly points out, the government, with the aid of the Hudson Institute, had defined the "correct" psychological profile as the willingness to carry out genocide or initiate the apocalypse.[17] If the plans of the military and the scientists in *The Andromeda Strain* had been carried out as intended, nuclear weapons would have turned the alien organism into a global pestilence. *The Andromeda Strain* calls ours the only species intelligent enough to have devised the means to destroy itself. And it shows that, like Frankenstein, we confront the products of our own brilliant creativity as alien monsters, beyond our control.

In the decades since *The Andromeda Strain*, although we have perhaps become more complacent about the nuclear threat, we may have become more disturbed by the biological threat. Today, the possibility of global plague seems to haunt our culture more than ever. Why?

One reason is that, thanks to Richard Preston's article in the October 26, 1992 *New Yorker* and his best-selling nonfiction book *The Hot Zone*, millions of people became aware of an incident not altogether different from the scenario of *The Andromeda Strain*. In 1989, a U.S. Army biological strike team had to take extreme measures to prevent one of the world's most virulent and infectious viruses from escaping from an Army biological warfare laboratory in Frederick, Maryland. Ridley Scott was directing a movie adaptation of the story, *Crisis in the Hot Zone*, starring Robert Redford and Jodie Foster, when that project got preempted by the 1995 movie *Outbreak*. In many ways, *Outbreak* looks like a slick, megabuck update of *The Andromeda Strain*, but with a team of medical doctors (Dustin Hoffman and Rene Russo) as quite innocent adversaries of the military version of Victor Frankenstein (incarnate in Donald Sutherland), who has been developing the virus as a biological warfare agent.

Another 1995 release, Terry Gilliam's brilliant *12 Monkeys*, is a far more innovative and incisive science fiction film about the possibility of planetary plague. *12 Monkeys* uses time travel to project human history from World War I through 2035 as a tableau of ever-advancing technology under the control of ever more demented and brainy lunatics. In a revision of Chris Marker's 1963 short film *La Jetée*, the doctors who run the nightmarish underground society of 2035 are trying to alter the past to prevent the outbreak of a viral plague in 1996 that made life impossible on the surface of the planet. The mad laboratory worker who had traveled around the world to release the virus globally is portrayed as only marginally more insane than the eminent scientist who had originally cultured it. Though intellectually and visually quite demanding, *12 Monkeys* turned out to be quite popular, perhaps because audiences recognized the accuracy of its vision.

Does the possibility of a madman releasing a plague nurtured in a laboratory seem far-fetched? Larry Wayne Harris, an Ohio well inspector and member of the Aryan Nations, in 1995 ordered from American Type Culture Collection, a company in Rockville, Maryland, three pure strains of the bubonic plague bacteria that wiped out one-third of the population of Europe in the fourteenth century. After he complained that his shipment, for which he had paid $240, was late, the Center for Disease Control was notified. When the FBI, police, public health officials, and emergency workers in spacesuits searched his home, they found blasting caps, smoke grenades, almost a dozen M-1 carbines, and white supremacist literature. In the glove compartment of his car, parked in his driveway, sat the three vials of plague still packed in two layers of glass, absorbent foam and a sealed metal canister. Since it is not illegal to own bubonic plague, Harris was convicted only on one count of wire fraud (based on the fact that he had made up a phony laboratory and used his employer's lab permit).[18] More recently, we have learned of another isolated fanatic who obtained a laboratory-developed form of anthrax and, for some reason, mailed it in a number of letters, killing several American citizens.

However, no one, so far, has deliberately released a plague of planetary proportions. No American town has been devastated by a microorganism nurtured by the military, as in *The Andromeda Strain* and *Outbreak*. So why our growing concern about a planet-wide plague? Because we already have one—AIDS.

As poverty deepens and health care systems disintegrate around the world, the human species is creating ideal conditions for a pandemic. Impoverished families in India and Thailand sell their daughters into prostitution, so the celebrated "one night in Bangkok" (or Bombay, "Asia's largest sex bazaar"[19]) is now spreading AIDS at a tremendous rate among heterosexuals. In the near future, by some estimates, one out of every six Indians will be HIV positive.[20] In South Africa there are now upward of two million AIDS patients. AIDS is now out of control in cities like the one where I teach, because the two main employment opportunities open to most of the population are prostitution and illicit drug selling. (More than half the prostitutes in Newark are HIV positive.) The United States, which currently imprisons a higher percentage of its population than any other country, has turned the prisons into perfect breeding centers for AIDS by denying prisoners condoms. As AIDS spreads, the overburdened health delivery system, already weakened by galloping Reaganomics, could virtually collapse for much of the population, especially if the virus were to mutate toward easier transmission.

No work of science fiction dramatizes the contradictions of contemporary disease and medicine more starkly than Norman Spinrad's *Journals of the Plague Years*, his extrapolation of a future society dominated by AIDS. Though the story was anthologized back in 1988 as a novella, Spinrad could not find a publisher for the novel until 1995, a fact he attributes to AIDS having "become more central to our lives . . . so central that denial is no longer a viable option."[21] He does, however, maintain one stricture originally imposed by his agent: the word AIDS never appears in the novel.

These *Journals of the Plague Years* describe a society where disease has shaped politics and the economy, and where sex has become equated with death. Some areas, such as San Francisco, have become Quarantine Zones, patrolled by the Sex Police to make sure that nobody ever leaves. The most vengeful victims of the Plague are recruited into the imperialist American Foreign Legion, better known as the Army of the Living Dead, to kill, rape, and plunder the Third World, stigmatized as the source of the Plague. Pharmaceutical companies keep developing new vaccines, but the Plague stays ahead of them by mutating, and so the same companies also turn out a stream of palliatives to prolong the lives of the disease's victims. Teenagers and adults are fitted with sex interfaces, mechanical devices through which they have orgasms with each other. Advanced technology has also produced arcades filled with sex machines for those who lack or don't want a partner. In this loveless society, sexual intercourse without a machine is known as "meat."

The complicated plot involves a sadistic soldier of the Army of the Living Dead; a religious maniac who holds the second highest political position in the nation—the lifetime Directorship of the Federal Quarantine Agency (FQA); a young Berkeley woman who becomes Our Lady of the Living Dead—dedicated to having sex with as many Plague victims as possible so that "natural selection" would eventually make the pathogen mutate into one no longer fatal to its host; and a medical doctor developing vaccines for one of the giant drug companies. When Doctor Bruno himself contracts the Plague, his feverish efforts succeed in creating a retrovirus that mimics and attacks every strain of the Plague and is spread through sexual contact. He injects himself with the virus, making readers expect him perhaps to become another Frankenstein. But absurdist black humor is of course one of Spinrad's trademarks. So Dr. Bruno dedicates himself to a quest quite the opposite of that of Frankenstein, who is so horrified by the thought of sex with Elizabeth: "The moral imperatives of the oath of Hippocrates and the fondest desire of any man coincided. It was my duty to have meat with as many women as I could as quickly as possible" (71).

What forces him to act quickly is that the heads of his corporation, realizing that his antidote would bankrupt the company and wreck the nation's economy, now overwhelmingly dependent on the Plague, are out to destroy his antivirus virus and all records of it. When Dr. Bruno links up with Our Lady of the Living Dead and they find refuge in San Francisco, the corporate moguls convince the fanatic Director of the FQA to drop a thermonuclear bomb on the city. In the nick of time, the Director discovers the outrageous truth. "You suppressed a total cure for the

Plague to preserve your own profits?" he asks incredulously. You "kept trying to get me to nuke San Francisco" just to keep your company "solvent"? (132) This is so grotesque that even he is shocked over the brink of sanity. The world is saved, and love is restored.

In Spinrad's novel, a writer from the middle of the twenty-first century can look back from "our happier perspective" to the sickness, mental and physical, of "the Plague Years." Let us hope that our own contradictions of disease and medicine have such a happy resolution.

Notes

1. Edgar Allan Poe, "The Facts in the Case of M. Valdemar," in Poe, *The Complete Tales and Poems of Edgar Allan Poe* (New York: Barnes & Noble Books, 1992), 663.

2. Mary Shelley, *Frankenstein, or, The Modern Prometheus*, ed. Johanna M. Smith (Boston: Bedford Books, 1992), 45, 54. This is an accurate text of the 1831 edition that I use since it incorporates relevant changes made by Mary Shelley from the original 1818 edition. Later page references in the text are to this edition.

3. Olaf Stapledon, *Star Maker* in *Last and First Men and Star Maker* (New York: Dover, 1968), 401–402.

4. Greg Bear, *Blood Music* (1985; New York: Ace Books, 1986), 94, 167. Later page references in the text are to this edition.

5. Octavia E. Butler, *Parable of the Sower* (1993; New York: Warner Books, 1995), 128.

6. Brian W. Aldiss, *Billion Year Spree: The True History of Science Fiction* (Garden City, NY: Doubleday, 1973), 23.

7. C. L. Moore, "No Woman Born," in Groff Conklin, editor, *Treasury of Science Fiction* (1948; New York: Bonanza Books, 1980), 200.

8. Barbara Ehrenreich and Deirdre English, *Witches, Midwives, and Nurses: A History of Women Healers* (Old Westbury, NY: Feminist Press, 1973), 12; Anne Llewellyn Barstow, *Witchcraze: A New History of the European Witch Hunts* (San Francisco: Pandora of HarperCollins, 1994), Chapter 6, "From Healers into Witches"; Monica Green, "Women's Medical Practice and Health Care in Medieval Europe," *Signs*, 14 (Winter 1989), 434–473; Leland L. Estes, "The Medical Origins of the European Witch Craze: A Hypothesis," *Journal of Social History*, 17 (1983), 271–284.

9. Mary Griffith, *Three Hundred Years Hence* (Philadelphia: Prime Press, 1950), 73.

10. Ehrenreich and English, 18.

11. Ehrenreich and English, 21–22.

12. Quoted in David Ketterer, *Frankenstein's Creation: The Book, The Monster, and Human Reality* (British Columbia: University of Victoria, 1979), 42.

13. *Frankenstein*, 41. In the 1818 edition, Elizabeth is the daughter of the sister of Frankenstein's father, who adopts her after her mother dies at some unspecified time.

14. *Frankenstein*, 47. In the 1818 edition, Elizabeth is already almost recovered when Victor's mother imprudently visits the sick chamber just to see her.

15. Mary Shelley, *The Last Man*, edited by Hugh J. Luke, Jr. (Lincoln: University of Nebraska Press, 1965), 167–169, 168.

16. Jack London, *The Scarlet Plague*, in London, *The Science Fiction of Jack London*, edited by Richard Gid Powers (Boston: Gregg Press, 1975), 327. Later page references in

the text are to this edition.

17. Michael Crichton, *The Andromeda Strain* (1969; New York: Dell, 1970), 110.

18. "Man Gets Hands on Bubonic Plague, But That's No Crime," *Washington Post*, December 30, 1995; "Bill Targets Bacteria," *Washington Post*, January 29, 1996.

19. "India's Shame," *Nation*, April 8, 1996, 12.

20. "India's Shame," 12.

21. Norman Spinrad, *Journals of the Plague Years* (New York: Bantam, 1995), 146. Later page references in the text are to this edition.

3

The Missionary Physician,
from Asclepius to Kevorkian

Frank McConnell

In confronting the topic of "disease and medicine in science fiction and fantasy," I am reminded of the title of J. D. Bernal's classic book, *The World, the Flesh, and the Devil*, all three of those terms being understood as the entrapments of history—money, sex, and sheer cussedness, say—that impede the soul in its ascent to the purity of union with godhead.

Now, that's a classically gnostic notion, implying absolute contempt for society, for the life of the body, and for the passions—what else can "the devil" mean?—in favor of a spiritual, immortal essence of the self, in eternal congress with what the Kabballah calls the "Ain-Sof," the Gnostics call "The Father" or "The Pleroma," and Paul Tillich calls "The Ground of All Being."

And that's pretty heady stuff. It can feel right, on a day when the sun is shining, the check is in the mail, you're convinced she really loves you, and your shoes don't hurt. Gnosticism, in other words, is a helluva good religion if you feel great. And if you *don't* feel great, it's got a lot of ways of convincing you that you actually *do*. Pain is only a delusion: the Buddhist *samsara* as opposed to *nirvana* (copies to Kurt Cobain, founder of the group with the latter name and suicide); pain is "redemptive suffering," the dodge of those Christians who, like Teilhard de Chardin and Pope John Paul II, want you to believe that Uncle Ernie's lung cancer is a suffering offered up—I love that phrase, "offered up"—for the salvation of, well, the world; or pain is an impolite imposition by that underbred fellow, Satan, easily overcome by proper meditation upon the scriptures—the answer of America's premiere writer of science fiction, Mary Baker Eddy.

Gnosticism, in other words, doesn't need doctors—or says it doesn't—just because doctors either heal or soothe the body, and gnosticism, whatever else it does, really hates the body.

Christopher Hitchens, in his grand *Buchlein*, *The Missionary Position*, relates a television interview with the late hospice-founding celebrity, Mother Teresa—or, as Hitchens has termed her on television, "the ghoul of Calcutta":

She described a person who was in the last agonies of cancer and suffering unbearable pain. With a smile, Mother Teresa told the camera what she told this terminal patient: "You are suffering like Christ on the Cross. So Jesus must be kissing you." Unconscious of the account to which this irony might be charged, she then told of the sufferer's reply: "Then please tell him to stop kissing me." There are many people in the direst need and pain who have cause to wish, in their extremity, that Mother Teresa was less free with her own metaphysical caresses and a little more attentive to actual suffering.[1]

I relate that anecdote, not only to chill you to the bone, but to make the point that what we call "mainstream" science fiction is, by and large, much more on the side of Mother Teresa than on the side of her unhappy charge. I have argued before that science fiction is essentially gnostic. I now insist, under the pressure of our common topic, that if it is a genre at all, it is so *only* because of its deep participation in the gnostic urge to be *elsewhere*: out of this time, out of this body, out of this iron chain of circumstance we call life. Jesus is kissing you. We are Men Like Gods. We are Last and First Men. We are Lazarus Long, or cowboys in the bodiless eternity of cyberspace. Or we are Thetans, spiritual beings from another dimension, entrapped in and drugged into forgetfulness by the MEST, or matter/energy/space/time lower cosmos. That is the essential teaching of Scientology, founded by an important colleague of Isaac Asimov, Frederik Pohl, and the whole Golden Age generation, and it is also, precisely, the plot of *The Pearl*, one of the earliest and finest gnostic poems. If mainstream sf has never noticed Mary Baker Eddy as one of its guiding spirits, it has blushed to acknowledge L. Ron Hubbard; but in all honesty, it can afford to do neither.

And these are really not visions of the future. I have always maintained that people—even that lovely man, Fred Pohl—who defend sf on the basis of its predictive power are missing the boat—like the guys in Vegas who fade the faders. I mean, what's the *point*? So H. G. Wells may have predicted the tank, and Hugo Gernsback described radar, and Arthur C. Clarke imagined a communications satellite. Big damn deal. Make enough wild guesses and you've got to be right some of the time. Stay at the table long enough, with a bottomless stash of cash, and you *will* roll triple sevens. That's, as the British say, a mug's game.

No. Far from being visions of the future, these are—in true gnostic fashion—anxious expressions of profound discomfort with the present. And that means profound discomfort with the body—for the body is our interface with the present. Let me explain.

Pohl once told me, jokingly, that all science fiction writers are ugly. The reason? Since they were ugly, they couldn't make friends on the playground at recess or get dates for the prom—so they had to retreat into a world of their own imagining, replete with pleasures only they could enjoy, and hence became writers of sf.

I don't think that was entirely a joke. Not that sf writers really *are* ugly—the field has, of course, matinee idols like Chip Delany and Gregory Benford—but that a certain fear and loathing of the body as the body is built into the form. Think about the heroes and heroines of classic space opera, the perfect bodies of Flash Gordon and Dale Arden or of the moon-voyaging couple in the film *Things to Come*

(1936), or of the statuesque male and female *Hitlerjuegen* who adorned virtually every cover of *Amazing Stories* and *Planet Stories* during the fifties. Granted, those covers, along with the covers of my grandfather's *Police Gazette*, were my own personal introduction to the brave new world of eroticism, and as such are remembered with sincere, nay Proustian, affection. But isn't the "perfect body" precisely the fatal will-o'-the-wisp of those who hate the body—the opiate of the anorexics?

"Anorexia" is derived from two Greek words: the prefix *an*, a privative meaning "not," and the verb *oregomai*, "I desire." It means, in other words, "desirelessness"— *not* simply aversion to food—rather like the state of *nirvana* or the state of perfect, disinterested contemplation aspired to by the gnostics. It is anti-life, and it is notoriously difficult to treat.

Anorexia is difficult to treat—actually, it's damned near impossible to treat—for the same reason that science fiction, on the whole, has a such a difficult time dealing with the idea of the doctor. (And you thought I'd never get around to the topic at hand, didn't you?)

According to the *Oxford English Dictionary* (henceforth *OED*), the first use of the term "anorexia" was in 1588—before William Shakespeare wrote *Romeo and Juliet*. Astonishingly, the first use of the word "anorexic" is not until 1907—twelve years after Wells invented those passionless, dreamy stoners, the Eloi, in *The Time Machine*. The condition was identified, that is, 400 years before it was necessary to come up with a name for the sufferers of that condition.

Why?

Because, I think, before the end of the nineteenth century, there simply weren't enough anorexics around to be worth the naming. And now, as anyone with access to a TV set knows, there are enough of them to populate the talk shows—all the talk shows—for a whole season; and, more heartrendingly, to populate all the campuses at which we teach. And what does that have to do with science fiction? Everything.

Think about Case, the problematic hero of William Gibson's *Neuromancer*. Like all cyberspace buccaneers, he entertains complete contempt for the body—for what he calls "the meat." (I am informed by some of my more advanced computer-weenie students, by the way, that it is common enough among them to refer to real-world, interpersonal encounters as merely "meat space"—the poor bastards!) At the beginning of the novel Case has been exiled from cyberspace, having been caught stealing information from the net. Surgically disabled from interfacing with the net, he is exiled to the punk hell of Chiba City. There he is visited by Molly, a beautiful, dangerous woman who enlists him on a risky enterprise, the reward for which will be his reinstatement as a cyberspace voyager, free again from exile in the mere dark wood or *selva oscura* of "the meat." They move to the Sprawl, the purgatorial mega-city extending from Boston to Atlanta, where Case is assigned a helper, the computer-generated personality construct of the "Dixie Flatline," the now-dead, greatest cyberspace jockey in history. Eventually Case, Molly, and Dixie ascend to the fabulous orbiting colony, Straylight, where the mission is successful. And the mission's ultimate purpose? To bring about the union of Neuromancer and

Wintermute, two gigantic mainframes whose union—yin and yang—produces the ultimate Artificial Intelligence, able to connect with other AI's throughout the universe. And Case is returned to full health, his liver, spleen, kidneys replaced, free as promised to cruise the net and indulge his contempt for "the meat."

Now, it should be obvious that, splendid as Gibson's novel is, in all conscience he owes 30 percent of his royalties to the estate of Dante Alighieri. *Neuromancer* is a dark book (George Slusser has written brilliantly about the extent of its darkness); but it is dark just because it is—not an inversion—but a gnostic skewing of *The Divine Comedy*, perhaps the most *anti*-gnostic poem in the Western canon. Case is Dante the pilgrim, Molly his Beatrice, and the Dixie Flatline his eminent precursor in the art, his Virgil. But the end of *this* comedy is not to behold the Multifoliate Rose of the Godhead and return to life *in* the body, *in* time, but rather to witness the birth of the purely abstract deity, Neuromancer/Wintermute, and return to the infinitely replaceable, therefore time-free body that is, really, only a vehicle to allow the mind to escape forever into cyberspace—not all that different, really, from the fata morgana "perfect body" of the anorexics. Man at his worst, as Kenneth Burke once observed, is separated from his proper life by instruments of his own devising, and rotten with the spirit of perfection.

In the world of the anorexic, doctors are sublimely irrelevant because the body is not a thing to be healed, or nurtured, but rather punished into ideality (which is to say, into abstraction). In the world of *Neuromancer*—and, I'd say, in science fiction altogether—doctors are relevant *only* because of what they can do, not *for*, but *to* the body.

As the *OED*, again, tells us, it's only comparatively recently that the word "doctor" came to mean, almost exclusively, "medical practitioner," with all the attendant mojo. (Here's an experiment you can try at home for fun: When I call the phone company to complain about a charge and identify myself as "Frank McConnell," the guy at the other end always responds, "Well, Frank, our records show . . ." When I identify myself as "Doctor Frank McConnell," though, it's always, "Well, yes, Doctor McConnell, just let me check our records here . . ." Dig? And I don't think he gives me the honorific and the politesse because he thinks I may be a Ph.D. in English Literature.)

"Doctor" comes from the Latin *doceo*, "I teach." So to be *doctus* is to be one who has been taught, and to be a *doctor* is to be a teacher: an expert, a professional, a *technician*: rather as to be a gnostic (Greek *gnosis*, "knowledge") is to be a guy in the know, a technocrat of the transcendent.

And to be that is to regard the body as a thing to be either overcome or improved upon—but *not* as something to be comfortable in on its own terms. Remember the opening voiceover of *The Six Million Dollar Man*: "Steve Austin, astronaut. We can *make him* stronger—faster." (I always want to add "hornier"— but that's precisely what the gnostic/medical orientation *doesn't* allow.)

It's an old delusion, the mind/body split, and it's probably all Plato's fault— although, as Friedrich Nietzsche understood, Plato didn't really *mean* to cause such a mess; really, now, no one who venerated Socrates can be all that opposed to horniness. Nonetheless, it's part of the bedrock of our culture, and it's been growing apace—if bedrock can grow—since Gabriel Harvey discovered in 1624 that blood is just lubricant and the heart is just a pump, since René Descartes in 1645 argued, epochally, that the body is just a machine with a bored spirit at the control panel, and since Luigi Galvani passed an electric current through vermicelli, causing his little dead worms to boogie, thereby inspiring not only Walt Whitman ("I sing the body electric") but the first ever authentic science fiction novel (written, significantly, by a woman).

Victor Frankenstein is surely the *capo* of all sf doctors. And what, precisely, *is* his real, unforgivable sin? This is like asking, what is the essential crime of Oedipus? Or what is at the core of Hamlet's *angst*? All three characters are so crucially, authentically mythic that they give us back an infinite array of answers to those questions, depending upon the angle of attack with which we *ask* them ("them" meaning the characters *and* the questions, since the characters *are* the questions).

In the present context—doctors, sf, and that old thing, the meaning of the universe—here's what I think about Victor Frankenstein's sin. He lost his beloved, madonna-like mother at an early age. He was raised with the family's adopted daughter, Elizabeth, as if she were his loving sister but also with the tacit understanding that she eventually would be his betrothed. And that's a kind of hygienic incest—incest, whatever else it is, being a passionate denial that the body of the beloved can be *other*—can, in fact, really be a "body" ("somebody") at all. He fed his young imagination on the works of Paracelsus, Cornelius Agrippa, and the other gnostic/alchemists, went to University at Ingolstadt, and heard from his kindly tutor in chemistry, M. Waldman, that the guesses of the mystics were becoming realities in the researches of the new scientists: the philosopher's stone could be achieved, after all: the transmutation of lead (body) into gold (spirit). So Victor set about to discover the secret of life, did so, and in the hope of creating a race of greater men, animated a giant body stitched together from corpses. And as soon as the animated creature opened his eyes, and stared at his creator, his creator stared back and, repulsed by the ugliness of his creation, fled.

And that's the sin: not to create life, but to be repulsed by the life you have created: to give symbolic birth to a "new man" and then to reject that birth, in a grotesque parody of parturition, because it is still a *body*. Think about Wells's Dr. Moreau; Robert Louis Stevenson's Dr. Jekyll; Rotwang in Fritz Lang's *Metropolis* (1926); the bloodless, passionless Dr. Susan Calvin of Asimov's overrated robot stories; the disinterested experimenters who make retarded Charlie Gordon a genius only to have him fall back into a worse retardation in the *really* best sf story ever, Daniel Keyes's "Flowers for Algernon"; or Ash, in Ridley Scott's *Alien* (1979), himself an android, contemptuous of the flesh and in love with the purity of the inhuman. To be "incarnate" means, precisely, to be "made flesh," to be of woman born, to live *in* time, in what W. B. Yeats calls "the frog spawn of a blind man's ditch";[2] and in that sense the gnostic urge is, precisely, anti-incarnational. It does not want the Word to be *made* flesh, but rather for the flesh to burn away so that the

Word can conquer, and by conquering escape, the world. At its terminus is the exaltation of the anorexic, the loathsome faith of Mother Teresa—at its terminus is the "dream begotten by the hatred of death upon the fear of true immortality, fondled in secret by thousands of ignorant men and hundreds who are not ignorant."

That last bit isn't me, by the way. It's C. S. Lewis, describing the folly of science fiction in his own great science fiction novel, *Perelandra*.[3] And Lewis helps us see how, while sf participates essentially in the gnostic urge, it also, by a blessed swerve of bad faith, refutes the doctrine. (This should surprise no one, since storytelling is always wiser than doctrine.)

As that crucial thinker and vile man, Michel Foucault, tells us, post-Enlightenment medicine ("sf" medicine, for our purposes) is, in its obsession with the improvement of the body, another objectification of the body, another inscription of power, another benevolent—or *faux*-benevolent—manifestation of the need to control. Philippe Ariès, in *Western Attitudes toward Death*, makes the same point, less shrilly than Foucault: The fact that we die now, by and large, in the antiseptic anonymity of hospital rooms rather than in our own homes is actually a technological blasphemy, a denial of the reality and dignity of death itself. The missionary physicians, who would save us from our own corporeality, have done great things, but they have also depleted what Alfred North Whitehead called the *enjoyment* of the very body they wish to exalt and refine. Really: aren't we the first culture in history to count calories, spot-check cholesterol, and make love with the sole purpose of not dying? We *are* a gnostic culture. Even our national obsession with pornography is a sign of it, since pornography—the fantasy of the "perfect body" again—defines the flesh as a purely objectified, scented, depillatoried scene of gratification—a "meat puppet," in Gibson's brilliant phrase—that, since it cannot respond, is as disposable as a condom and as insignificant as a wet dream. We glorify out intellectuality by making sexuality a trivialized commodity. Our pornographers are not lyricists of the flesh. They are Anabaptists with Leicas.

But notice. All the missionary physicians from sf I enumerated are failures, their gnostic voyages wrecked on the shoals of the intransigent flesh. They discover that we *are* mortal if we are to be human, and that our life is, must be, in Alexander Pope's astonishing phrase, only—only!—"this long disease."[4] Science fiction at its profoundest denies the very gnosticism for which it yearns, and that conflictedness is its great value for our increasingly conflicted era, and its inestimable gift to such almost-sf writers as William Burroughs, Thomas Pynchon, Don DeLillo, and Jonathan Lethem.

For sf—mythology, not theology—cannot forget what Whitehead, again, calls "the witness of the body."[5] And since it cannot forget, it is forced to remember another kind of medicine, another kind of doctor, who existed before doctors usurped the term.

Pharmakos is the Greek word for what I mean, and though masculine in declension, it is taken to be feminine in syntax. The source of our "pharmacy" and "pharmacology," it is usually translated as "witch." But that is a male imposition upon the history of female healing. *Pharmakon* means, equally, "drug," "medicine," and "poison." So a *pharmakos* is, basically, a "wise woman," skilled (*not* learned) in the life and death of the body, or, simply, a "healer." In Mexico today—if you know the right people—you can find a *Curandera*—a healer, almost always a woman—who will give you roots and teas for your pain, not to deny it or transcend it, but to soothe it so you may reenter your own life.

Mind you: I would not go to a *Curandera* about a broken tooth or an attack of gout. But I would also not go to a doctor—or, to be realistic, an HMO—to be reassured about my possession of *my* body, *my* own life. I'm simply discussing alternate, and essential, attitudes toward life in time. And mind also: I do not wish to be called a "feminist" any more than I wish to be called a "Marxist," say, or a "Rosicrucian." All firm opinions, as the divine Oscar should have said and certainly believed, are vulgarities.

Nevertheless, it is undeniable that the tradition of the healer—the *yin* side of the circle—has been overshadowed by the exploratory, experimentalist, *yang* heritage. Ever live in a small town and try to find a female ob-gyn? Women—the women's tradition of medicine—knows birth as no male ever can and therefore understands death as no male ever can. Men are puzzled and frightened by both, and therefore are driven to transcend or deny the riddle: "You nurse the kids, honey—I've got to go slay a dragon." As Thorstein Veblen suggested long ago, that may be the heart of all male narratives.

Thus, the god of healing, Asclepius, is really more on the *yin* side of things. His power is to guide the body through its dying life to a human death, accepting the body as, not the carapace of the self, but the self *itself*. And thus Jack Kevorkian—whom I regard as a rather heroic fellow—is a legitimate heir of Asclepius, defending the right of humans to possess their lives and their lives' ends away from the desiccation of life-support plumbing and so-called "heroic measures." It's a different kind of medicine, a different kind of mission. Like storytelling itself, it seeks to lead you into, rather than away from, your life. It's why Socrates's last words, in the *Phaedo*, are a reminder to make a sacrifice to Asclepius: for a life well and truly lived.

Science fiction boasts less healers than it does doctors, just because its concern is—whether it recognizes it or not—with the anxiety, the inescapable *malaise*, of the gnostic urge. Fleeing the body, it always returns to the body. And that paradox is not just its real glory, but its connection with the central myths of our culture. As G. K. Chesterton says, there are two ways of getting home, and one of them is to stay there. Sf, gorgeously, takes the long way around. Let me conclude with two texts without comment.

The last written, and my least favorite, of the gospels, that of John (circa 120 C.E.) gives us a gnostic Jesus, a strange visitor from another planet, who would be quite at home in sf. John's Jesus is a luminous being, hardly *there* save for his *obiter dicta*: in John's Last Supper, there isn't even a sharing of the bread and wine among the twelve, just a long, rather tedious monologue by the Christ. Food, after all, is a tawdry thing for the true gnostic to much about with. John's Jesus, effectively, is a resurrected being even before the resurrection.

In the Gospel of Luke (circa 90–100 C.E.), on the other hand, the *most* narrative of the gospels, Jesus is a figure in and of the world, in and of the body. It is Luke alone of the evangelists who tells the birth of the babe; Luke alone who sets the Sermon on the Mount not on a mount (an exalted place) but on a plain (a man speaking to men); and Luke alone who tells the most wonderful of the post-resurrection narratives. Listen:

The tomb has been found empty, and no one knows what that means. The next day, two disciples are walking to the town of Emmaus. A stranger—Jesus, of course—joins them, talking with them about the things of God and man, but they don't recognize him. They urge him to come to dinner with them. They recline to eat. And, in Luke's sublime phrase, "they recognized Him in the breaking of the bread": in the life of *this* body, in the body of *this* life, in the holy complexity of human time. Luke's risen Jesus is less "the Christ" than he is the ratification of our life as we live it. I think Luke's Jesus could have shared a cup or two with Plato's Socrates.

And sf—like us all—is torn between the two gospels, and fortunately falls back from John's transcendence into Luke's immanence, keeping us sane (a word which in Latin also means "healthy," in the only sense of "health" that makes sense). Early legends about Luke, of course and rightly, described him as a physician.

"The imperfect is our paradise," says Wallace Stevens.[6] The fallible, dying, and sensuous body is our only real Pleroma. And like the travelers to Emmaus, we recognize God—and ourselves—in that most gloriously mortal of activities, the breaking of the bread.

Notes

1. Christopher Hitchens, *The Missionary Position: Mother Teresa in Theory and Practice* (London: Verso, 1995), 41–42.

2. W. B. Yeats, "A Dialogue of Self and Soul," in Yeats, *The Collected Poems of W. B. Yeats* (1933; New York: Macmillan, 1956), 232.

3. C. S. Lewis, *Perelandra* (1944; New York: Macmillan, 1964), 82.

4. Alexander Pope, "Epistle to Dr. Arbuthnot," in Pope, *Alexander Pope's Collected Poems*, edited by Bonamy Dobrée (London: Everyman's Library, 1956), 257.

5. Alfred Lord Whitehead, *Process and Reality*, Corrected Edition, edited by David Ray Griffin and Donald W. Sherburne (New York: Free Press, 1978), 5.

6. Wallace Stevens, "The Poems of Our Climate," in Stevens, *The Collected Poems of Wallace Stevens* (New York: Alfred A. Knopf, 1954), 144.

4

No Cure for the Future: How Doctors Struggle to Survive in Science Fiction

Kirk Hampton and Carol MacKay

Is There a Doctor in the House?

Our study focuses on what might be considered the classic mode of science fiction—stories projecting a technologically advanced future, or those in which change takes place through a signal scientific discovery or contact with an alien race; these were stories in which we felt medical doctors might be instrumental or problematical. Of less interest to us were worlds in which little or no chronological or scientific advance is featured, such as parallel universes, alternate histories, settings less advanced than present-day Earth, post-apocalyptic futures, horror, and fantasy. Within our parameters, we wanted to see what happens to doctors as technological healers of the body—and as characters. Doctors in our present-day lives and in mainstream fiction are intriguing figures, men and women whose activities are often crucially important in shaping individual lives at the most intimate level. Doctors outside of science fiction loom in our minds as powerful and complex figures—healers and decision-makers who apply both technical knowledge and a degree of craftsman-like intuition to their work; flawed figures who seem alternately arrogant and compassionate, hated and admired, ignorant and wise.

However, when we began searching the field, we immediately ran into some peculiarities. First of all, it was a good deal harder to find doctors as potent, three-dimensional characters than we had expected, and we found a much greater population of such doctors in film and television than in fiction. Moreover, the stories involving doctors usually take place in the present or only a small step into the future. In more far-reaching accounts, doctors virtually disappear, and even the stories in which doctors attain stardom have certain unusual qualities. This fact suggested that the science fiction future is bad for doctors, so we looked more closely to find out why. We found a plethora of doctors helpless in the face of mysterious plagues or invulnerable aliens, faceless villains, technicians using magical devices to cure denizens of the future, and machines, robots, and holograms replacing human doctors altogether. What we did *not* find was an abundance of healers—high-tech doctors employing futuristic techniques on futuristic diseases, wielding speculative medical tools to heal humans with invented diseases or ailing aliens.[1] And intriguingly, when we found such elements, certain qualities attached themselves to the stories, as if a special protective environment were required for such events to occur.

The problematic universe that science fiction creates for doctors is well-illustrated by Groff Conklin and Noah D. Fabricant's anthology, *Great Science Fiction about Doctors: Eighteen Choice Tales of the Outermost Worlds of Medicine*, in which relatively few medical doctors actually appear. Many of these short stories were apparently selected because they were written *by* doctors, and several do not fit within the genre of science fiction in the first place. Even when doctors are present, they are usually not the focus of the story, and only five or so examples treat doctoring as central.[2] Another case in point is Ward Moore's *Caduceus Wild*, a novel in which physicians rule the world. Yet the novel is not really about doctors—it concerns a group of "Abnormals" and their efforts to escape their dystopian world. By and large, the physicians are peripheral, existing as ghostly, horrific villains.

Later in this chapter, we develop a theory of the symbology of "classic" science fiction that will show more precisely why doctors are an endangered species, if they dare to show up in the confines of the genre. For now we can generalize, borrowing an idea from Frank McConnell, that doctors rarely dominate the world of written science fiction because their business is with the body—and science fiction is a world almost never concerned with the issues of physical frailty and malfunction. By the same token, however, the science fiction universe is clearly one in which medical problems might conceivably occur; the people and other creatures in science fiction generally grow old and can be wounded. Illness may not be often mentioned, but here again, the average science fiction universe at least theoretically has diseases. Because even the most rapid-fire works of written science fiction occur in virtual slow-motion as compared with television shows and films, a look at the rhetorical techniques of several works can give us a preliminary view of how—and to some extent why—the science fiction environment might be toxic to doctors.

When entering the slow-moving, extrapolated universe of textual science fiction, the reader instinctively wonders about the role and importance of the physical bodies of the characters (most especially the protagonists), and science fiction authors betray a corresponding intuition that this is a question that must be disposed of—usually, the more quickly the better—a fact which is made evident, as often as not, on the very first page. This phenomenon might be called "the disposal of the body question," and science fiction writers employ a variety of rhetorical devices to answer our unconscious query about why we will not need to think about physicality—and hence, medicine. The general technique is to disarm the reader by first making an issue of physicality and then rhetorically dismissing the issue. This moment generally occurs quite early in the work, if not at the very outset. The method serves as an explanation of why the story is not going to be concerned with the body question.

Several passages from landmark texts can demonstrate this procedure at work. Larry Niven brings off the effect in his usual elegant fashion on the first page of *Ringworld*, where the central figure, Louis Wu, is described as having "pearly, perfect, perfectly standard teeth." He has sneaked out of his 200th birthday party, and we are told that any partygoers who might miss him would probably assume "that a woman had gone with him."[3] As the opening of the novel continues, it becomes even clearer that Louis's concerns are not physical. He is in fact suffering from the boredom and ennui that precede most quest stories. Niven's highlighting of Wu's age, perfect health, and ongoing virility succinctly presents, then dismisses, any concern with physicality—and hence, with any need for medical care to be addressed. The body question is efficiently laid aside. Isaac Asimov's *Foundation and Empire* accomplishes the same task by using the opposite tack. Instead of being perfectly well, Emperor Cleon II is perfectly sick. "I live," he says, "if you can call it life where every scoundrel who can read a book of medicine uses me as a blank and receptive field for his feeble experiments."[4] Once Cleon vents his complaint, he and the novel get on to more important matters. Whether unneeded or ineffectual, doctors—through the implied dismissal of the body question—are laid quickly and resolutely aside in both of these science fiction yarns.

Intriguingly, Poul Anderson's *Mirkheim* sets up an intense awareness of the body by placing its human hero on a heavy-gravity planet—a setting where, presumably, an awareness of and trouble with the body might become a perennial motif of existence: "Leaving his spaceship, Benoni Strang grew violently aware of weight. . . . Flesh strained against the burden of itself." But dramatic and emotional concerns take over almost immediately. By the end of the scene—less than two pages later—the story's true dynamics have completely reversed the concern with physicality and weight that began the segment. "The dream in Strang flared upward," Anderson writes, and the passage closes in a world of weightless thought forms.[5] In similar fashion, John Brunner in *The Shockwave Rider* takes a view of physicality apparently as extreme as Anderson's—but the illusion disappears just as rapidly. His novel begins with a stark description of a man in a "bare steel chair . . . as naked as the room's white walls."[6] Immediately after this description, however, the focus turns to the man's remarkable career as creator of an endless number of cybernetic personae, and within a few paragraphs we dip briefly into one of his fantasies, then another, then yet another—till the vivid fleshly existence we saw at first has been utterly laid aside and the novel propels us into its true areas of interest.[7]

Doctors as Greek Chorus

Science fiction doctors are most often denizens of the present or near future, and they would seem to be a hapless lot. Usually minimal characters, they frequently serve as Greek chorus in films dealing with alien invasions. They proclaim the mystery and power of the situation at hand, in statements such as "I've never seen anything like it!" "This renders medical science totally obsolete!" or "It has healing powers beyond anything we can understand!" The physician in *The Blob* (1958) barely has time to recognize the mystery embodied in the creature before he is eaten by it. The doctor in *The Incredible Shrinking Man* (1957) tells the shrinking man that he is shrinking—for reasons unknown, and with no known cure. The ship's physician in *Forbidden Planet* (1956) formally announces the evolutionary impossibility of the monster. This helplessness permeates the genre. Even Dr. McCoy's oft-repeated "He's *dead*, Jim!" in the original *Star Trek* series has some of this quality. After all, coming from a doctor, it is a statement of total defeat.[8] One especially poignant example is a briefly seen doctor in *The Day the Earth Stood Still* (1951). An alien from an advanced civilization heals a bullet wound in himself with a touch of ointment from a ridiculously tiny vial. The flabbergasted physician shakes his head at this feat and declares he's either going to give up medicine or go out and get drunk. Besides proclaiming the magnitude of the alien's technology, this doctor is painfully aware of his imminent uselessness. We haven't even stepped into the future, and already the doctors are irrelevant.

The doctors who do elbow their way to center stage—those who try a little harder—do not often enjoy illustrious careers and comfortable retirements. *Au contraire.* Some of them have achieved mythological status for the very magnitude of their failures—or else the ironic consequences of their successes. Dr. Frankenstein, Dr. Jekyll, Dr. Tyrell in the 1982 film *Blade Runner*—all are split, shattered, and crushed by their own medical audacity. Notice, too, that these characters have somewhat lost their precise definition as doctors, and seem rather to be hybrids, such as doctor-researcher, doctor-entrepreneur, and doctor-lunatic. Even Murray Leinster's Med Service hero, Calhoun—a much more freewheeling figure—would seem to compound the amalgam; Conklin and Fabricant refer quite casually to his combined designation as "physician-pilot-sociologist-teacher" (198). Science fiction seems to cause doctors to morph into other roles.[9] And like doctors, the technicians who so often replace them are systematically diminished—betraying the fragmented and disconnected qualities we see in bona fide science fiction doctors.

The dominant pattern of impotence and irrelevance, disintegration and obliteration, suggests that doctors of the science fiction universe are in contact with some highly destructive substance or energy, against which they are grossly overmatched. As if aware of their situation, these harried physicians reveal some psychological oddities. For example, they do seem somewhat anal retentive. The doctors in *The Andromeda Strain* (1970) must scrub down any number of times and operate behind protective shields, gloves, mechanical devices, and plastic suits. The interstellar doctors in James White's Sector General novels must maintain both physical and psychological purity at all costs. The space hospital is crammed with hermetic seals and buffers, and even stray thoughts or (heaven forbid) emotions trying to rise up from the subconscious must be spotted and sanitized—lest they endanger the ship's clean-running efficiency. Even McCoy has such a moment in the 1968 *Star Trek* episode where he has to re-implant "Spock's Brain." At first—artificially jazzed with superhuman abilities—he does fine, but as the effects wear off he freaks out over the impossible tidying-up job he has to do. There is a similar, rampant anxiety about disorder in the well-populated subgenres featuring mutant viruses, plagues, and alien invasions—three contexts that invariably marginalize doctors, as they are rendered innocuous or forced to abdicate their power to the military posthaste.

If the doctors' world drives them toward neurosis, it also exacts masochistic forms of self-protection from them—a partitioning off, denial, or even destruction of portions of their most intimate emotional being. Thus, while sexuality sometimes makes an initial appearance in these stories, the doctors often have to enact a radical separation from their own sexuality—an especially painful part of the doctors' isolation. The doctor's sexuality in *Invasion of the Body Snatchers* is split off from him in the course of the 1956 film; the scene in which he pitchforks the pod version of his lover effectively ends it. In the 1931 film, *Dr. Jekyll and Mr. Hyde,* Jekyll's sexuality is initially central to his relationship with his fiancée, but is split off from him in his persona of Hyde. Even Hyde's possession of the lower-class woman is sadistic rather than sexual, so once again, images of psychological sundering proliferate around science fiction doctors. In one episode of *Star Trek*, "The Man Trap" (1966), a past love of McCoy's makes an appearance—but turns out to be an illusion-projecting monster sucking the life from humans and using its disguise to manipulate McCoy; in the climax of the episode, McCoy is forced to shoot the apparency of his former lover. This story shows the doctor violently rending his sexuality from himself. In these stories, the split occurs in relation to an exact duplicate of the lover. Other works—such as Robert Louis Stevenson's *The Strange Case of Dr. Jekyll and Mr. Hyde*—employ a second character who seems to serve as a shadow of the first. The double or shadow image in these cases is a crystallization of science fiction doctors' need to psychically break themselves apart.[10]

Some doctors have their sexuality divorced from them in less direct ways. The heroes of *Outland* (1981) and *Outbreak* (1995) suffer separation and literal divorce. Tyrell's huge, lonely bedroom was known on the set of *Blade Runner* as "the Pope's bedroom," conveying a virtually asexual connotation. In *Fantastic Voyage* (1966), the doctor is a philosophical dreamer, so caught up in his inner world that he doesn't even notice that his assistant is an admiring Raquel Welch. For a male doctor, the love of a good and attractive woman establishes his credentials as a worthwhile person, even if the relationship cannot develop or last. And this connotation renders the necessary separation even more poignant. The woman's frequently seen status as an illusion or alien serves as a symbol for the science fiction physician's relationship to his sexuality, to bonding social institutions such as family, and to other humankind in general. Two of the women doctors in the genre—Dr. Lazarus in *Outland* and Dr. Reynolds in *Brainstorm* (1983)—also seem to be separated from their sexuality, but in a nonviolent manner. Each woman is in contact with an attractive male, but no physical love is implied. Sexual implications are further offset by the demeanor and visual presentation of these characters, which seem to suggest that sex is irrelevant to them. Drs. Lazarus and Reynolds both have substance-abuse problems, which may be a subdued variation on the self-violence or self-damage often necessary for the science fiction doctor.

Another epidemic among science fiction doctors also has a psychoanalytic ring—an immense concern about inadequacy. Recall the crestfallen physician in *The Day the Earth Stood Still*—dismayed at the potency of the space visitor's tiny vial—or Bones worrying about losing his touch. It is often the doctor's job to declare, "Our weapons are useless!" But this anxiety about order, containment, and adequacy reveals something more significant than these psychological allusions. It suggests the science fiction doctor's instability of self. This precariousness sometimes takes the form of rigid overinsistence ("I'm a *doctor*, damn it!"), sometimes obsessional fixation—as with Victor Frankenstein and Nathaniel Hawthorne's Aylmer in "The Birthmark." And despite such mechanisms, the minds and personalities of these doctors do undergo sudden changes, shifts, and splits, suggesting that whatever they are up against has the psychological power to warp their very selves. The hero in *Invasion of the Body Snatchers* mentally and emotionally disintegrates from the strain of his experiences. James White's Sector General surgeons are subject to schizophrenia and nightmares. And Stevenson's Dr. Jekyll develops literature's most famous split personality.

This sundering of selves—brought about by the constant time pressure, isolation, and need for suppressive behavior—amounts to literal insanity. As Gary Westfahl points out elsewhere in this volume, the doctors of Sector General in their remote space hospital have problems maintaining their sanity. So does the harried, sleep-deprived physician-hero of *Invasion of the Body Snatchers*. In the movie *Lifeforce* (1985), one unlucky doctor has a complete mental breakdown as the corpse on which he is performing an autopsy suddenly reanimates and starts sucking the life out of his colleagues—a graphic instance of a mysterious force destroying science fiction doctors. Even success can threaten these unfortunate practitioners, as we see in James Whale's 1931 film *Frankenstein*; at the hair-raising moment when the creature gains life, his creator goes briefly but transcendently mad. A large percentage of the mad scientists in the field could be—and often are—called "mad doctors."[11]

Inside the Bell Jar

Usually irrelevant or destroyed by the end of the stories they are in, science fiction doctors of the mid-twentieth century only rarely survive the trip into the twenty-first—and the physicians we happen to meet in that more distant future have two distinct mechanisms that seem to protect them. One is what we call their "time bubble" or "anachronistic shield." The time bubble surrounding these featured doctors symbolically and psychologically connects them to the past—when doctors could more safely exist—and the association with more hospitable times seems to protect them against the pressures so prevalent to their kind. L. Ron Hubbard's Ole Doc Methuselah is treated as a curmudgeonly, walking anachronism, a wandering frontier physician (Leinster's Calhoun is clearly modeled after Hubbard's character). The planets Doc and Calhoun travel to are generally more primitive than our present-day Earth, so these swashbuckling doctors move freely in a very large bubble of past time. Like Doc Methuselah, the crusty Dr. Lazarus in the movie *Outland* is fittingly named.

Dr. McCoy ("Bones") of *Star Trek* is, as his nickname implies, a man resolutely out of his time. His safety bubble exists in his own irascible personality, which stands in stark contrast to the gung-ho denizens of the twenty-third century like Kirk and Spock. This aspect of Bones's character is played up in *Star Trek: The Motion Picture* (1979), where his first appearance suggests that—free of the enforced modernity of Star Fleet—he has reverted to an old-time, country doctor, complete with bushy beard and rustic attire. Terrorized by the glitchy transporter, he seems to see it as a newfangled contraption he's glad to have been away from, and he must be drafted into the adventure that Spock and Kirk are beside themselves to plunge into. In a later film, *Star Trek III: The Search for Spock* (1984), McCoy's protective association with the past makes him an appropriate repository for the deceased Spock's disembodied memories.

Their necessary bond with the past exacts from these futuristic physicians a severe price in the form of *isolation*—yet it simultaneously serves as their second protective mechanism. Isolation seems to afflict science fiction doctors in whatever century they work, but like the time shield, it also seems somewhat necessary for them. They may actually need seclusion in order to function; certainly they think they do. Consider Frankenstein in his laboratory, Tyrell in his huge bedroom, or the virus-hunters of *The Andromeda Strain* in their hypersterilized hideaway. And to return to McCoy's constant assertions that he's "a *doctor*, damn it," we can perceive a humorous touch of isolation in that line, as if the doctor needed to reaffirm that he is not playing some other role—one that might connect him to the future folks he has fallen in with. In its more extreme forms (as with Frankenstein, Aylmer, and their ilk), this isolation melds into obsessiveness and insanity, ever-present perils for the doctor of tomorrow.

Dr. Crusher of the television series *Star Trek: The Next Generation* seems superficially to be a thoroughly contemporary woman, but like most futuristic medical doctors, she is essentially characterized in terms of the past (in Crusher's case, the loss of her husband). She is never fully in the present, and the episodes featuring her emphasize the extreme isolation that comes with being out of one's time. It is Crusher who spends an entire episode ("Remember Me," 1990) locked in an alternate *Enterprise* where other members of the crew gradually disappear—until she is alone in a universe which is running out of time and will soon cease to exist. As for the nameless "Emergency Medical Program" in the *Star Trek: Voyager* television series, a mere holographic projection, he disappears when there's no one to treat—out of time much of the time. And his charmingly priggish personality has some of the old-fashionedness of McCoy. The EMP's anonymity suggests a high degree of isolation, and two episodes featuring this character have thrown him into alternate universes which only he can enter. It is fitting that one episode deals with a confusion between reality and illusion—the stuff of insanity—while the other casts the doctor into the thoroughly anachronistic world of knights and swordplay.

Of Timelocks, Energy Vacuums, and Pariahs

Turning now to those specialized stories where doctors actually take center stage or dominate the action, their ubiquitous diffusion and marginalization are countered by an unvarying pattern of three interlocking features—an *energy vacuum*, a *timelock*, and a state of *social ostracization*. First of all, the physician-heroes exist in extremely moribund surroundings. There's plenty of excitement in *Fantastic Voyage*, but it does take place within the body of a comatose man, on the verge of death, whose body has been cooled as much as possible to further slow down his metabolism, and whose heart must even be stopped so the minuscule voyagers can scurry through it. In one scene, full-sized doctors and nurses have to hold their breath while the microscopic crew sail through the inner ear. That's what you call a low-energy environment. *The Andromeda Strain* occurs in a deeply buried tomb of sterility and silence, so void of vitality that the doctor-hero becomes romantically involved with the voice of the computer. *Invasion of the Body Snatchers* takes place in a nightmarish psychological and emotional void; whole identities—bodies, minds, and emotions—are absorbed by the invaders, creating a radical vacuum of communication and relationships. The hero finds himself cut off from the world, isolated emotionally, and finally pursued by soulless zombies.

In addition to taking place within an energy and emotional vacuum, these unique stories feature a distinct time pressure or timelock. An extension of the anachronistic shield, this urgency seems to protect the doctors in these stories—or even enhance their (temporary) powers. Both *The Andromeda Strain* and *Fantastic Voyage* employ a highly defined, strict time limit on the protagonists' activities, as does Arthur Porges's tale starring a microscopic alien surgeon, "Emergency Operation." The "heart-stopping" scene in *Fantastic Voyage* even functions as a timelock within a timelock. *Body Snatchers* is a paranoid extravaganza of haste and constant flight—a nightmare world where you can't even take time to sleep. *The Andromeda Strain* employs the timelock to ironic, as well as dramatic, effect, since the isolated physicians are deceived about how much time they have. Incorrectly thinking that the spread of the virus has been halted aboveground, they are aware only of the smaller, inner time constraints they subject themselves to, while a huge time bomb ticks away upstairs. The time pressure thus exists as another indication of the fundamental irrelevance of the doctors in this story. Other stories where doctors can be the heroes tend to parallel this absence of vitality combined with a timelock—as, for example, the doctors in Alan E. Nourse's *Star Surgeon* and Lee Correy's *Space Doctor*, with a limited time before the plague planet dies or the stranded survivors run out of oxygen. The cramped, almost parodic quality in the "vacuum" stories suggests that doctors require diminished surroundings to look good.

The environments in which science fiction doctors can briefly thrive have to be carefully engineered, for these physicians cannot survive in a complete vacuum, any more than they can thrive in a future world bursting with advanced technology and vital energy. Even in their narrow ecological niche, these doctors (and others who play a merely supporting role) have been cast out, disgraced, or ostracized, and their wounded natures are often expressed by an addiction to drugs or drink. *Alien3* (1992) occurs in a time, energy, and emotive vacuum so intense it makes the preceding movies of the trilogy seem like musical comedies by comparison. Clemons—the first human physician of the series—is serving time for fatal blunders committed while on a drunk. Likewise, the doctor with the appropriately *déclassé* name of Spider in the film *Johnny Mnemonic* (1995) has been cast out of society and his profession. A similar painful isolation surrounds Dr. Heidegger in Hawthorne's "Dr. Heidegger's Experiment" (his ministrations killed his fiancée on his wedding night) and the protagonist of *Body Snatchers*, whose former friends and neighbors become zombies trying to track him down, while the two men hearing his story are fitting him for a straitjacket. The doctors in *Fantastic Voyage* and *The Andromeda Strain* seem to be under suspicion, while obsessive figures such as Drs. Frankenstein, Rappaccini, and Jekyll suffer a similar fate, existing in an asocial netherworld. In most of these cases, the doctor's role as outcast has come about through a fatal excess of heart. Science fiction doctors can play briefly significant roles in their vacuum worlds—so long as the vacuum isn't too intense—but they have a superfluity of anachronistic emotions that renders them vulnerable. Even the vacuum that keeps them alive hurts them.

Symbolism and Displacement

Having developed this rather sad view of doctors in science fiction, we came upon another intriguing phenomenon. Nonmedical characters in the genre—particularly groups of them—can often be interpreted as symbolic doctors. For example, the Jupiter expedition at the end of Stanley Kubrick and Arthur C. Clarke's *2001: A Space Odyssey* (1968) is like a symbolic M.D. probing a mysterious growth. Dave Bowman, the isolated survivor of the expedition, has to contain the epidemic of death—as it has metastasized to HAL, the psychotic computer—by performing time-reversing brain surgery on HAL from the protective isolation of his spacesuit. His medical career doesn't last much longer, of course, as he soon encounters the ambivalent "disease" and is completely absorbed. The scientists at the climax of *Close Encounters of the Third Kind* (1977) try to conduct a physical exam, but are overwhelmed by the vitality of their patient. They act much like the literal doctors we have seen—hiding out in a sealed environment where no one can see them (the area around the ground is literally and lethally sprayed) and arranging their tools very neatly, but their most important exploratory instrument, the electronic organ, is abruptly removed from the player's hands as greater forces take over. In this eminently happy medical encounter, the past literally walks onto the scene, as abductees from bygone eras emerge from the ship—pure symbols of the past into which doctors revert.

Similarly, in *Blade Runner* the series of genetic engineers we meet function as a communal if fragmented doctor, from whom their creation, the "replicant" Roy Batty, is seeking medical attention (i.e., to extend his four-year lifespan). In both Terminator films (*The Terminator*, 1984, and *Terminator 2: Judgment Day*, 1991), two figures from the future arrive in our world—one good and one evil —and in both stories, the virtuous time-traveler engages in activities parallel to those of doctors. Having reversed time—always helpful to the science fiction doctor—each has to forestall a terminal illness without being "infected." Like literal doctors in the genre, both of these terminator-fighters obsessively leave no stone unturned (the second one even has himself destroyed, to prevent contamination), and both develop an intimate relationship with the past they have traveled to—in keeping with science fiction doctors' natural affinity with the past. As for the evil terminators, they seem able to incorporate people into themselves and to mutate (vocally in the first movie, physically in the second) like viruses.

Even alien invaders function as symbolic "super-doctors." They usually heal themselves miraculously and sometimes perform physicals on the people of the target world. The sentient varieties often impersonate and even duplicate us; at the very least, they seem to know everything about us. The genre is also full of alien races whose entire interest in earth is medical, such as handling sterility problems (*I Married a Monster from Outer Space*, 1958; *Mars Needs Women*, 1966) or saving a dying world (*This Island Earth*, 1955). Machines can make the grade, too, comporting themselves like doctors. In *2001*, HAL sees himself as sterilizing the ship for the health of the mission. In *Alien* (1979), the android poseur, Ash, performs a physical on an ailing crewman—but is really acting as midwife for the dormant alien. The robot Gort in *The Day the Earth Stood Still* conducts a lifesaving medical procedure on the man from space, who then goes on to warn earth about the health risks it is about to take. His visit is clearly prophylactic in nature.

Dwelling in a universe filled with displaced symbols of themselves may contribute to the uncertainty about self-definition we have observed in science fiction doctors. In *Body Snatchers*, the hero keeps making strangely self-deprecating remarks about his relationship to his profession; fittingly, his friend asks him if he can forget that he is a doctor—and then immediately calls upon his expertise *as* a doctor. (The film is more elliptical about this situation than is the novel.) The *Star Trek: Voyager* holographic physician is himself an embodiment of self-definition and mutability problems. Sometimes changing shape and size, he recurrently disappears, partially or wholly, and the issue of finding a name for himself keeps popping up. Even the egotistical Tyrell demarcates himself from his handiwork. At Roy's appearance, he first utters the classic doctor's line, "What seems to be the problem?" Roy replies "Death," and Tyrell suddenly divorces himself from the proceedings by saying, with uncharacteristic modestly, "I'm afraid that's a little out of my jurisdiction."[12] We also see considerable self-esteem problems in *The Day the Earth Stood Still* for the doctors who are studying the unearthly visitor, Klaatu: "He was very nice about it, but he made me feel like a third-class witch-doctor." Understandably, a recurrent emotion amongst science fiction doctors (subsisting in a world teeming with fragmented images of themselves) is despair.[13]

Mary Shelley's prototypical science fiction tale *Frankenstein* does it both ways, symbolically embodying the shattering of a doctor's psyche in the literal image of the creature. If Victor's quest is initially the penetration of the mystery of life, it soon turns into a ghastly project of combining out-of-scale body parts. Condignly, the monstrous embodiment of this quest isolates Victor from his fellow humans and possibly from himself (i.e., from his sanity, as his personality disintegrates), and ultimately destroys his marriage, his great attempt to bond with another. In point of fact, the creature's motley construction is an ironic symbol for the struggle of medicine within science fiction. Pieced together out of individuals who have already broken apart, the monster becomes alive in a parodic sense—it is itself radically isolated, radically disintegrated, and destructive of Frankenstein's own coherence and connectedness.

The Vital Force

Our theory took shape when we hypothesized that the factor minimalizing doctors—dispersing them into symbols, or tearing apart their psyches—might itself constitute the subject matter of the genre. Our contention is that science fiction doctors are indeed up against something very powerful, overwhelmed or absorbed by a principle which dominates the genre and is often treated as if it were the mightiest force in the universe. In its pure form, this force manifests itself in some of the most sublime and awesome images in the genre—images such as the Mother Ship in *Close Encounters*; Stanislaw Lem's protean, sentient planet Solaris; the mindblowingly huge machine "V'ger" from *Star Trek: The Motion Picture*; the monolith in *2001: A Space Odyssey*; and the machinery of the Krell in *Forbidden Planet*.[14]

This idea is quite difficult to represent. Its depiction in film requires inspired artistry and technical expertise; its depiction in literature requires exceptional imaginative and verbal power. A good textual example can be found at the climax of Clarke's novel *2001: A Space Odyssey*, when astronaut David Bowman encounters an almost unimaginable alien technology:

[H]e literally could not describe what he was seeing.
    He had been hanging above a large, flat rectangle. . . . But now it seemed to be receding from him. . . . Impossibly, incredibly, it was no longer a monolith rearing above a flat plane. What had seemed to be its roof had dropped away to infinite depths; for one dizzy moment, he seemed to be looking down into a vertical shaft—a rectangular duct which defied the laws of perspective, for its size did not decrease with distance.

Still under the spell of this force, Bowman later looks on in awe:

He knew . . . that he was watching the operation of some gigantic mind. . . . [He] moved into a realm of consciousness that no man had experienced before.
    At first, it seemed that Time itself was running backward. . . . The springs of memory were being tapped; in controlled recollection, he was reliving the past.[15]

Entities such as Clarke's mystical monolith share some important qualities. First, they are *mind-bending*—alluring yet possessed of deadly power, evoking disturbing connections to repressed memories, possibly possessing an ambiguous, alien intelligence, and sometimes invading characters' minds. Secondly, these images *bend space*, as it were, with their ability to change form, to project different forms, and to absorb things, often merging discrepant qualities within themselves or even holding within themselves microcosmic versions of reality. And thirdly, they seem to *bend time* by causing or else undergoing rebirth, dormancy, and reverse movement in time—sometimes amounting to an "erasure" of things or events.

    This recurrent image is a profoundly ambivalent, ultimately incomprehensible power that embodies life, but is not contained by it. Primal and pervasive, beautiful and threatening, it constitutes the essential force of life and of intelligence, but it is also the power of horror and death. It is not hard to see the fascination with these qualities in science fiction; they resonate with associations to the human psyche and also suggest intriguing parallels to technology itself. Indeed, this complex and compelling symbol is an archetype specific to the technological age. It appears in overt form in *Forbidden Planet* and *2001* and reaches its apotheosis in some of the Promethean texts and films of the 1970s, such as *Close Encounters* and *Star Trek: The Motion Picture*. The images of these works seem to combine qualities of the quest, the shadow, the tempter/temptress, the mother, and the trickster, and are best interpreted as an expression of our complex attitudes toward technology—and technology's relationship to our own minds and emotions.[16]

    Before showing how embodiments of this factor affect doctors in science fiction, we should note that it appears not just as intense crystallizations like Solaris and the Mother Ship, but in fact pervades the genre—at times almost to the point of obsession. The creature in *Alien*, for example, carries implications of dormancy, rebirth, shape-changing and inhuman intelligence, with possible connotations of psychological repression. Monsters in general are endlessly reborn, and a large percentage of them change shape and/or merge with other entities. In both the TV series and films of *Star Trek*, Mr. Spock is seen sometimes as an alien intelligence, sometimes as a seething mass of repression, other times still as being split between opposing halves. He can merge with other minds, and his body is reborn in *The Search for Spock*—a process that involves a sort of time-reversal, as he has to recapitulate the stages of biological growth. The terminators of both films also bristle with these ambiguous features—time-traveling, polymorphous, apparently sentient. Darth Vader from the *Star Wars* saga seems like a walking embodiment of repressed emotions, and his nefarious deeds include freezing Han Solo (dormancy and rebirth) and attempting to absorb Luke Skywalker into his dark world, animated by a mighty but alien intelligence. And Ringworld, Larry Niven's breathtaking extrapolation of hard science, has a mysterious, alien intelligence behind it, suggests a lost or frozen past, and contains within itself full-scale "maps" of Earth and the other planets. And even E. E. "Doc" Smith's Lensman series— whose stories comprise among the most gung-ho exemplars of staggering future technological progress—presents a succinct crystallization of some undefined yet potent energy which animates the universe he has created:

The Lens is a lenticular structure of hundreds of thousands of tiny crystalloids, built and tuned to match the individual life force—the ego, the personality—of one individual entity. While not, strictly speaking, alive, it is endowed with a sort of pseudo-life by virtue of which it gives off a strong, characteristically-changing, polychromatic light as long as it is in circuit with the living mentality with which it is in synchronization. Conversely, when worn by anyone except its owner, it not only remains dark, but it kills; so strongly does its pseudo-life interfere with any life to which it is not attuned. It is also a telepathic communicator of astounding power and range—and other things.[17]

We call this meta-archetype "the vital force," a name which itself recalls many motifs and titles of the genre—the "force" of *Star Wars*, countless mysterious energy sources or threats, and resonant movie titles such as *Lifeforce* and *The Lifeforce Experiment*.[18] One episode of the television series *Star Trek: The Next Generation* is entitled "Force of Nature." (We saw a *Star Trek* yarn on the Internet called *Primal Forces*.) The term has a familiar ring because its basic qualities permeate the science fiction stories we are exploring to a remarkable degree. As for doctors, their symbolic job within the realm of science fiction is usually that of portioning out small, precisely measured quantities of the vital force. Science fiction—understandably enraptured by the possibilities of this possibly infinite energy—is not very interested in such a nitpicking vocation. In fact, the job of doctor runs against the very grain of the stories they find themselves in. No wonder they want to quit or get drunk! But at least doctors are somewhat familiar with the vital force, and this modest expertise explains their oft-seen role as Greek chorus.

They are able to recognize the vital force in its untamed state and authoritatively pronounce it as such. The Dr. Frankensteins and Tyrells of the science fiction universe release excessive quantities of the vital force—and are unable to contain it. Doctors of a more distant future, where the vital force really cuts loose, can exist only as out-of-time figures within a protective bubble of anachronism.

As we have already noted, various characters and groups of characters seem to take on the quality of doctors in science fiction, and we can now explain this occurrence. Handling a tricky substance like the vital force necessitates certain recognizable, and even extreme, forms of action, so virtually anyone dealing with it will tend to act in a manner parallel to that of doctors. But in high-tech futures, where healing is unnecessary (or in the dystopias, where it is not an option[19]), science fiction's fascination with extreme environments all but precludes the meaningful presence of literal doctors as substantive characters.

Variations on the Theme

Doctors in science fiction resemble overspecialized animals or plants that can survive only within a very narrow range of conditions. Stories such as *Fantastic Voyage*, *Invasion of the Body Snatchers*, and *The Andromeda Strain* supply the highly specific environment that these characters require. These stories comprise a subcategory of science fiction which provides a time, energy, and emotional vacuum that protects doctors on a large scale much as the anachronistic bubble protected them on a small scale, but is not so intense as to rule out that necessary quantity of the vital force the doctors need to fulfill their specialized functions. If their vulnerable roles sometimes force science fiction doctors to behave in an overly meticulous fashion, the requirements for their optimum survival seem to be similarly precise. As if existing in carefully constructed terrariums, the doctors of these stories play out shrunken-down, mock epics—parodic quests that are undercut by their isolation, their stature as wounded outcasts, and by various ironies related to reality/illusion, self-definition/identity, and scale.

There are peculiarities of scale in these vacuum-worlds. The doctors in *Invasion of the Body Snatchers*, *Fantastic Voyage*, Porges's "Emergency Operation," and *The Andromeda Strain* have tremendous difficulty completing absurdly small journeys—ones that are effortless under normal circumstances. These short trips become mock-quests which work quite well dramatically, but seem absurd in retrospect. The hero of *Body Snatchers* is basically trying to leave town—and a small town at that. At the climax of *The Andromeda Strain*, the key figure is just trying to get from one floor to another; and of course the "fantastic voyagers" and the alien micro-micro-surgeon of "Emergency Operation" are traveling the shortest distances of all.

Within this pressurized environment, doctors seem to be saving the world, but their success is undercut by problems of identity, definition, and the blurring of illusion and reality. Definitional questions—particularly as applied to the doctors themselves—come to the fore, and the viewer or reader may not feel certain about who is who and what is really accomplished. The very surgeon sent to save the day in *Fantastic Voyage* may be a traitor, so the incredible efforts and fantastic technology that constitute the material of the story may be marshalled for the purpose of killing the patient. The qualifications of Dr. Mark Hall, the medical doctor in *The Andromeda Strain*, are questioned (he is accepted by the team leader, Dr. Jeremy Stone, "with the greatest reluctance" [55]), and his ambiguous identity is in fact the basis for his importance to the mission. Hall is forced upon Stone because he fulfills the Defense Department's "Odd Man Hypothesis"—his social and familial isolation makes him the most likely team member to activate the failsafe self-destruct mechanism with which the underground laboratory is equipped. To add to the irony, the doctors in *The Andromeda Strain* turn out to be irrelevant, as the virus aboveground abruptly mutates to a harmless form and, we are told, will be washed into the ocean by the rain. Apparently, the situation at the end of the tale would be the same had the doctors not been involved at all—except for one life lost as an indirect result of their efforts and, presumably, lives disrupted and a lot of money spent. *Invasion of the Body Snatchers* is a nightmare of misidentifications, the line between reality and illusion further blurred by the necessity to avoid sleep indefinitely, and the success of the quest remains disturbingly ambivalent.[20]

In keeping with a universe of delusion, shifting identities, and parodic downscaling, doctors meddling with the volatile, shape-changing aspect of the vital force often warp into medical versions of the trickster archetype.[21] The plots of doctor-centered science fiction stories frequently turn on trickery with a medical edge. For example, the characters in *Caduceus Wild* employ all manner of medically-oriented subterfuge, as non-doctors deceive doctors with phony medical records while trying to escape the Medarchy, and doctors murder other doctors in the name of surgery or feign friendship with the "patients" while secretly calling in the Medcops. Hubbard's Ole Doc Methuselah effortlessly manipulates others' perceptions of the facts, while again and again, Leinster's Calhoun deceives whole planets in his efforts to heal. Even Dr. Full, a washed-up doctor of the present day who receives high-tech medical equipment from the distant future in C. M. Kornbluth's 1950 story, "The Little Black Bag," dupes the world, his miraculous medical skills wholly contained within his futuristic tools--which, as the story makes clear, any idiot could employ.

There is an intriguing subvariant of these quests in a vacuum, in which a doctor's powers are temporarily magnified by some outside force such an advanced race or a visitor from the future. One classic example is "The Little Black Bag"; McCoy's operation on Spock's brain is another. And the ship's doctor in *Forbidden Planet* has his intelligence vastly but fatally intensified by alien technology— significantly, at the only point in the story where he plays an essential role. The medical knowledge of James White's space surgeons in his Sector General series is temporarily enhanced by the use of "Educator tapes" containing the recorded memories of the greatest physicians of various species. An intense and pivotal scene in *Brainstorm* employs a thought-recording device to make death an enhancement of the woman doctor-researcher's perceptions and communicative abilities. In this story, as in our other examples, the elements of the "enhanced doctor" story become immediately evident. Isolated (the stricken Dr. Reynolds is working at odd hours, so her calls for help go unheard) and faced with a severe and terminal timelock in a form of a massive heart attack, the dying doctor undergoes a miniature odyssey, reaching the recording device on the other side of the room with incredible difficulty. The degree and quality of her "amplification" then proceed to animate the rest of the film. In these stories the timelock is usually built-in (the increased abilities will only last so long), but the mechanism is different. Instead of an energy vacuum formed around the doctor, the doctor is protected from the vital force in what usually proves to be a risky manner, through the extraordinary enhancement of his or her inner energy level.

The scenes and stories involving a temporary augmentation of a doctor's capabilities resemble the "vacuum" types inasmuch as their dramatic effectiveness masks an undercutting irony—and once again it is an irony of scale. If the vacuum stories are mock quests, the "zapped doctor" stories are like mock tragedies, in which the doctor oversteps his or her bounds and is condignly punished—fatally, in two of the cases just discussed. But there is a disproportion in these microtragedies that parallels the shrunken-down journeys of the doctors in a vacuum. In *Forbidden Planet*, Doc Ostrow's rise and fall is absurdly short; he dies within minutes of receiving his gift of super-intelligence. In "The Little Black Bag" the doctor's tragic flaw is ridiculously petty; he yields just once to the lucrative lure of cosmetic surgery. McCoy's moment of hubris is comical rather than fatal, as he declares the operation on Spock so easy "a child could do it," then later on pronounces it impossible. And the condign punishment of the Sector General doctors for exceeding their human bounds is relatively paltry: they're subject to alien nightmares. So even as we look at the most prominent doctors in the genre, we see almost-hidden ironies which invert, minimize, and demean their stature.

Caduceus Wild and William Morrison's short story "Bedside Manner" exemplify another variant on the "vacuum" motif. In these inverted tales, the *nonmedical* characters experience what science fiction doctors usually do. In *Caduceus Wild*, the doctors are presumably outside the bell jar, ruling the world, free of any timelocks. It is the characters in this novel who find themselves living in a vacuum (at one point in a vault), faced with innumerable pressures and timelocks, being forced to play the trickster, having enormous difficulty making extremely small journeys, and constantly dodging destruction. For example, the protagonist Larch and his companions are isolated by their anachronistic beliefs, which render them social outcasts, renegades living in a perpetual timelock of pursuit. Larch, his knee injured, can barely traverse a quarry; he thus experiences the science fiction doctor's challenge of traveling a minuscule distance.

The inversion of the doctor-in-a-vacuum formula in "Bedside Manner" places the alien physician far outside the restrictions that limit ordinary science fiction doctors. In this short story, we encounter an almost anagogical extrapolation of the qualities normally experienced by physicians in science fiction. The radically injured woman, Margaret, has no perceptions except those granted by the seemingly omnipotent alien physician, whom she never sees. Without his ministrations, neither she nor her husband could possibly survive. The mystery of her continued existence creates in her a powerful anxiety and urgency, which constitute a subjectively crushing timelock. Like doctors in a bell jar, she cannot assay a single movement, much less a journey. And except for occasional visits from the alien, she is unconscious and in a state of sensory deprivation, isolating her even from her own body. In a sense, her entire universe is a vacuum.

Two final examples project the inversion formula into the moral realm—J. R. Shango's "A Matter of Ethics" and Niven's "The Ethics of Madness." Yet another alien-enhancement story, the former partakes of some of the qualities of this inverted subtype as the elite heart surgeons, with their high-tech, alien scalpels, put the medical students and interns through some of the paces a doctor commonly experiences. These evil doctors are themselves excised when the hero makes their secret available throughout the galaxy. "The Ethics of Madness," like so many science fiction tales, all but replaces doctors with machines and technicians, and the result is another world whose inhabitants suffer from timelocks, energy vacuums, and the like. The "autodoc" literally surrounds its patients, like the "projected" doctors we have just seen, but in Niven's story, Douglas Hooker is also pressured by a strict timelock. A potential paranoid, he is warned that he must never be away from the autodoc, which can treat him for his inherited disposition, for more than two weeks. Fate tricks him when the warning bulb of his small desk autodoc burns out. By the end of the story, Hooker's madness and consequent actions isolate him, sending him outside the galaxy itself, pursued by the wronged man whose sole purpose is to kill him. At this point, he is an ancient shell of a man, tens of thousands of years old, cared for, ironically, by his shipboard autodoc.

Physician, Heal Thyself

Can science fiction doctors survive outside the bell jar—perhaps by inverting their nature as administrators of the vital force, and becoming villains, extracting the essential energy from their victims? But doctor-villains ultimately fare no better than the entrapped, virtuous practitioners on whom our study has focused. The faceless figures who want to dissect E.T., for example, are in our terms little more than specialized thieves, using their knowledge of the vital force to draw it out from the alien—whose charm and glowing forefinger mark him a rich repository of the vital force. Yet as such wicked physicians "vivisect" their victims, they suffer a parallel fate. They are often treated as fragmented or incoherent—fitting punishment for their perverted use of the vital force. The malevolent doctors (who, typical of the genre, elide into scientists) in Aldous Huxley's *Brave New World*, Anthony Burgess's *A Clockwork Orange*, *Caduceus Wild*, the 1996 film *Phenomenon*, and countless other science fiction stories exist not so much as characters as soulless, faceless fragments. In one extreme example, *Star Trek: Voyager* presents an entire race of evil "surgeons" who require a constant supply of organs from healthy species, which they obtain with gun-like medical devices. Physically, these horrific creatures are chaotically disfigured. The sequence of this sundering process is reversed in Jekyll and Hyde, where the doctor's misguided effort to segregate his own psyche results in his Hyde persona sucking the life from others. And the quasi-science fiction film *Coma* (1978), as opposed to the novel, employs a symbolic motif of division, where the unmasking of the villain comes about through a fractionated name.[22]

But if survival remains problematic for members of this beleaguered profession, the genre offers them an unexpected, anagogical triumph after all, for not just characters, but embodiments of the vital force themselves often act like doctors. It is the nature of powerful exemplars of the vital force such as V'ger and the Mother Ship to either obliterate or absorb human beings. In other words, they heal us as if we were afflicted bodies, or exterminate us as if we were the affliction itself. V'ger sees itself as a purifying doctor ridding the universe of "carbon units": a thoroughgoing specialist, Dr. V'ger scans the Enterprise once and probes it twice, taking samples and closely examining its interior before deciding which procedure to use. The similarly huge and menacing probe of *Star Trek IV: The Voyage Home* seems intent upon wiping out humanity in its efforts to locate the only form of life it is interested in, humpback whales. Clarke's *Childhood's End* and *2001* suggest that the vital force is nurturing us like sickly children. One of the characters in *Solaris* opines that the planet is performing psychic surgery on the people studying it. And the supernal technology of the Krell in *Forbidden Planet* seems to function as a general practitioner for the whole planet, constantly monitoring and safeguarding its health.

These examples of "the vital force as doctor" bring us full circle in our discussion, for despite everything, the healing profession seems to possess its own special immortality, with its features preserved and appearing everywhere. If ordinary human doctors are quickly destroyed by the vital force, they ultimately experience a rebirth within it.

Notes

1. The invention of mindblowing, futuristic diseases—along with medical people of comparable magnitude to deal with them—is a course almost wholly neglected by science fiction writers. Whether in Larry Niven's world of "autodocs" or *Star Trek: Voyager*'s realm of all-knowing computer-run holograms, the matters of sickness and health that so affect our lives are rarely mentioned.

2. Groff Conklin and Noah D. Fabricant, M.D., editors, *Great Science Fiction about Doctors: Eighteen Choice Tales of the Outermost Worlds of Medicine* (New York: Crowell-Collier, 1963); later page references in the text are to this edition. Here are the contents of this out-of-print anthology, with italics designating the five titles where physicians are *bona fide* central figures: Miles J. Breuer, M.D., "The Man without an Appetite"; Arthur C. Clarke, "Out of the Cradle, Endlessly Orbiting"; Clifton Dance, Jr., M.D., "The Brothers"; Sir Arthur Conan Doyle, M.D., "The Great Keinplatz Experiment"; Harold Fink, M.D., "Compound B"; Nathaniel Hawthorne, "Rappaccini's Daughter"; David H. Keller, M.D., "The Psychophonic Nurse"; C. M. Kornbluth, *"The Little Black Bag"*; Murray Leinster, *"Ribbon in the Sky"*; Winston K. Marks, "Mate in Two Moves"; William Morrison, *"Bedside Manner"*; Alan Nelson, "The Shopdropper"; Alan E. Nourse, M.D., "Family Resemblance"; Edgar Allan Poe, "The Facts in the Case of M. Valdemar"; Arthur Porges, *"Emergency Operation"*; J. R. Shango, *"A Matter of Ethics"*; F. L. Wallace, "Bolden's Pets"; J. A. Winter, M.D., "Expedition Mercy."

Even the publication history of the collection supports our thesis regarding the scarcity of science fiction doctors. Conklin acknowledges that his collaboration with Fabricant arose out of a challenge from Anthony Boucher (editor of *The Magazine of Fantasy and Science Fiction*), who recognized the difficulty of assembling such a specialized collection (344). Moreover, once Conklin and Fabricant had their compilation in hand, they did not know quite what to make of it: "We have made no effort to arrange these stories in any medical or literary pattern; to do so would have been both forced and futile" (10). Apparently the task of finding patterns has fallen to us. Lastly, on the subject of such anthologies, we should point out the publication by Alan E. Nourse (himself a physician) of his own stories, *Rx for Tomorrow: Tales of Science Fiction, Fantasy, and Medicine.*

3. Larry Niven, *Ringworld* (New York: Ballantine, 1970), 1.

4. Isaac Asimov, *Foundation and Empire* (1952; New York: Avon, 1966), 32.

5. Poul Anderson, *Mirkheim* (New York: Berkley, 1977), 2–3.

6. John Brunner, *The Shockwave Rider* (New York: Ballantine, 1975), 3.

7. In those stories where medicine is featured, the author often seems compelled to formally justify its importance, as if placing medicine at the heart of a science fiction universe violated some unstated "natural law" of the genre. This rhetorical task parallels that of dismissing the body question in nonmedically oriented works. Such statements tend to evoke a past marked by a forced inversion of the natural state of affairs. "Ribbon in the Sky," from Murray Leinster's Med Service series (in Leinster, *Quarantine World* [New York: Ace, 1983]), has its hero Calhoun articulate medicine's significance in terms of the physicians' ethical responsibility for the situation they created:

"We medics," said Calhoun, "made it necessary for men to invent interplanetary travel because we kept people from dying and the population on old Earth got too large. Then we made interstellar travel necessary because we continued to keep people from dying and one solar system wasn't big enough. We're responsible for nine-tenths of civilization as it exists today, because we produced the conditions that make civilization necessary." (226)

In contrast to Leinster's world, where the forced inversion emerges from the pressure of too much life, the grim past evoked by Ward Moore in *Caduceus Wild* posits the destructive, contractive pressure of worldwide disease. This time doctors have undergone a less subtle ethical inversion. Once heroes, Moore's doctors now function as villains:

Upon this very fear [of disease] rested the whole interwoven fabric of world government: the Medarchy.

Supreme authority vested in a select few. For at the time of the exploding of the aerosol germ bombs in the last stages of the war, the ascendancy of physicians went unquestioned. Doctors had to be in complete charge of survivors in order to prevent further epidemics, dietary mistakes, and total chaos. Doctors' orders thus became the only legal and legitimate orders. Unchallenged. (Moore with Robert Bradford, *Caduceus Wild* [Los Angeles: Pinnacle, 1978], 8; page references in later notes are to this edition.)

8. Given the multiple instances of McCoy's signature remark in so many episodes of *Star Trek*, it is no wonder it assumed a humorous edge in a retrospective television show on the series. Cutting a succession of clips so that they rapidly juxtapose one another further confirms the impression of the doctor's helplessness in the face of so many unknowns.

9. In the unique science fiction novel in which doctors seize control, the world-governing physicians take overt steps to avoid any such hybridization. Trying to eliminate mongrelization—or even a collegial relationship with other medical scientists—results in the following scenario in *Caduceus Wild*:

The word "Iatrarchy" itself had taken on a specialized meaning in the new medical culture. It now designated the North American quarter of the four main geographically arranged sections of the World Medarchy, the American doctors having opted for a purist rendering of two Greek roots meaning "government by doctor" rather than the Latin-Greek mongrel word which might be misinterpreted as meaning government by the science of medicine. Which might in turn leave room for biochemists, metabolic physiologists and godknows-what other borderline professionals to begin giving orders too. (12)

10. Other examples of shadow-pairings in the field include Aylmer and his servant Aminadab in Nathaniel Hawthorne's "The Birthmark," Frankenstein and his Creature (not to mention Captain Walton and Frankenstein), and possibly, Doctor McCoy and Spock of *Star Trek* fame.

11. Technically speaking, Victor Frankenstein is not a doctor, as H. Bruce Franklin notes elsewhere. Nonetheless, Franklin himself participates in some of the same slippage that we all fall prey to. See his section entitled "Medicine Men" in *Future Perfect: American Science Fiction of the Nineteenth Century*, rev. ed. (New York: Oxford University Press, 1978), in which he refers to the period in question as "the century of Drs. Frankenstein, Rappaccini, Chillingsworth, Heidenhoff, and Moreau, and of Drs. Oliver Wendell Holmes and Silas Weir Mitchell (not to mention Dr. Arthur Conan Doyle)" (219).

12. For more information on the background of the film (including its source, Philip K. Dick's novel, *Do Androids Dream of Electric Sheep?*), see Paul M. Sammon, *Future Noir: The Making of Blade Runner* (New York: HarperCollins, 1996); another useful resource for our on-the-set observations is the special *Cinefex9* issue, *Blade Runner—2020 Foresight* (1982).

13. Appropriately, synecdoche—the fragmented form of symbolism in which a part stands for the whole—creates an abstracted, almost dissociated, embodiment of medicine. The reduction of medicine into technology appears in several grotesquely comedic examples from the *Star Wars* saga and Frank Herbert's *Dune*—namely Darth Vader's noisy helmet (which conceals, replaces, and "empowers" his disfigured head), and the body-lifters for the fleshy immensity of Dune's megalomaniac potentate.

14. In *Billion Year Spree: The True History of Science Fiction* (New York: Schocken, 1974), Brian W. Aldiss reminds us of Edmund Burke's definition of the sublime, which "inspires awe and terror and, with pain as its basis, disturbs the emotions." Burke speaks of "delightful horror"—"the most genuine effect and truest test of the sublime" (*On the Sublime and the Beautiful* [1756]). When this quality is crystallized into an image of

technology, we have the vital force. As always, Mary Shelley was there first, with her potent image of science creating life. Clearly, the vital force as it appears in twentieth-century science fiction embodies the ancient concept of the sublime. Verbal depictions of the sublime recall Dante Alighieri's *Paradiso*, John Milton's Heaven (*Paradise Lost*), and the visionary poems of William Blake. With the rise of modern technology came the artist's ability to extrapolate technological advance to the point of infinity.

15. Arthur C. Clarke, *2001: A Space Odyssey* (New York: Signet Books, 1968), 190, 216.

16. These images constitute quasi-scientific devices that symbolize the emotions—an attempted fusion of two conflicting yet essential purposes of science fiction. Perhaps this bifurcation stems from science fiction's problematic relationship to melodrama. In his article, "'Man against Man, Brain against Brain': The Transformation of Melodrama in Science Fiction," Gary Westfahl quotes Peter Brooks's typification of melodrama as featuring "full emotional indulgence" and points out how—despite its dependence on melodrama to provide vitality—the scientific agenda of science fiction brings it into simultaneous conflict with melodrama (*Themes in Drama 14: Melodrama*, edited by James Redmond [Cambridge: Cambridge University Press, 1992], 195–196). The resultant mixture of emotion-based melodrama and intellect-based science in science fiction has inevitably turned it into a genre obsessed with the relationship of emotion and intellect; in fact, the formal conflict has developed into a thematic meditation. Science fiction stories can profitably be analyzed as explorations of this theme, and the structures of the tales emerge as attempts to resolve the emotion-intellect dichotomy. *Star Trek: The Motion Picture* is an overt example, in which the mind-based V'ger literally merges with a passionate character. *2001* performs a similar, if less polarized operation, combining images of the vital force with the archetype of rebirth to accomplish a fusion. In contrast, *Solaris* fixates on the conflict itself, as the planet's nature vis-à-vis emotion and intellect remains ambiguous to the end. Despite science fiction's effort to fuse emotion and intellect through imagery, they retain an ineluctable ambiguity; their double nature as both good and bad embodies our uncertainty about emotion, intellect, and technology (the expression of both aspects of the human psyche).

Alien creatures can be read as a more or less successful effort to symbolize the absence of this conflict (that's what truly makes them "alien"). "Good" (usually technologically advanced) aliens tend to present a flawed harmony between emotion and intellect. For example, the aliens in *Close Encounters of the Third Kind* invite the human race to join them in their musical coalescence of mindblowing technology and big-heartedness, while the aliens in *The Day the Earth Stood Still* politely inform us that we are being drafted into their machine-assisted truce between mind and emotions. More disturbingly, evil aliens (i.e., "monsters") imagistically strip away either intellect or emotion altogether, removing one of the twin elements we instinctively sense as essential to our humanity. Where the benevolent races were social, these creatures are isolated, or else exist in hives or clusters. Generally nonverbal, their behavior is ceaselessly oriented toward a single goal—a characteristic of insanity, as either reptilian voraciousness or an incessant mechanical intellect. The alien in *Alien*—possibly the most brilliantly developed extraterrestrial monster in science fiction— symbolically destroys (or preempts) both human emotion and human intellect in its horrific double birth. First it clouds its victim's mind, covering his organs of perception and placing him in a coma; it then horrifically breaks his heart, indelibly establishing the creature as the potent embodiment of all that is negative in the human psyche. Inevitably, technology is one with the creature in this nightmare vision. All of the ship's mechanisms, from the air shafts to the computer, unhesitatingly ally themselves with and act to nurture the alien.

17. E. E. "Doc" Smith, *Second Stage Lensman* (1953; New York: Pyramid, 1975), 11.

18. *The Lifeforce Experiment*, a 1994 film made for Canadian television, is based on the Daphne du Maurier novella, "The Breakthrough," available in her short-fiction anthology, *Don't Look Now* (Garden City, NY: Doubleday, 1966).

19. In cyperpunk, post-apocalyptic, or dystopian works such as *Johnny Mnemonic* and the TV series *Max Headroom*, the vital force appears as a parodic irritant, manifesting itself within or alongside the minds of protagonists who have little connection with the warped, volatile analogs of their intellects. These implanted or projected dwarves display a sometimes intricate interplay of the qualities of the vital force together with its opposites. For example, the eponymous quasi-character of *Max Headroom*—perhaps the most sophisticated development of the inverted vital force—is presumed to be a duplicate of the hero, but displays infantile qualities that sardonically recall the rebirth and reversal-of-time aspects at work in the vital force. In a travesty of the supernal magic of the vital force in full flower, where malfunction is unimaginable, Max stutters. His antic silliness burlesques the mind-bending aspects of the vital force. Spatially, Max is a crudely projected two-dimensional version of the hero (cartoonish in quality), an utter inversion of the vital force's ability to contain whole minds and universes within itself. And while Max might be assumed to be an enhancement of the hero, with the hero's resourcefulness and courage augmented by a vast computer network, he is instead a clown, a mockery of the mysterious alien intelligence that seems to animate the vital force.

20. The variations on our paradigm can assume subtle forms. For example, the 1995 film *Outbreak* (whose status as science fiction versus mainstream thriller depends on our beliefs about viruses and their potentialities) places the protagonist in the ascetic vacuum of military life and the emotional vacuum of divorce. The hero, Sam Daniels, spends most of the film in more literally vacuous environments—hypersterilized "clean zones" and suits (à la *The Andromeda Strain*), a plague-stricken town, or literally up in the air. Breaking the repressed and repressive rules of his military milieu, Daniels instantly becomes a hunted outcast; isolated with his assistant, he assays the prototypical mini-quest—trying to leave a small town, like the hero of *Body Snatchers*. The story is propelled by a severe timelock, and its climax shows the tiny, frail helicopter containing the doctor trying to head off a gigantic bomber, an emblem of the vital force in an overwhelmingly destructive form.

21. For further examples of how archetypes operate in science fiction and other forms of popular culture, see *Patterns of Popular Culture: A Sourcebook for Writers*, edited by Harold Schechter and Jonna Gormely Semeiks (New York: Harper & Row, 1980), which contains Ursula K. Le Guin's article, "Myth and Archetype in Science Fiction" (442–448), reprinted from the journal *Parabola: Myth and the Quest for Meaning* (1976).

22. The heroine assumes that a shifty, minor character with the last name "George" is the villain, but a tension-filled revelation scene shows the villain to be the hospital chief of staff, Dr. *George* Harris, who was preparing to suck the vital force out of her via unexpected, involuntary surgery.

5

From Dr. Frankenstein to Dr. McCoy:
M.D.s and Ph.D.s in Science Fiction

Joseph D. Miller

A few years ago, a story arc on the television series *ER* involved the internship of an M.D./Ph.D. This represents the only time I have ever seen an individual with the "double degree" portrayed in a doctor show. This particular character was the ultimate nerd—absolutely no interest in patients, no knowledge of the most rudimentary of social interactions, and capable of fainting dead away at the sight of blood. Yet this same character had his own extremely well-equipped laboratory in molecular biology, to which he retreated at any possible opportunity. The entire story arc seemed to say that somehow the acquisition of an academic doctorate changes the "good old boy" doctor, typically lionized by TV's doctor shows, into some kind of poorly socialized mad scientist—a mad scientist nonetheless equipped with laboratory facilities that most of us do not see until we have completed many years of graduate school and postdoctoral research.

I began to wonder whether this is simply a reflection of series creator Michael Crichton's own conflicted attitude toward medical science. Crichton received his medical degree from Harvard, an institution that places far more emphasis on basic science training than most medical schools, generally to the dismay of first- and second- year medical students. But Crichton has never practiced medicine; rather he segued directly into a career as a science fiction writer. Much of his work, including his novels *The Terminal Man* and *Jurassic Park*, betrays considerable ambivalence and often frank hostility toward modern science. Interestingly, Crichton does not consider himself to be a science fiction writer and has turned down invitations to appear at science fiction conferences on such grounds.

It is tempting to suggest, then, that Crichton's history has produced a personal psychodynamics characterized by a fawning admiration for the unattainable love object, medical practice, coupled with a somewhat paradoxical distaste for medical science. Clinical competence requires the mastery of laboratory technique; if deficiency in such technique was the reason for Crichton's decision not to pursue medicine, laboratory science then takes the psychological role of the rival preventing access to the love object, that is, medical practice. If this interpretation is correct, it is easy to see why Crichton's self concept would not allow him to consider himself a science fiction writer, all evidence to the contrary. One wonders what Crichton would say if he were accused of being a "medical fiction writer," to coin a term? If there is any truth to this psychological interpretation, it would follow that an M.D./Ph.D. should be beneath Crichton's contempt, because the M.D./Ph.D. has sullied the "good" of humanistic medical practice with an evil lust for the pure knowledge of basic science.

Such speculation leads to broader questions: Are scientists and physicians portrayed differently in science fiction? Do television and the movies portray scientists and physicians differently than does the science fiction novel? Are there historical antecedents for this supposed differential portrayal of the scientist and the physician?

In the Beginning

Brian W. Aldiss and other critics believe Mary Shelley's *Frankenstein* to be the original science fiction novel. Victor Frankenstein, then, is the primordial "mad scientist." However, the first caveat here is that Frankenstein is more of a medical doctor than an academic Ph.D. The M.D., in his attempt to defeat death, can be seen as a Promethean mediator between God and humanity. Frankenstein's attempt to reanimate dead matter is a Faustian extension of the medical project; the hubris of Frankenstein guarantees that the success of this project will be paid for in the coinage of personal suffering, in particular the death of Frankenstein's brother, friend, and wife at the hands of the Monster.

But Frankenstein must also be seen in terms of the scientific ferment of the Victorian era. While Shelley's novel predates Charles Darwin's *The Origin of Species*, it is contemporaneous with the work of Erasmus Darwin, Charles's grandfather. Even in 1818 the position of humanity at the center of the biological universe was beginning to be challenged by the fossil record. This blurring of the border between humanity and the rest of the animal kingdom is apparent in both *Frankenstein* and other speculative works of the period. The harvested tissues that constituted the Monster were not solely of human origin; the slaughterhouse and the charnel house contributed equally. The Monster is a chimera, possessing the intellectual powers of the most rational of humans, but also inhumanly base desires and emotions beyond the control of the sociocultural conditioning Sigmund Freud called the superego. This conflation of the rational and the bestial is seen in numerous Victorian and post-Victorian works, including of course Robert Louis Stevenson's *The Strange Case of Dr. Jekyll and Mr. Hyde*, in which the physician actually is the Monster. Edgar Allan Poe's short story, "The Murders in the Rue Morgue," hinges on the expectation that the story's murderer is human, rather than the eventually revealed simian character. H. G. Wells's *The Island of Dr. Moreau* turns the tables by imbuing non-human characters with human abilities.

In each of these works there is a kind of horror at the realized potential for bestiality in humans, the pinnacle of creation. This horror echoes the fear of the shape-shifter, the vampire, the werewolf. But the true horror results from the knowledge that the shape-shifting is imposed by humans and their machinations, as opposed to the bite of the bat or wolf. And it is typically the physician, particularly the surgeon, who is responsible for the hybridization of human and beast. All these works suggest a revulsion at the revealed, bestial, Darwinian origins of humanity, as well as anticipating the ego/id distinction of Sigmund Freud that was destined in a few short years to extend the bestial attributes of humanity from the biological to the psychological sphere.

In *Frankenstein* it is also easy to see the replacement of eighteenth-century vitalism, the belief that a life force invests all living creatures, with a defined physical mechanism. Luigi Galvani's work, showing that electricity could induce muscular contractions even in dead organisms, was well-known to the Shelleys and Lord Byron. Shelley recalled, in her introduction to the 1831 revised edition of *Frankenstein*, that "galvanism had given token of such things: perhaps the component parts of a creature might be manufactured, brought together, and imbued with vital warmth." In this same introduction Shelley recalls an amazingly precognitive dream in which she sees the Monster invested with life through the action of a "powerful engine."[1] In the novel Frankenstein "collected the instruments of life around me, that I might infuse a spark of being into the lifeless thing that lay at my feet." Upon reanimation, "A convulsive motion agitated its limbs" (57,58). This is a revolutionary departure from the Cartesian separation of mind and body; a thinking creature may be produced from inanimate matter simply by the application of the "powerful engine," presumably akin to an electrical generator. For this reason I have argued elsewhere that *Frankenstein* is not only the first science fiction novel, but also the first fiction of neuroscience, in which the modern notions that mind is a function of matter (admittedly highly organized matter) and that mental activity is ultimately electrical in nature, are paramount, although implicit.

Is Frankenstein a mad scientist? After all, the defeat of death, even at the expense of the quality of life, is the major project of modern medicine. In fact, it may be argued that Frankenstein was a stimulus for the invention of one of the most effective devices for the prolongation of life. But what of the horror at the use of body parts from deceased individuals? Today, we cannot reanimate dead matter, but we are able to extend animation through blood transfusion and organ transplants into living humans and we experience no horror at the prospect, in spite of its Frankensteinian resonances. But what of the use of non-human tissue? Xenotransplants have been repeatedly performed with some success; for example, the baboon heart is of the appropriate size for transplantation into the chest of newborn infants in the case of neonatal cardiac dysfunction, and we routinely genetically transplant the human immune system into transgenic mice. But there is a popular horror at this genetic cross-species miscegenation, illustrated by rules from the National Institute of Health against genetic manipulation of human fetal tissue or introduction of non-human genes into such tissue. In the science fiction literature the theme of genetic miscegenation is often treated less histrionically than in the movies—compare Cordwainer Smith's "The Ballad of Lost C'Mell" with the fourth "Alien" movie, *Alien Resurrection* (1997). But in general the 20/20 vision of hindsight from the viewpoint of the twenty-first century is that the madness of Frankenstein and other medical doctors of nineteenth century "medical romances" may hinge on the conflation of the human and the bestial.[2]

The Scientist as Hero

A very different trend begins in the 1860s, with the publication of *Journey to the Center of the Earth* (1863) and *From the Earth to the Moon* (1865) by Jules Verne. For the first time in a scientific romance the protagonists are actual scientists, rather than physicians. And these protagonists are explorers, with no hint of the Faustian angst that characterized so many earlier works of the nineteenth century. But another 30 years must go by before the publication of Wells's *The Time Machine* (1895), followed by *First Men in the Moon* (1901). Finally in 1912, Arthur Conan Doyle's *The Lost World* cemented the position of the scientist in science fiction. Professors Cavor and Challenger, as well as the anonymous Time Traveller of Wells's story, are the prototypical scientist heroes.

What was responsible for this "sea change" in the history of the scientific romance? *Fin de siècle* science fiction was strongly influenced by the media popularity of the great scientist-inventors of the day: Louis Pasteur, Thomas Alva Edison, and Albert Einstein. Thus we begin to see stories like Garrett P. Serviss's sequel to Wells's *The War of the Worlds*, *Edison's Conquest of Mars*. Fourteen years after the publication of *The Lost World*, the first issue of *Amazing Stories* was published, followed a few years later by the first issue of *Astounding Stories*. The pulps under editors such as Hugo Gernsback and John W. Campbell, Jr. probably were the strongest contributing factor to the solidification of the scientist-hero trope in science fiction, particularly as the Golden Age authors matured in their writing skills. Heroes like E. E. "Doc" Smith's Richard Seaton, Campbell's polar scientists in "Who Goes There?," Isaac Asimov's Susan Calvin and Hari Seldon, and Robert A. Heinlein's Waldo personified the Golden Age scientific super-hero. The evil scientist is also in evidence; there is the occasional Marc DuQuesne to balance the Richard Seatons. But by and large Golden Age science fiction is synonymous with hero worship of the scientist.

New Wave portrayals of the scientist in science fiction, however, were less sympathetic than those of the Golden Age. Often the protagonist is not a scientist at all, but a "common man" reacting to the excesses of off-stage evil scientists. Nonetheless, the scientist-hero persisted, albeit in more complex terms. And the scientist-hero is still present in the *fin de siècle* science fiction of this century. Character development is more complex, but we still have the physicists of Ursula K. Le Guin's *The Dispossessed*, Gregory Benford's *Timescape*, and Greg Egan's *Quarantine*; the geologists of Kim Stanley Robinson's Martian trilogy; the astronomer of Carl Sagan's *Contact* (offering interesting resonances with Fred Hoyle's earlier astronomers in *A for Andromeda* and *The Black Cloud*); the many computer scientists in works like Greg Egan's *Permutation City* and Rudy Rucker's *Software*; and the biologists of Greg Bear's *Blood Music*, to name just a few.

The physician in the science fiction novel is perhaps not as evident following the advent of the pulps. But there are still sympathetic portrayals such as Samuel Lann in A. E. Van Vogt's *Slan* and James White's various alien physicians in the Sector General series. The truly evil, Faustian medical doctor has become as rare in the science fiction novel as the mad scientist (although thrillers such as Robin Cook's *Coma* still make use of the evil physician archetype). Evil knowledge has largely been replaced by the evil usage of knowledge, be it by the government, the military or multinational corporations.

Ph.D.s and M.D.s in Cinema

The Faustian physician was a standard element in early cinematic presentations. The first horror movie was Edison's production of *Frankenstein* in 1910. A second Frankenstein movie, *Life without Soul*, followed in 1915. *Dr. Jekyll and Mr. Hyde* was filmed seven times in the first decades of the twentieth century, including John Barrymore's classic portrayal in 1920. *The Monster*, in 1925, was another thinly disguised take on Frankenstein. The first dystopian science fiction film is probably *Metropolis* in 1926, but this too exhibits a Frankenstein subplot. Instead of a mad physician we have a crazed inventor, Rotwang, who creates a mechanical, rather than biological, simulacrum of the female lead, Maria. The robot's actions result in a kind of populist revolt that destroys Metropolis and results in the immolation of the robot, perhaps the stimulus for any number of subsequent Frankenstein movies in which the Monster is destroyed by fire. The parallels with Frankenstein are obvious, but here the rising of the commons is not aimed at the destruction of an aristocrat, but rather the social structure itself. The subtext is that socialist revolt is monstrous and ultimately self-destructive, consistent with the developing political situation in pre-Nazi Germany.

In 1931 we get the Boris Karloff *Frankenstein* and the Frederick March *Dr. Jekyll and Mr. Hyde*. And 1932 saw a production of *Murders in the Rue Morgue*, as well as *Island of Lost Souls*, a cinematic revision of *The Island of Dr. Moreau*. The year 1935 saw *The Raven* with Bela Lugosi as a crazed surgeon, *Bride of Frankenstein*, and *Mad Love* with Peter Lorre as yet another insane surgeon. Finally we get *Son of Frankenstein* in 1939 with Basil Rathbone in an unlikely lead role. All of these movies are characterized by the mad physician, typically the mad surgeon, but rarely the mad Ph.D. Perhaps the only major exception is *The Invisible Man* (1933). But this too is a Faustian melodrama: The enticing potion of knowledge produces a grandiose hubris as a side effect, leading to the ultimate demise of the protagonist. Once again, knowledge is overwhelmingly dangerous, its acquisition implies a hubris that challenges the natural order, and the ultimate payment for that knowledge is suffering and death.

But the thirties also produced a change in the role of the scientist/academic Ph.D. reminiscent of what occurred in the scientific romance thirty years before. *Things to Come* (1936) is perhaps the first science fiction film to take an optimistic view of the future. The scientist, in particular the rocket scientist, is lionized in this film. Of much greater popular success were the Buck Rogers and Flash Gordon serials between 1936 and 1940. It is difficult from the vantage of sixty odd years later to understand the grip that Flash Gordon had on the public. *The Purple Death* was banned from movie theaters in Kansas because of the intensity of the special effects. The most wrenching of these special effects showed crowds of people (presumably in New York) succumbing to what amounted to purple blotches on the forehead! Flash, the protagonist of the series, was an adventurer and explorer, yet it was up to the academic scientist, Dr. Zarkov, to save his hash on virtually every occasion, generally through the invention of an invisibility ray or other technological marvel. Zarkov is the first scientific hero of the big screen, but is unremarked even by most students of the obscurantia of science fiction.

How can one explain this admittedly brief spring of the scientific hero in cinema? One contributing factor had to be Orson Welles's *The War of the Worlds* broadcast of 1938. This broadcast was initially considered to be literal truth by many of the same citizens impressed by the exploits of Flash Gordon. The Martians were a scientific menace; only a scientific hero could hope to overcome such difficulties. Faustian physicians could be of no help in such dire circumstances!

But this spring of the scientific hero was destined to be of short duration. In the science fiction literature, pre-World War II anxieties about the misuse of technology, particularly nuclear technology, were becoming manifest in stories like Heinlein's "Blowups Happen" (1940), Lester del Rey's *Nerves* (1942) and Cleve Cartmill's prescient short story "Deadline" (1942).[3] Perhaps the climate of the times can help to explain movies in which the evil physician has been replaced by the evil scientist. For instance, in *Dr. Cyclops* (1940) the mad scientist utilizes atomic rays to miniaturize unwilling subjects. Karloff plays no less than five mad scientists between 1939 and 1943 in *The Man They Could Not Hang, The Man with Nine Lives, Before I Hang, The Devil Commands,* and *The Boogie Man Will Get You.* Lugosi plays the mad Ph.D. in *The Phantom Creeps* (1939), *The Devil Bat* (1941), *The Ape Man* (1943) and *Return of the Ape Man* (1944). Other mad academic scientist movies of this era include *Man Made Monster* (1940) with Lon Chaney, Jr. and *The Mad Ghoul* (1943) with George Zucco.

The mad physician doesn't completely disappear in the forties; Lugosi plays this role in *The Corpse Vanishes* (1942), in which he steals blood from young women to create an anti-aging potion. And the Frankenstein movies continue with *Ghost of Frankenstein* (1942) and in 1944 with *Frankenstein Meets the Wolfman* and *House of Frankenstein.* But it is clear by 1950 that the mad Ph.D. has largely displaced the mad M.D. on the big screen.

In the post-Hiroshima era the academic scientist continues to be the fall guy. In *The Thing (from Another World)* (1951) an academic scientist foolishly ensures the (temporary) survival of James Arness's fabled Giant Carrot, in very great contrast to Campbell's original story. In *Forbidden Planet* (1956) it is scientific hubris that leads to considerable murder and mayhem at the invisible "hands" of the Monster from the Id. In *The Fly* (1958) we see again the conflation of the rational and the bestial, but here the Faustian character is an academic scientist, presumably a physicist. There is still the odd mad doctor, as in *Donovan's Brain* (1953) and *Frankenstein 1970* (1958) and even the rare scientific hero in the British Quatermass movies. But the British have never suffered the degree of nuclear guilt that we have, so perhaps they better tolerate the idea of the scientific hero.

The association of madness with nuclear energy is seen in *Bride of the Monster* (1955) in which Lugosi as mad scientist tries to create a nuclear superhuman. But it is in the "giant creature" movies of the fifties and sixties that we can most clearly see the equation of scientific, in particular nuclear, hubris with death and destruction. Thus we have giant ants (*Them!*, 1954), lizards (*Godzilla*, 1956), moths (*Mothra*, 1961), spiders (*Tarantula*, 1956), crabs (*Attack of the Crab Monsters*, 1957), amoebas (*The Blob*, 1958), and even giant bunny rabbits (*Night of the Lepus*, 1972), as well as more mundane homicidal birds (*The Birds*, 1963), frogs (*Frogs*, 1972), and zombies (*Night of the Living Dead*, 1968). The assumption here is that nuclear physics is as Faustian an occupation as Frankensteinian reanimation. Nuclear knowledge is an arrogant presumption and intrusion into God's domain. Invariably, nuclear knowledge is monstrously applied as weapon and the byproduct monsters wreak death and destruction, fulfilling the Faustian bargain. And of course it is possible to remove the middleman—we don't really need giant atom-engendered monsters to destroy humanity; we can do an excellent job all by ourselves, as in *On the Beach* (1959). Thus we have no scientific heroes because our flagship scientists, the physicists, have "known sin."

The sixties begin with another insane surgeon with a taste for disembodied heads (*The Brain That Wouldn't Die*, 1959) lingering in the theaters. But scientists continue to be the major target for ridicule, whether mild, as in *The Absent-Minded Professor*, charmingly but spacily portrayed by Fred MacMurray (1961) and the Jekyll and Hyde Jerry Lewis vehicle *The Nutty Professor* (1963). The scientist as eccentric bumbler is later seen in *Back to the Future* (1985) and in the incredibly stupid Steve Martin vehicle *The Man with Two Brains* (1983), as well as in the comic parapsychologists of *Ghostbusters* (1984) and *Ghostbusters II* (1989). But the greatest satirical interpretation of the mad Ph.D. is Peter Sellers's portrayal of *Dr. Strangelove* (1964). Strangelove is a peculiar amalgam of Nazi scientist, Frankenstein, and horny bureaucrat obsessed with the notion of underground fallout shelters as breeding grounds for the repopulation of the human race, a notion which is the direct "fallout" of the anticipated detonation of the movie's Doomsday Device. In contrast, *Fantastic Voyage* (1966) is a rare positive portrayal of science in which a miniature submarine must course through the circulatory system of a stricken scientist and save his life by breaking up a blood clot, before the submarine returns to normal size.

In this same period the scientist is also held responsible for a new sin never ascribed to the medical doctor—the enhancement of natural or artificial intelligence. In *Charly* (1968) based on Daniel Keyes's novel *Flowers for Algernon*, a new neurological procedure imbues a retarded janitor with genius.[4] Charly rapidly becomes a scientific prodigy, but the Faustian price he pays for this knowledge is not only his soul (read intellect), but the ironic, self-gained foreknowledge that his genius has a definite termination date. After all, the horror of senility is not senility itself, but the premonitions and intimations of loss that occur while we are still in our "right minds."

Films in this era also burden the scientist with the new sin of creating artificial intelligence. HAL in *2001: A Space Odyssey* (1968) is the obvious example of the evil fruits of this insane labor, but there is also computer as dictator in *Colossus: The Forbin Project* (1968) and later computer as rapist in *Demon Seed* (1977) and robotic computer as suburban wife in *The Stepford Wives* (1974). But perhaps the most paranoid extension of this scientific sin occurs when the global satellite communications network, SkyNet (read the Internet), is imbued with intelligence and promptly becomes genocidal in *The Terminator* (1984). It is of some interest that Bill Gates appropriated the name SkyNet for a proposed network of 50 communications satellites, which may ultimately handle the bulk of high speed Internet communications.

Two of the best-known science fiction films of the seventies and eighties, *Close Encounters of the Third Kind* (1977) and *E.T.* (1982), illustrate yet another scientific sin: the withholding of scientific information by government scientists, a theme that can be traced at least as far back as the suppression of information about the lunar monolith in *2001* and as far forward to the paranoid government conspiracies of *The X-Files*. This theme of suppression is also apparent in the film *Independence Day* (1996) in which Area 51 scientists have been suppressing Roswellian UFO technology for 50 years. While this film does have a scientific hero in the computer scientist played by Jeff Goldblum, he is an outcast and an outsider only called upon by the government in their hour of desperate need.

Psychologists know sin in *A Clockwork Orange* (1971) in the guise of institutionalized brainwashing for sociopaths. Crichton's *The Terminal Man* (1974) suggests that electrical stimulation of the human brain can be used to elicit psychotic behavior, thus inventing the evil neurophysiologist. Pharmacologists are tagged in *Scanners* (1980) in which pregnant mothers are treated with the psi power-inducing drug ephemerol, with brain-busting consequences. But perhaps of greatest significance is the new scientific sin of genetic manipulation. Dr. Mengele is the evil Hitler cloner in *The Boys from Brazil* (1978) and the later "Alien" movies combine alien and human genes in a manner that both invokes a new scientific horror while echoing the beast/human hybridization that is in part the sin of the mad M.D.s in *Frankenstein*, *Dr. Jekyll and Mr. Hyde*, and *The Island of Dr. Moreau*. In *Blade Runner* (1982) the off-screen genetic sin is the creation of short-lived androids. But the greatest molecular sin to date is the cloning of dinosaurs in *Jurassic Park* (1993), based on Crichton's novel, a Faustian sin with the usual gory repercussions. And so the molecular biologist has come to know sin, at least in the cinema.

The mad physician never completely disappears from this latter period of science fiction film. Thus we have the *nouveau* Frankenstein in *Reanimator* (1985), the organlegger doctors of *Coma* (1978) and Hannibal Lecter, the psychotic serial killer physician of *Silence of the Lambs* (1991) and *Hannibal* (2001). But they are far outnumbered by the mad Ph.D.s of this era. In all fairness, the scientist is occasionally portrayed in a sympathetic light; thus we have the heroic microbiologists of *The Andromeda Strain* (1970) and *Outbreak* (1995), the ethnopharmacologist of *Altered States* (1980) who eventually achieves oneness with the universe, the space scientists in orbit around *Solaris* (1971), and of course the incredibly sympathetic character of the SETI astronomer portrayed by Jodie Foster in *Contact* (1997).

Why, as a sinner, is the scientist ever portrayed in a sympathetic light in the movies? A number of possible answers spring to mind. For one, post-Hiroshima nuclear angst probably colors the American view of the scientist much more than the European view; thus the Quatermass movies and *Solaris* are quite sympathetic to the scientist. Movie adaptations from books have something of a chance of portraying characters in the way they were written, particularly if the author has the clout of an Asimov or Sagan; thus we have intact scientist heroes in *Fantastic Voyage* and *Contact*. But most importantly, it seems to be all right to have a scientist hero if the threat is from without, as is the case in almost every movie in which there is a recognizable scientific hero. Reactive science is acceptable; thus Zarkov can build Flash an invisibility ray to save Dale, Flash, and ultimately the entire Earth from Ming, Emperor of Mongo. But active science is disallowed because it is arrogant, Faustian, and unnatural. Thus, Wells's scientist who invents the invisibility potion in *The Invisible Man* cannot be treated as a hero in the movie. In other words science applied for the good of humanity is fine and heroic; pure research only for the sake of knowledge itself is self-indulgent and ultimately evil. As is said in umpteen B movies, "There are some things Man is not meant to know!"[5]

The Good Doctor in TV Land

It is easy to talk about the role of the scientist in science fiction on television simply because there is so little that can even be called science fiction. There was a reasonably sympathetic portrayal of an academic scientist in the series *Sliders*. The British series *Dr. Who* also presented the scientist in a heroic role, although Dr. Who is of course an alien scientist. In contrast, John Lithgow reprised the Nutty Professor in *Third Rock from the Sun*, though he was funnier than Jerry Lewis. Perhaps the only thing of critical interest that could be said of Lithgow's portrayal of a physics professor is that it shares with the Nutty Professor the Jekyll and Hyde trope; instead of scientist and lounge lizard in the Lewis vehicle and its Eddie Murphy remake, Lithgow does scientist and alien. In contrast to Dr. Who as alien scientist, we have Dr. Solomon as scientist-alien. Much of the show's humor derives from this continual juxtaposition of the Alice-in-Wonderland-like alien and the stuffy, pompous academic professor.

The best of what passes for science fiction on television are *Star Trek*, its various successor series, and *Babylon V*. In the original *Star Trek*, there is a science officer, Mr. Spock, and in *Star Trek: The Next Generation* we have essentially the same role played by Lieutenant Data. These are essentially heroic portraits of the scientist, although in both cases the subtext is that the scientist lacks emotion and humanity, presumably sacrificed at the altar of cold rationality. But the scientists were dropped in *Star Trek: Deep Space Nine*, *Star Trek: Voyager*, and *Babylon V* (though a scientist was brought back on board for the "prequel" *Star Trek* series *Enterprise*). In contrast, however, there is always a ship's doctor: Dr. James "Bones" McCoy in the original, Dr. Beverly Crusher in *Next Generation*, Dr. Bashir in *Deep Space Nine*, the hologrammic Doctor in *Voyager*, and Dr. Franklin in *Babylon V*. These characters are always "good old boys"; McCoy in particular is the archetypical old country doctor. These doctors can be arrogant at times, but they are always heroic, often emotional and thoroughly human. In fact, this is exactly the way doctors have always been portrayed on television, from *Dr. Kildare* to *ER*. Perhaps the only exception is the cowardly, and at times traitorous Dr. Smith of *Lost in Space*. It is as if television simply skipped the mad physician phase which characterized the early years of science fiction in literature and in cinema.

The final television work to consider is *The X-Files*, which during its classic years saw Scully playing Sancho Panza to Mulder's Don Quixote. It is important to see Scully as an M.D. and Ph.D., since she holds a doctorate in physics. In contrast to the M.D./Ph.D.(perhaps we should say Ph.D./M.D.) of *ER* considered at the beginning of this chapter, Scully represents the emotional and the rational and is never ridiculed in the series. Perhaps this is because Scully is the quintessential M.D., occasionally masquerading as a scientist, as opposed to the physician poseur of *ER*, who is primarily cast as arrogant basic scientist. Scully, in the series's early years, was the counterpoint to Mulder's often pretentious and generally gullible predilection for paranormal explanations. But she was gradually co-opted to Mulder's viewpoint, following the implantation of an alien technology transmitter in her brain and various other adventures that largely sapped her skepticism, once one of the best features of the show. But *The X-Files* often gets at least the background science right, and Scully as scientist hero is the most realistic portrayal television has managed so far. This makes good psychological sense since the physician is typically venerated on television; it would then be very difficult to paint the Ph.D. side of Scully with the same satirical brushstrokes applied to Mr. Spock and Lieutenant Data, the previous avatars of the scientist hero on television.

Conclusions

Some preliminary conclusions are possible. It is clear that the earliest science fiction literature typically employed the mad physician as protagonist. Jules Verne was the first prominent author to introduce the academic scientist as hero, although it took some thirty years for this trope to displace the medical doctor. The medical doctor has played a much smaller role in the science fiction novel since the turn of the century. Science fiction literature is fairly even-handed in its treatment of the scientist; the scientist may be good or evil, and often comes in moral shades of gray.

In the cinema, the same early stage of the mad medical doctor is apparent. In the thirties there is a brief spring in which the scientist hero comes into vogue. But the forties see the rise of the mad scientist, perhaps as a result of nuclear angst. Heroic scientists make occasional appearances in film from then on, but they are greatly outnumbered by the Strangeloves.

Television largely skips the mad physician stage, but segues directly into an almost unremitting characterization of the scientist as autistic at best, evil or insane at worst. Since physicians are universally worshipped on television, the only hope for sympathetic portrayal of the scientist seems to be hybridization with the humanistic medical doctor, a juxtaposition of the rational and the emotional that resonates with the theme of *The Strange Case of Dr. Jekyll and Mr. Hyde.*

Finally, while I have suggested that the scientist hero in cinema was short-lived due to a developing prescient fear of the uncapping of the "Nuclear Genie" in the early forties, it is unlikely that this will be the last time that the scientist knows sin. Just as Cleve Cartmill's story "Deadline" presaged the use of nuclear weapons, the current literary and cinematic focus on the resultant horrors of the application of molecular biology, as in movies like *Jurassic Park* and *Blade Runner*, suggests that the Biological Accident is yet to happen—and of course, international developments in biowarfare guarantee that "Accident" may not be the appropriate term. In any event, no matter what sorts of evil doctors have perpetrated in the past, the Dr. Strangelove of the twenty-first century will most likely be a molecular biologist.

Notes

1. Mary Shelley, *Frankenstein, or, The Modern Prometheus*, ed. Johanna M. Smith (Boston: Bedford Books, 1992), 23. A later page reference in the text is to this edition.

2. There is at least one other aspect of Frankenstein's behavior that is absolutely sane and consistent with the tenets of sociobiology. Frankenstein's refusal to create a mate for the Monster, though it results in the loss of his own bride, guarantees that the Monster will not reproduce. Considering the strength and intelligence of the Monster, characteristics that presumably would be present in his progeny, such progeny would be formidable competitors with Homo sapiens. Thus Frankenstein's action may be the first example in literature of social altruism at the species level.

3. Many years later, *The China Syndrome* (1979) echoes *Nerves* and "Blowups Happen" in the cinema, putting the physical scientist on the same moral plane as the mad M.D. of the Victorian era. Oddly, the movie was released within weeks of the Three Mile Island reactor accident, the closest the United States has ever come to an enactment of the China Syndrome.

4. *The Lawnmower Man* (1993) is an interesting combination of the Frankenstein theme and the Charly theme. The Faustian scientist here is a computer scientist who uses virtual reality techniques to raise the intelligence of his somewhat retarded handyman to genius level. The handyman eventually becomes a kind of cyber-God and Frankensteinian retribution is visited upon the computer scientist.

5. Is Indiana Jones a scientist hero? *Raiders of the Lost Ark* and its sequels always present Jones as the archaeologist one step up from grave-robbing. Jones is an academic professor, but as an archaeologist he must be a reactive, rather than an active scientist. Nevertheless, in each of the movies he gains some degree of "forbidden knowledge," generally of a religious nature—yet he never pays the Faustian price. The explanation may be that he is generally in reaction against the much more arrogant Nazi archaeologists—these are the scientists who cancel the Faustian debt for their hubris. They constitute the necessary external threat in their desire to use mystical powers to rule the world; without them Frankensteinian logic decrees that Jones would have to pay for the knowledge he gains.

Part II

Case Histories

6

The Immunology of Science Fiction: Maupassant's "Horla," the Medical Frame, and the Evolution of Genres

George Slusser

When we examine the forces, cultural and generic, that lead to the emergence of a "science" fiction in the nineteenth century, the following elements create a puzzle of sorts. The first element is the increasingly acute question about what the external world is and how we can know and represent it. The Positivists, whose ideas dominate much of this century, are said by John Stuart Mill to follow Hume in this regard: "We have no knowledge of anything but Phaenomena; and our knowledge of phaenomena is relative, not absolute. We know not the essence, nor the real mode of production, of any fact, but only its relations to other facts in the way of succession and of similitude."[1] If we can know only facts, and if "facts," by the origin of the word, are things "made," then who made these occurrences—some force in the world out there that we, *a priori*, cannot know? Or, as Hume would have it, insofar as we organize in our own minds the phenomena we register, we create our own categories of order—ideas like "causality" that we believed an inherent element in the external physical world, but which turns out to be simply a mind form. This might remain an academic exercise, were it not for the way positivist knowing impacts a second element of the puzzle—medical science. For here, in the domain of our personal bodies, in terms of sickness and health, "facts" are not content to exist out there. Instead, they invade and destroy the organism.

These elements interact in interesting ways. Positivist medicine was perhaps the major biological science in the nineteenth century, at least in France, and as such tended to be "biological philosophy." Instead of operating as an inductive, experimental physiology, its focus increasingly turned to the creation of categories and frames, the classification of facts. As science, it sought more perfect taxonomies of the already known, and thus tended not to push the envelope beyond these limits, to engage "new" entities at the interface between body and extended "world." For example, Comteans dismissed "darwinisme" as superfluous: "Le vrai problème biologique consiste à articuler structure et fonction" (The real problem of biology consists in delineating structure and function).[2] Second, this positivist mania for increasingly rigorous framing may contribute to its own shift of emphasis, in the later part of the century, from physiological to "psychological" concerns. Positivist medicine, in light of this shift, appears to reverse the old dictum *mens sana in corpore sano*. The body will remain healthy if balance is restored to the mental forces. This in turn will shield the patient from the possibility of invasion by alien elements without, because these elements are simply declared unclassifiable, hence unknowable, thus finally nonexistent. If such a view seems too radical, let us examine the evidence supplied by the two versions of Guy de Maupassant's "Le Horla." We see here a shift from one form of medical frame to another, as "science" places itself between subject and possible incursions of the "out there" (as the name "hors-là" literally states). The first is the "madhouse" or psychiatric ward; the second is psychoanalysis itself. If we can say that across this century various closed forms that both represent and protect the hegemony of the human subject are increasingly assailed by forces of material transformation, then we have in our medical frames a consummate final form of "governor," overlooked because it arises from inside the scientific enterprise itself.

If John Stuart Mill clearly admires Comte and the positivists, in his *Auguste Comte and Positivism* he challenges the limits of their method in a manner analogous to Maupassant's questioning of the medical frame in his two versions of "Le Horla." Mill praises positivism for its attempt to remove the activity of human agency from the process of observing and presenting "facts." This is in line with scientific endeavor from Francis Bacon and René Descartes to Isaac Newton. But the strength of the Comtean method is, for Mill, at the same time a serious weakness. For Comte, by confining knowledge to facts, and in further stating that [the] "essential nature and their ultimate causes [of these facts], either efficient or final, are unknown and inscrutable to us," radically limits scientific activity. First, there are deeper levels of causality—the positivist "fails to perceive the real distinction between the laws of succession and coexistence . . . and those of . . . the action of Causes: the former exemplified by the succession of day and night, the latter by the earth's rotation which causes it" (57). Second of all, such causes often lie beyond the frames of logic that occlude our view of them.

Instead, Comte follows Descartes, substituting "an extraordinary power of concatenation and coordination" for what Mill calls the "independent thought" needed to engage deeper causes beyond the organized web of facts. Positivism, for example, cannot deal with the supernatural: "Positive philosophy maintains that within the existing order of the universe, or rather of the part of it known to us, the direct determination of every phaenomenon is not super-natural but natural" (15). Such logic simply declares the "horla," because it lies beyond the domain of known facts, nonexistent: "If the universe had a beginning, its beginning, by the very conditions of the case, was super-natural; the laws of nature cannot account for their own origin" (14).

What Mill ultimately finds in positivist science is a "mania for regulation" that denies the independent thinker access to phenomena outside its frames of order. Following Mill's Cartesian argument, one could argue that the ultimate realm to regulate is the mind itself. However rigorous the systems and institutions of medicine in place, the disordered psyche remains the entry point that lets the "supernatural" penetrate the medical frame. Once admitted, its power to subvert the control mechanisms of positivist medicine is great. Maupassant's internee, in the first version of "Le Horla," blames his doctors with their control experiments, for opening the mental doors to the possibility of this "other": "Et tout ce que vous faites vous-mêmes, Messieurs, depuis quelques ans, ce que vous appelez hypnotisme, la suggestion, le magnétisme—c'est lui que vous annoncez, que vous prophétisez" (And everything you have been doing, Messieurs, for the last several years, what you call "hypnotism," "suggestion," "magnetism"—it's *he* you've been announcing, prophetising all along).[3] One might parallel the efforts of psychonalysis to regulate the entry of external phenomena into the brain with Comte's desire to elaborate a new system of phrenology. Comte, Mill tells us, traced a grid in *a priori* manner over the exterior of the brain, a structure "grounded on the best enumeration and classification he could make of the elementary faculties of our intellectual, moral, and animal nature; to each of which he assigned an hypothetical place in the skull" (185–186). The deeper causes, inside that skull, are untouched by this system, just as, with Maupassant's doctors, any connection between the deep mind and outside forces, remain occluded, "out there." Beneath the taxonomies and grids we trace upon the surface, inside the brain, lies the place of possible interface between human and "alien." This is not necessarily a place of sickness or health. What it may offer is even greater, intuitive scientific exploration. For the scientist Pascal, "le coeur a ses raisons que la raison ne connaît point" (the heart has its reasons that reason does not know).[4]

As Tzvetan Todorov defines the "fantastique," it is a genre that cultivates (but cannot sustain) hesitation between knowledge within the frame of known laws of phenomena, and experience outside that frame where these laws do not hold. Again however, Todorov's neatly traced schema does not touch the deeper activity of genre formation beneath. When Todorov addresses the evolution of his genre beyond the nineteenth century, he reveals the positivist limits of his formulation. The idea of hesitation with its supposed tensions, we discover, is disingenuous. There is no tension at all except that needed to maintain the stasis of Todorov's theoretical frame, his grid of internal relationships. To either side of his "fantastique" lie those areas of causality Comte would occlude from scrutiny. The side of the "étrange" is that of the causes of known nature; the side he calls "le merveilleux" relegates, with some disdain, the move to reach out to new causalities to the realm of fairy tale.[5] Rather than admit that his "fantastique" might evolve or transmutate into new forms, Todorov merely places it in a new medical frame—that of psychoanalysis: "Allons plus loin: la psychanalyse a remplacé (et par là même a rendu inutile) la littérature fantastique. . . . Les thèmes de la littérature fantastique sont devenus, littéralement, ceux-là mêmes des recherches psychologiques des cinquante dernières années" (Let's go farther yet: psychoanalysis has replaced [and in doing so made useless] fantastic literature. . . . The themes of fantastic literature have become, literally, those of psychoanalytic research during the last fifty years).[6]

Maupassant's two versions of "Le Horla" appear at first glance to confirm Todorov's generic model. Version One seems to be an example of *l'étrange*, the eighteenth-century category of the supernatural explained, in which strange occurrences are in the end reframed within the realm of consensus reality. The events the protagonist recounts are weighed by the doctors, indeed even become plausible to one of the examiners: They might be worth considering. The larger body of medical experts however remains silent: The possible existence of a "horla" has been uttered, the doors of the institution close upon it. If this is no longer a case of individual madness, it might be one of multiple or mass hallucination. We cannot imagine our prudent board of doctors, despite difference of opinion, moving away from their stand of rational skepticism.

In Version Two, the overt frame of medical authority is removed. This, apparently, moves the reader from the strange to the realm of the fantastic. Not only is there no institution or doctors present, but the story itself is no longer rationally organized by a patient seeking to persuade the experts. We have instead a first-personal journal account, one that records day-by-day reactions to phenomena. This narrator is as emotional and confused as the first narrator was logical and persuasive. If at first we think that this new speaker, not restrained by the hospital setting, is freer to engage the possibility that this "horla" really exists, we soon think again. The increasing mental instability of the narrator, as it appears, tells us we might be reading the diary of a madman after all. Doctors at this time encouraged patients to express themselves in art, or to keep diaries of this kind as therapeutic methods. The medical frame then, though covert, may be still present, with the narrator recording step by step his descent into madness. Though there is no overt intrusion of a doctor into this tale, the reader still senses in the narrator's account a silent narratee who, if not directly addressed, at least overhears his gropings to explain what is happening to him. This listener is the psychoanalyst.

This is the usual reading of Version Two. I wish to read it however in the contrary sense, not as an affirmation of the medical frame, but as an attempt to expose and reject that frame in favor of the possibility of open-ended investigation of alien phenomena—an investigation that, in terms of the scientific establishment, must necessarily operate outside the consensus, as it involves the breaking of its comfortable boundaries. What emerges instead, from this solitary narrator's account, is a gradual sense of the inadequacy of Cartesian or Comtean categories to explain the "facts" of possible alien encounter. As with Comte's phrenological calque on a living brain, "psychoanalysis" becomes little more than a holding action, the affirmation of "can't know" in the face of possible material incursion on human existence. Maupassant's narrator in fact, as we will see, increasingly challenges the frame of his psychoanalyst-listener. In doing so, he actually devises a method of engaging the material world more in tune (in terms of nineteenth-century French science) with that of Claude Bernard's "médicine expérimentale," where "A l'aide des *sciences expérimentales actives*, l'homme devient un inventeur de phenomènes" (aided by active experimental science, man becomes an inventor of phenomena, not just someone who classifies them).[7]

Todorov, in the parallel realm of genre formation, may appear (like Maupassant's narrator in Version Two) to demand more "scientific" latitude. But compared with a genuinely open-ended analysis, Todorov's claims are purest facade. He chides Northrop Frye's efforts at defining generic categories as yielding merely taxonomies or "catalogues." What he proposes however, as "scientific" alternative to the messy historical genres Frye flounders in, are "theoretical genres," more Comtean frames: "De toute évidence, les genres historiques sont un sous-ensemble de l'ensemble des genres théoriques complexes" (given the evidence, historical genres are simply a sub-set of the larger set of complex theoretical genres) (25). Thrown over Version Two of "Le Horla" however, Todorov's "theoretical" frame, like the psychoanalytical frame in the story, fails to resolve the disruptive tensions at work beneath the surface. In light of such frames, Todorov tells us that because of psychoanalysis we no longer need, as example, the vampires of fantastic literature to reference our fascination with cadavers. Yet, in terms of the Horla, and of the slightly later Dracula, these vampires do not represent, on some theoretical or symbolic level, so much as incarnate an alien physical force—they *are* the plague, the pathogen, the invisible man or man from Mars. As such they cannot be met by what Claude Bernard calls "abstractions," but rather by an "active" science willing to admit and engage such unknown forces.

What begin to emerge on the level of genre as Maupassant rewrites his story—as he wrestles within the positivist framework with the hypothesis of an alien that may be *successor* to the present human form—are forms akin to what we call horror and science fiction. Both of these require that we take the alien possibility *literally*, as a material not a figurative menace. By doing so, the person facing the alien breaks the mind circle, in which all sense of an "out-there" becomes a figment of the imagination. Within the medical frame, accepting the Horla is madness. Outside, it becomes the higher "madness" of the visionary scientist, alone against the world of his narrative. As such he acts against his narratee, the addressee within the text who belongs to the consensus reality he begins to challenge. His new addressee is the reader who, as he re-perceives the world through the narrator's sole eyes, begins to override the old order and grapple with the Horla himself. Beyond psychoanalysis, this new reader is no longer limited to dichotomies such as "sick" or "healthy," "good" or "evil," but is now free to consider the phenomenon before him as neutral, a case of the evolutionary struggle for survival.

Before reading Maupassant's Version Two, we must examine the generic continuum in which the story operates. First, the origin of the medical frame in early Romantic literature reveals the nature of the transgressive force it must contain. It was with the figure of the artist that the Romantics revived the ancient association between "madness" and divine inspiration. Notably, it is in the public dimension of music (or more precisely the conflict between private "inspiration" and public performance) that artists first take on, for writers like Hoffmann and Balzac, the potential for social disruption. In Honoré de Balzac's story "Gambara" (1834), a "doctor" and his medicine protect the boundaries of society from aggression by Gambara's music. The music Gambara thinks is sublime, is to ordinary ears grating cacophony. But Gambara when drunk plays music that is accessible, even sublime, to the normal ear. When Count Andrea realizes this, he explicitly takes the role of social doctor, and treats Gambara with this "medicine" to cure him of his folly. Balzac, if ambiguous about the role of art in society, appears to favor the medical frame.

Another important source for Todorov's "fantastic" however, E. T. A. Hoffmann, appears to revel in the disruptive force of the antisocial artist, his ability to elude the frame. Hoffmann's central figure, Johannes Kreisler, seems but another fugitive from that "Irrenhaus" that has held so many Romantic musicians from Wackenroder's Joseph Berglinger to Ken Russell's Tschaikovsky in *The Music Lovers*. For Hoffmann, however, the physical madhouse can yield to the ubiquitous social frame, where all good citizens are invited to assume the role of "doctor," even the philistine cat in the novel *Die Lebensansichten des Katers Murr* (*The Life and Opinions of the Tomcat Murr*, 1818). The very form of this novel is a supposed act of "healing," whereby Murr recycles the very medium of Kreisler's sublime (and by that token criminal) ravings by using the backs of torn-out sheets of the artist's music and diary to write his healthy and wise reflections on life. The reader however awaits the "mad" fragments of Kreisler as they resurface amidst Murr's clinical efforts to suppress them.

A shift in Kreisler's direction comes in the later nineteenth century—and ironically from within that realm of middle-class pragmatic "health" fostered by social doctors such as Andrea—with Jules Verne. Verne's visionaries are now scientists and inventors, their "madness" the desire to push the physical envelope— to travel faster, or farther, than mankind ever has, to open human beings to new, potentially alien encounters. In response perhaps to these challengers—Nemo, Ardan, Barbicane—exploring their "mysterious islands" in real seas and cosmic places, the "alienists" like Jean Charcot (and ultimately Sigmund Freud) shifted focus from wonders without to abnormalities within. If there is to be an alien encounter, it is better to locate it, not at the center of the Earth, but at the core of the human mind, in the subconscious, where one can hope to rectify the inbalance. The result of course is to stifle any possibility of change or transformation. We can be healed; but we must not risk situations in which we can either diminish or grow.

How this situation plays out in the 1950s, with viewers acclimatized to the new generic labels "horror" and "science fiction," is seen in the two endings of the 1950s film *Invasion of the Body Snatchers*. In the film, the people of Santa Mira are physically possessed by alien creatures. The takeover is pointedly more than just mind-snatching; there are "pods" that presumably shape themselves into the exact form of the victim, to become indistinguishable in all things except individual will. Dr. Miles Bennett gradually sees everyone dear to him succumb to the pods and become one with the "group mind"—a popular version of (or aversion to) the positivist taxonomies and psychoanalytical grids of the previous century. In the first ending Miles escapes to the freeway, banging frantically on cars as they pass, seeking to give news of the invasion. But no one stops. No one within the frame of the film believes Miles, or is given the chance to do so; the pods will spread, and mankind may be doomed. The doctor has become the "madman" within the frame of his fictional world; to the viewers however he is sane. There can be, in this case, no covert frame. The viewers have seen the whole story, and they know Miles is right, that there is an alien taking human bodies, that action must be taken to stop it.

Miles's experience within his frame is horror; his audience, however, is in the realm of science fiction. The second (accepted) ending merely transposes the sf vision back into the film's frame. In this version, the police pick Miles up and interrogate him. At first, they do not believe his story, and even call psychiatrists. Then, there is a report that a truck carrying strange "pods" has overturned on the road. The "quick-thinking" police captain puts two and two together, calls the army, and we are on the way to a physical response to a physical threat. One can argue of course that such "serendipity" is but another frame, meant to protect our cherished anthropocentric "individualism." For, logically, why cannot the next step in human evolution be a group entity? This ending however must be accepted as a re-enactment of the sf ritual of discovery and action. In a sense, the first ending is also a re-enactment of an earlier stage on the road to sf—this time of the situation of the narrator of Maupassant's Version Two. But where the viewer's gaze makes this a ritual, Maupassant's rendition   presented in the words of an isolated narrator, through which truth and fiction are filtered, never directly seen—places us in the middle of the process of discovery, ourselves encompassed by the covert frame, struggling with the narrator to break free to accept, and engage, the Horla. Maupassant's rendering "from within" of this crucial step in the formation of the sf genre is masterful.

The opening pages of Version Two seem to position us for discovery of its narrator's psychosis. Once the reader becomes an amateur psychologist, he identifies with the narratee, the covert analyst. By this means, it seems, a medical frame is constructed where none is overtly visible. There are no statements of "facts" from this narrator, in contrast to the narrator of Version One, who (though in the end he remains an inmate at the asylum) has learned to master the rhetoric of rational science. This narrator instead offers emotional effusions. To the attuned ear these, ranging the field of Romantic cliché from nature to Rouen's gothic spires, echo the *Schwärmerei* of Hoffmann's Nathanael in "Der Sandmann." Such a discourse is manic-depressive, full of inexplicable *Ahnungen*. An example is his immediate reaction to the passage of the Brazilian three-master, which in Version One, through logical deduction, was only in the last pages revealed to be the possible vector for the Horla's penetration of France. This narrator, on seeing the boat, cries out: "Je le saluai, je ne sais pourquoi, tant ce navire me fit plaisir à voir" (I saluted its passage, I don't know why, I felt such a thrill at its sight) (422). As these fevers of the intellect *precede* his outbreaks of physical fever and insomnia, the reader tends to locate their cause within the mind, and not any valid reaction to physical phenomena. The reader thinks here (as he does with Hoffmann's Nathanael) of a mind addled by too much Romantic literature and art. Indeed, the language and images used issue from literary hauntings. There are echoes of Charles

Baudelaire's "spleen" ("I await sleep the way one would await the executioner" / "J'attends le sommeil comme on attendrait le bourreau"). Or of Füseli's famous painting "The Nightmare": "Je dors. . . . [E]t je sens aussi que quelqu'un s'approche de moi, me regarde, me palpe, monte sur mon lit, s'agenouille sur ma poitrine, me prend le cou entre ses mains et serre" (I sleep . . . and I also feel that someone approaches, is watching me, touches me, climbs onto the bed, kneels down on my chest, takes my neck in his hands, squeezes) (424).

Maupassant adds more scenes to the opening pages of Version Two, all echoing a Romantic "sublime," which in their frenzy appear to suggest a psychopathology of the overwrought imagination. The narrator's first entry expresses a near-Oedipal fixation on his native "soil": "J'aime ce pays, et j'aime y vivre parce que j'y ai mes racines, ces profondes et délicates racines, qui attachent un homme à la terre où sont nés et morts ses aïeux" (I love this region, and I love to live here because I have my roots here, those deep and fragile roots that attach a man to the ground where his ancestors were born and died) (421). His clinical acumen awakened, the reader now has the account of a walk in the nearby (familiar) forest. What occurs seems a Romantic commonplace, where man is overwhelmed by nature. But the heightened, "fantastic" mood of the account suggests other dimensions. Inexplicably, the narrator begins to turn on his heels, "very fast, like a top." Few readers at the time could escape the reference to Hoffmann's Nathanael in "Der Sandmann," overtaken by a similar automatism. To the psychoanalyst, there can be no question of alien possession; this can only be an example of "alienation," a Cartesian category where mind loses control over its extended body, thus allowing it to revert to the condition of "machine" or automaton. The Hoffmann reference however, for the careful reader, points at the same time in a different direction, outside the medical frame. In Hoffmann's story, the rational mind is clearly no more capable of locating the boundary between self and other, than is Romantic "intuition." Freud's "explanation" of Nathanael's actions as "Oedipal," for example, does little more than reveal the inadequacy of medical rationalism, for it reduces the hypothesis of alien incursion to experience of the "unheimlich," a case of mind decentered from its familiar "home" environment. Hoffmann, on the other hand, clearly shows Nathanael, like Maupassant's narrator, reaching beyond the frame of mind and convention. An example is the episode where Coppola tosses a welter of eyeglasses before Nathanael, and he picks up a pair, and sees the world not only anew, but in a clear inversion of the Cartesian and "scientific" co-optation of the extended world. For gazing on the automaton Olimpia, she becomes to him (but to none other around him) an independent "alien" being, as with Frankenstein's creature artifice brought to "life." In similar manner Maupassant's narrator, in meditating on his experience, begins to turn the psychoanalytical model around, pointing his analysis outside the frame, toward a living "presence" no one can see. In Version One, it is only in concluding his argument that the protagonist offers a reason why we cannot see the Horla. Offered in a Cartesian perspective, it is an explanation meant to be taken as "rational" by his clinical audience. "Notre oeil, Messieurs, est un organe tellement élémentaire" (our eye, sirs, is such a primitive organ) (418), he says, mind is dependent on its material senses for information of the outside world, and these are of necessity problematic.

The lone narrator of Version Two raises this problem instead in an early entry. And he turns the Cartesian proposition around. Where the sense of sight cannot perceive the too small or too large, might not cultivating the more physically direct senses (as with Pascal's "le coeur a ses raisons que la raison ne connaît point," offer points of contact between our being and invisible presences around us: "Tout ce qui nous entoure . . . tout ce que nous frôlons sans le connaître, tout ce que nous touchons sans le palper" (everything that surrounds us . . . that brushes up against us without our knowing it . . . that touches us without our feeling it) (422). Maupassant's narrator thus moves closer to a Fontenelle, who in his concept of "plurality of worlds" challenges Descartes on reason's necessary isolation. A spinning body is not necessarily a body alienated from mind, creating a mechanical "double" that is mind's distorted mirror image. It may be literally what it seems—a body visited (a possibility Hoffmann leaves open) by a material alien being. It is something to be apprehended palpably, by reaching physically beyond the Cartesian frame of "images," "shadows," "symbols," in order to touch it physically.

We find like ambiguity of experience, with subsequent reversal of a promised psychoanalytical frame, in the next episode—that of the narrator's visit to Mont Saint-Michel. Here, in this archly Gothic site, the narrator seems to fall prey to its unbalancing phantasms. Surrounded by "bêtes fantastiques" (the word appears multiple times in his account), he hears a superstitious monk tell of cavorting monsters who assail humans—an "invisible realm" that can exist—positivist science tells us—only in a deranged mind. And indeed, the narrator seems prey to such delusion by auto-suggestion, for that night the strangler of his dreams takes the form of one of these beasts: a succubus. Yet again a subtle shift takes place. For we see the narrator reaching out, taking an initiative that is scientific in nature. Pushing the monk to see if he believes in these creatures of legend, he discovers an agnostic ("I don't know"). Pushing further, he elicits from the monk a disquisition on the wind as neutral and nonhuman force, and discovers another person who touts alternate ways of perceiving the unseen: "Voici le vent, qui est la plus grande force de la nature, qui renverse les hommes . . . l'avez-vous vu, et pouvez-vous le voir? Il existe, pourtant" (Consider the wind, which is the most powerful force in nature, that knocks down men . . . have you ever seen it, can you see it? And yet, it exists) (427). Happenings that, at first sight, seem to reinforce the medical frame, suddenly point beyond the Cartesian boundaries of the visual, toward the possibility of literal alien contact.

Ensuing scenes—the milk-drinking visitations, telekinesis of the plucked rose, the self-turning page of the book, finally the vanishing of the narrator's mirror image—all again might seem, in the context of the narrator's excessive, neurotic-seeming self-examination, to chronicle the onset of madness. Increasingly, there occurs a fatal doubling in which mind separates itself from its mechanical simulacrum. First, there is somnambulism, where two parts of a same self operate without knowledge of each other; diagnosed as schizophrenia, this leads to homicide, and finally suicide, where the avenging automaton turns, first against other integral humans, then against his own body as seat of the alienated mind. Driven in the final pages not only to capture an image of the Horla, but physically to trap and destroy it, the narrator fits his house with iron shutters and doors. Enticing the Horla, in its invisibility a perverted "image" of the lost union of mind and body, to his reading room, he locks the doors, pours kerosene on the downstairs floor, sets the house on fire, and flees to the forest to watch it burn. Only the screams of his trapped servants seem to awaken him. Like the somnambulist, the man who lost his image in the mirror, he had "forgotten their existence." He is so fixated on this phantasm that he has forgotten the existence of normal beings. More troubling yet to one seeking proof of alienation, this scene is not narrated in its immediacy. Event and human response are themselves separated, as he recollects it from the distance of the next day and the "Hôtel Continental, Rouen." His sole concern here is that "it" escaped. With the Horla coming to get him, he has but one option: suicide, obliteration of man and image alike. Following the logic of the covert medical frame, the only verdict we can have is madness. If we accept this verdict, we have to deny the presence of the Invisible; the Cartesian perimeters of man's world are secure.

But if this is so, why did the covert doctor let the situation go this far? Why did he not step in, help the sick man recapture his mirror image, reverse his mad automaton plunge? Maupassant's narrator, alone to the end, can rely on no theory or institution; he can only count on his own, unaided reason. This however, the absence of doctors and asylums, is the point at which weakness is free to become strength. The "medical" verdict here is one that, in turn, ignores the presence, in the narrative, of literary secret sharers—characters created by the "mad" Hoffmann, who prove (like their author) equally slippery when enclosed in the medical frame.

As with Nathanael's narrative, that of Maupassant's protagonist just as well (if we accept to step beyond the frame and view it anew) can be seen to chronicle liberation from the tyranny of science's "case histories," reductive scenarios of mirrors and doubles that only lock him in turn in another burning building, that of mental derangement. Let us take another, Hoffmannesque, image: both Nathanael and Maupassant's narrator are spinning beings. As such, they turns so fast that they erase their image from the mirror. Doing so, they obliterate all sign of an "ego," the socially constructed self within that posits an unconstructed or monstrous self without, in the extended world. This act of image snatching acts to place them outside the Cartesian pale; they become objects without a subject. If we look at the actions of Maupassant's narrator in this light, we see developing in his gropings beyond the frame an independent mode of thinking. As such, this narrator must lose his image or shadow, for only by doing so is he free to engage the alien beyond the limits of conventional order.

We see this liberation occurring in the long added scene with Dr. Parent, who offers a demonstration of the positivist science of "magnétisme" and hypnosis. Already, as lone individual seeking to understand the milk drinkings and inexplicable movement of objects, the narrator has hit upon the hypothesis of somnambulism. He weighs the possible meanings of the term: "Alors, j'étais somnambule, je vivais, sans le savoir, de cette double vie mystérieuse qui fait douter s'il y a deux êtres en nous, ou si un être étranger . . . anime, par moments . . . notre corps captif" (I was a somnambulist then, I was living, without knowing it, that mysterious double life which makes one ask whether in fact there are two beings in each of us, or rather whether some alien being does not, in certain moments, take and hold captive our whole being) (428). The narrator has already become lucid enough to consider two possibilities: one, within the frame, where the body strays from mental control; the other, outside the frame, where we are taken over, body and mind, by some alien force. What Dr. Parent's actions reveal are the double nature of science itself. For in purporting to present, in objective fashion, an example of mental alienation, he is himself acting the role of alien invader of a human body, creating through hypnotism a state of division in the subject. The purpose of this "experiment" is not objective knowledge; it is an exercise of the power of science, which divides the human being so as to control its actions.

The name Dr. "Parent" is not innocent, nor is the name of the hypnotized cousin, Mme Sablé. The French title of Hoffmann's "Sandmann" is "L'Homme de sable." If a purpose of psychoanalysis is to resolve conflicts with parents, then Dr. Parent (working like Freud within this narrow frame) must analyze away the possibility there is a real, physical "sandman" out there. This he does by taking an external role himself, by displaying his own physical power to divide the self, then restore it to wholeness. Parent is vocal in his positivist diatribes against Voltaire's "infamy" of superstitious religion, indeed he cites from that author's *Sottisier*: "Rien de plus vrai que cette parole de Voltaire: 'Dieu a fait l'homme à son image, mais l'homme le lui a bien rendu' " (Nothing is more true than these words of Voltaire: God has made man in his image, but man has more than given that image back to God) (431). But what Voltaire meant, ironically, is offered (in a neat double irony) seriously by Parent, in the sense that the relation of man to God, or man to alien, is reduced to a neat mirroring, one capable of relocating this other being awakened by hypnosis, naming it a projection of some inner imbalance, man like God simply rendering his image back upon nature. Science then, looking on the mysteries of the external realm, need only extrapolate these within the internal, mirroring subject. By doing so, it refuses to seek beyond the frame, for external causes, in this case the possibility of "possession" by a being from out there.

Dr. Parent, however, in manipulating Mme Sablé, acts not only like god with his image, but like a cruel god. The narrator offers a protracted account of how her hypnotized "second self" first begs him, her cousin, for 5,000 francs, then is humiliated the next day when, now returned to her original state, he brings her the money she has no recollection of asking for. It might seem that the narrator is all too willing to participate in this mini-drama. Is he himself acting as double of the doctor-torturer? Or is this rather the expression of his desire, not only to participate, but to expand his investigative reach beyond that of the doctor, to test the limits even farther? Where the narrator in fact seems most eager to participate is in Parent's demonstration of *double vue*. But what the doctor reveals here is rather an inability to control images, to manipulate the subject through their control. Parent holds up a calling card. He asks his hypnotized subject to gaze into its blank surface and tell him what the narrator is doing behind her. Curiously she is able to do so: "Elle voyait dans cette carte . . . comme elle eût vu dans une glace" (She saw in this card . . . just as she would have seen in a mirror) (432). In this "double sight," a nonreflecting surface replaces the mirror. What this suggests is the possible intervention of some alien force within the mirror system itself. Blankness becomes visible, suddenly we are outside the frame. The doctor however, smug in his "science," does not realize this.

The narrator however seems to have learned this lesson, as we see from the later trap he sets to catch "sight" of the Horla now moving this time behind *his* back. The narrator sits at his desk and writes. Behind him is an *armoire* with a full-length mirror. Sensing he has attracted his visitor, he closes his door. Then, *certain* the alien is reading over his shoulder, he whirls around: "Je ne me vis pas dans ma glace! . . . Elle était vide, claire, profonde. . . . Mon image n'était pas dedans . . . et j'étais en face, moi!" (I didn't see myself in the mirror any more! . . . It was empty, clear, deep. . . . My image was not there . . . and I was standing right in front of it) (446). Fixed on the empty mirror, he sees his image gradually begin to reappear: "Tout à coup je commençai à m'apercevoir dans une brume . . . il me semblait que cette eau glissait de gauche à droite . . . rendant plus précise mon image, de seconde en seconde" (All at once I began to see myself in its cloudy depths. . . . It seemed to me this cloudy water was shifting from left to right . . . and as it did so my image became more distinct, from second to second) (446). Just as the blank greeting card allowed Mme Sablé to "see" what was behind her head, sight is again a function of blankness. Vision of the alien, it seems, can occur only when the interfering image of self is removed, when we cease to be thrall to this "other self" the doctors can control. The narrator is now free to draw the "mad" conclusion that the Horla's "corps imperceptible avait dévoré mon reflet" (the Horla's imperceptible body had devoured my image) (426). The rational hegemony of sight yields to literal, tangible contact.

Hoffmann's Erasmus Spikher, in "Die Abenteuer der Silvester-Nacht," also lost his mirror image. Hoffmann's variation of the fate of Chamisso's Peter Schlemeihl, who lost his shadow, is most significant. Schlemeihl's shadow is taken by the Devil. This is a Devil however whose sin is now the Romantic worship of self, whose fatal (and punished) pride would fill every mirror with its sole image. Such a devil, condemned to function in the positivist system that succeeds Romantic excess, takes in turn from potential rebels like Schlemeihl their shadow. To lose this, as tangible sign of their fallen condition, is a double Fall, for to appear *without* a shadow, as undivided being, incurs the wrath of a world where each being must bear the image of his second self as stigma.

Hoffmann, well aware of the medical frame building up in his time to reinforce this stigma, has his protagonist Spikher lose not a shadow but a mirror image. Such a loss is more intimate, first perceived not by others but by the sole self. To escape detection, Schlemeihl dons seven league boots, striding above the world of cast shadows. Spikher in contrast seeks internment, places where mirrors can be covered, an asylum. He thus submits to "mind forg'd manacles," strictures that psychoanalysis only reinforces in its pretense to "cure" its patient. As with Spikher, the narrator's first sense of this loss of image is one of terrible isolation of the subject, a helplessness akin to that of Pascal's thinking reed. In like manner, Maupassant's narrator feels physically crushed: "Tous les ressorts de l'être physique semblent brisés. . . . Je n'ai plus aucune force. . . . Je suis rivé à mon siège . . . de telle sorte qu'aucune force ne nous soulèverait" (All the mainsprings of the physical being seem to be broken. . . . I no longer have any strength, I'm stuck to my chair. . . . in such a manner that no force whatsoever would be capable of raising me up) (439–440). The persistent references to Pascal—note the generalizing "nous" in the preceding quote and in "Nous sommes si infirmes . . . si petits . . . sur ce grain de boue qui tourne délayé dans une goutte d'eau" (We are so weak, so small . . . stuck on this tiny fleck of mud that dissolves as it turns in a drop of water) (441)—offer another subtext, one that asks the reader to reconsider his "madness" as a new form of vision. In Pascalian fashion, if the universe that crushes him does not know, he, in coming to know he is crushed, achieves a new sense of the order of things. As he comes to see it, on one extreme lies Cartesian lucidity and with it madness ("Certes, je me croirais fou . . . si je connaissait parfaitment mon état" (Certainly, I would have to believe I was mad . . . if I knew my state of being perfectly) (437). On the other extreme is the Pascalian act of faith. Seeing this impasse, he is free to choose a third path: the median, science-fictional way expressed in Voltaire's famous twenty-fifth *Lettre anglaise contra Pascal*, of a gradual, physical evolution of things on earth. What the narrator expresses is Voltaire corrected by Darwinian "tooth and claw": "Un être nouveau! Pourquoi pas? . . . Pourquoi serions-nous les derniers? . . . C'est que sa nature est plus parfaite, son corps plus fin et plus fini . . . que le nôtre si faible, si maladroitement conçu" (A new being! Why not? Why should we be the final step? . . . What we have is a creature who is more perfect, with a better crafted and more perfect body that ours, which is so weak and badly conceived) (444). Given the hegemony of this human form on our modes of thought, in both Descartes and Pascal, is not this self-demeaning a necessary step if we are to admit, against all human science and logic, the possible existence of a genuine alien?

In the final scene the narrator, now absolutely certain of the Horla's existence, devises a ruse to trap it in his house and set fire to it. In doing so, he "forgets" his servants trapped inside. Maupassant places his reader at a final crux here. The verdict can be that this narrator is now totally insane, his burning the house schizoid. Or the reader, already pointed outside the medical frame by the undercurrent of references to Hoffmann, sees emerging here a new, single-minded visionary, a "scientist" with sole focus on contact with the alien. Working against the backdrop of Cartesian positivist system-building, Maupassant takes us through the steps that lead to this new epistemological stance: first, the cosmic isolation and helplessness of Pascal's thinking reed as condition for new *prisede conscience*; then, Voltairean relativism, displacing human centrality along a chain of being that includes the certainty of *higher* forms of existence this side of absolute Godhead;

finally, the condition of this obsessed hyper-investigator who foreshadows Bram Stoker's Van Helsing, or more recently Roy Neary (Roy Schieder) in *Close Encounters of the Third Kind*. The latter is, significantly, a lineman, thus one who has a hands-on knowledge of grids of power the rationalist scientist can "grasp" only in theoretical manner. Neary also destroys his house by obsessively building in its living room, out of all sorts of objects from sedate middle-class life, the huge model of Devil's Tower, the place where he goes alone to contact the alien, leaving the rationalist Lacombe (François Truffaut) behind, unable to act, looking on in awe.

Maupassant's narrator follows his own path. It is however, for those who read beyond the frame, the path of a visionary surely more scientific, in the modern sense, than that of his doctors. Maupassant makes subtle changes in Version Two to present the procedure of his investigator. For example, now as in Version One he does not simply come across the account of the Brazilian "incident" in a newspaper clipping. Very early in the story, he tells of his presentiment about the three-master coming up the Seine. Then, in the final pages, he presents an "objective" recounting of the same incident, this time from a scientific journal, the *Revue du monde scientifique*. It is paranoia that now becomes a doubtful hypothesis. For (rather than just a doctor brought to doubt by a skillful argument) there is convergence of evidence, the formulation of a now plausible hypothesis: "Je le trouvai si joli, si blanc. . . . L'Etre était dessus, venant de là-bas, où sa race était née" (I found the ship so beautiful and white then. . . . The Being was on that ship, coming from over there, from where his race was born) (443). This is an act of mind that, in accepting the physical possibility of a Horla, moves outside the frame of scientific authority, even that of the journal in which the events are recounted. The narrator is now free to turn to the marginal text of Dr. Herestauss, philosopher and theogonist. What was thought pseudo-science now can become, as with Dr. Van Helsing, hyper-science, the *supplement* needed to reach successfully beyond the frame. The name of this German appears as another mirror to catch a madman, here a double of the word Horla itself. The name however, if we look carefully, is not a simple German doubling of the French. In fact, by using this German substitute, we move from a "hors-là," a thing that needs to be pointed at, the out-there as brute object of terror, to a "her ist aus," "it is out there," which is syntactically closer to an act of gesturing outward, an impetus to engage in investigation, to meet the alien rather than retreat in fear of its possible existence.

Finally, Maupassant adds elements to his ending that mitigate the sense of closure in the narrator's final, agonizing "what if I didn't kill it?" If we assume the narrator simply kills himself, then the medical frame that has judged him criminally insane has triumphed. Maupassant makes it, however, that if this is so and the frame holds, then we all (because we have been drawn to identify with this narrator's search for a method of understanding) become inmates. Or worse, must share the fate of those locked in the narrator's house, in which we recognize Pascal's description of the *condition humaine*. If we closely examine the narrator's final words however, we discover stirring within them a new generic field, one defined by what we call horror and science fiction. These forms appear in the interstices of the old generic frame—that of the fantastic resolving itself in rational explanation of a pathological case—that no longer quite fits. The narrator is *certain* he did not trap the Horla, reiterating "sans aucun doute" several times. His judgment now bears the scientific authority of one who has seen the alien, not in his mind but out there, has hunted it, tried to destroy it, but realizes he cannot. This is a scenario that has subsequently played over and over in horror, witness John Carpenter's *Halloween* (1978), where psychiatrist turned alien hunter shoots the thing, it falls out the window, but when he looks there is no body there. But, just as the narrator's madness may not be real, his suicide may not prove final either. His final words, "Alors . . . il va donc falloir que je me tue, moi!" (Me then, it's going to be necessary that I kill myself!) (449), thrust a pronoun to the end in which the subject has objectified itself. This is more than another mirror, for it effectively moves the narrative beyond the thematic frame that Todorov sets for the fantastic. In Todorov's system, with its "thèmes du *je*" and "thèmes du *tu*," the "I" subject is not an actor but a looker-on (these are what he calls "les thèmes du regard"). Moreover, this looking is itself reflexive, not outward but inward within the mind theater, where it is deflected away from objects and toward another form of subject, the desiring "tu." This again is a mirror that inflects the potential scientific gaze into a frame defined by the "relation de l'homme avec son désir, et par là même avec son inconscient" (the relation of man with his desire, and thus with his inconscious) (146).

Maupassant's narrator does not merely look or desire; finally he acts. The results of his actions are destructive, the prospects horrific, for the alien, once recognized, escapes, to return again to prey on the compartmentalized and institutionalized minds of our culture, in the way Dracula could enter even the most closely guarded hospital, by means of those minds' unpreparedness for its assault. In Maupassant however, mind escapes its circle, and once this happens horror gives rise to the complementary genre of sf. If Todorov can equate the fantastic to psychoanalysis, cannot (keeping the medical metaphor) sf be equated with a form of immunology? Sf is literature's immune response to horror, to the string of menaces from outside the human frame, from Hamlet's warning of things beyond Horatio's ken to Dracula's infecting of the blood of a nation, things long in coming, long ignored: plurality of worlds, vectored plagues, unseen menaces, testing our defenses, finally arriving with the Horla. The response to this Horla may be science beyond the edge, as with Van Helsing. Or it may be mutagenesis itself, as in H. G. Wells's *The War of the Worlds*, where the invaders can no longer be repelled by individual human efforts, but where the human organism itself must realize its evolutionary capacity to resist invasion by becoming immune to those very pathogens that once confined it to hospitals and the narrowest of mortal limits. Nor is this mutagenic struggle of science fiction against the horrific necessarily defeat. For Maupassant's narrator escapes his frames. As do the survivors of Wells's Martian invasion, for despite carnage and fear of more invasions (which they in their insularity suddenly see for the first time), the invaders leave behind objects that strengthen human resistance, from which new knowledge can be derived. It is this drama of immunization that allows human beings, in science fiction as in life, to change and adapt in order to move to new domains of encounter.

Notes

1. John Stuart Mill, *Auguste Comte and Positivism* (London: N. Trübner & Co., 1865), 6. Later page references to Mill in the text and notes are to this edition.

2. Yvette Conry, *L'Introduction de Darwinisme en France au XIXe siècle* (Paris: Corti, 1974), 416, my translation. See also Harry W. Paul, *From Knowledge to Power: The Rise of the Science Empire in France, 1860–1939* (Cambridge: Cambridge University Press, 1985), 60–92.

3. Guy de Maupassant, *Le Horla et Autres Contes Cruels et Fantastiques*, edited by M.-C. Bancquart (Paris: Classiques Garnier, 1976), 419. All future references to both versions of "Le Horla" are to this edition, and all translations are mine.

4. Blaise Pascal, *Penses*, #277, in Pascal, *Pensées and The Provincial Letters*, translated by W. F. Trotter (New York: Random House, 1941), 95.

5. As Mill says, "The constant resemblances which link phaenomena together, and the constant sequences that unite them as antecedent and consequent, are termed their laws. The laws of phaenomena are all we know respecting them. Their essential nature, and their ultimate causes, either efficient or final, are unknown and inscrutable to us" (6).

6. Tzvetan Todorov, *Introduction à la littérature fantastique* (Paris: Editions du Seuil, 1970), 169. Later page references in the text are to this edition.

7. Claude Bernard, *Claude Bernard's Revised Edition of His Introduction à L'Etude de la Médecine Expérimentale*, edited by Paul F. Cranefield (New York: Neale Watson Academic Publications, 1976), 14; author's italics.

7

Surgical Evolution, or, The Scalpel as Shortcut: The Doctor as Interface between Science Fiction and Horror

David Hinckley

The secret humans were not meant to know is both a standard device and a major theme of horror fiction, which often originates in a conservative reaction to radical change in what is perceived as the "natural order" of reality, an order that Stephen Jay Gould would term "anthropocentrism," or a human-centered view, as opposed to the decentered picture of the universe, which he argues modern science compels us to accept.[1] It is no accident that the rise of horror fiction as a popular art form corresponds with the rise of science and industrialism during the latter part of the Enlightenment, for it is rooted in traditional notions of natural order which are ultimately human-centered and opposed to the positivism which informs much science fiction.

The positivistic researcher believes that he can, through the use of his reason, eventually subdue and dominate natural forces. Treating nature as impersonal object of study rather than as sacred and mysterious chain of being, he regards the imposition of external or technological order as sometimes necessary for the progress of knowledge. Science fiction horror suggests a causal connection between this scientific objectivity and the misuse of technology, and a paradigmatic case has always been that of the doctor as mad scientist. In Mary Shelley's *Frankenstein* and H. G. Wells's *The Island of Dr. Moreau*, such a ruthless visionary attempts to carve out a niche for himself in the quivering flesh of Nature, only to sever the sinews that bind him to humanity, and Nature, far from being reduced to tormented subservience, rises in fanged and clawed fury to devour him.

The irruption of the irrational into the process of supposedly rational scientific advancement is the defining characteristic of this particular variant of the horror genre, which undercuts a basic scientific optimism about the ability of human beings to understand and control natural forces within and without the human personality. To appreciate the close relationship between science fiction and horror, it is helpful to observe that the definition of science fiction offered by Darko Suvin, "the literature of cognitive estrangement,"[2] also applies to horror fiction to some extent, in that horror presents us with the hidden (repressed) fears and desires of our culture in a familiar context. There is a definite sense of alienation in the return of the repressed, where the everyday and familiar, in Sigmund Freud's famous phrase, the *heimlich* or homely, becomes unfamiliar or *unheimlich*, uncanny.[3]

The difference between sf horror and sf proper lies in the attitude toward the progress of science. Sf views science as the road to knowledge and a brave new world of prosperity and peace for all humanity; opponents of technological progress are treated as superstitious and regressive. Horror, on the other hand, regards progress with a jaundiced eye, pointing to the mistakes of the past and the potential terrors of present and future technological advances. Humans are often viewed as the irrational and dangerous disturbers of a quasi-mystical order, or at the very least as unearthing natural and unnatural secrets better left decently buried. While science fiction horror shares many of horror fiction's traditional attitudes toward technology, it also may advance a more sophisticated thesis than either of its parent genres; while acknowledging the potential for human beings to better themselves through the cautious application of technology, it also critiques the disorienting and dehumanizing tendency of certain scientific attitudes, most notably the notion of the perfectly objective observer/researcher.

The doctor serves as a perfect interface between horror and science fiction because he is at once homely and reassuring yet strange and threatening, the man who probes with cold steel the "tremendous secrets of the human frame." The traditional office of healer is fraught with ambivalence; even in the early twenty-first century the association of the doctor with the syringe and the scalpel, instruments of torture as well as healing, remains a potent horror device. Doctors preside over the agonies of birth and death, and as coroners dissect the human body with absolute detachment. While none of these tasks in itself a sociopathic monster makes, part of what sf horror suggests is that it is far too easy for clinical objectivity in the service of a "higher good" to result in disengagement from humanity altogether.

The nineteenth-century idea of the intellect as a cleaver that "murders to dissect" expresses this idea aptly: In treating the natural order as an object of conquest rather than cautious study, the mad scientist/doctor aborts all possibility of understanding his own place in that order. All scientific endeavor is of course not a process of raping Nature, but sf horror begins with the historically verifiable observation that the pursuit of science for its own sake is never really objective or dispassionate, and that all too often the scientist sees fit to take a shortcut. Such meddling with the natural order leads inevitably to Nature's vengeance, as the irrational reemerges in the horrific results of the obsessed doctor's surgical prestidigitations. The scalpel is therefore both tool and emblem of the mad doctor's relationship to the universe: in cutting, he is also cut off, isolated from the rest of humanity, even from a part of himself. This leads inevitably to a denial of social responsibility, even of reality, for in amputating his conscience he has effectively removed the capacity to consider the viewpoints of others.

Frankenstein is a work of Gothic horror also often cited as the original science fiction novel, emphasizing the affinity of the two genres. Victor Frankenstein professes a boundless curiosity for "natural philosophy"[4] or biology, which originates when he is thirteen and stumbles across the works of the alchemist Cornelius Agrippa. He becomes obsessed with discovering "the metaphysical, or in its highest sense, the physical secrets of this world" (43). Both Frankenstein's age and the connection with black magic via alchemy suggests the dangerous irrationality of his quest, and the correspondence of his monomania with the onset of puberty implies the twisting of natural adolescent desires into necrophilic dabblings in unhallowed arts, a common horror theme, in which the social outcast gains power through antisocial means. The connection of the scientist with the magician is also a common device, suggesting the supernatural (read unnatural) power of science in general.

Though ostensibly an attack on Christianity, the novel never fully abandons the mythic in language as well as plot and character. This ambivalence extends to the nameless creature, who rebukes Frankenstein with the classic lines from his Biblical and Miltonic self-education: "Remember, that I am thy creature; I ought to be thy Adam; but I am rather the fallen angel, whom thou drivest from joy for no misdeed" (90). The longing for affection and acceptance is expressed in deliberately religious language; the creature demands that Frankenstein recognize his duty in terms of the central mythology of his culture, ironically not remembering that Adam, too, was driven forth from Paradise. If Christianity is dismissed as a monstrous insult to human reason, the spirit that animates religion is never entirely exorcised; the novel's conflict arises from the struggle of the desire to attain mastery over nature with that part of human nature that must be sacrificed to attain that mastery, compassion, which forms the basis of social and religious values.

The creature wishes his creator to provide him with a mate, but Frankenstein is unable to complete the frightful labors that birthed the creature in the first place, so we have an Adam without an Eve, who quickly devolves into a Satanic monster. Like Frankenstein, whose "workshop of filthy creation" (56) isolates him from his family and his academic peers, the creature is isolated by his horrifying appearance, even as his creator can never return to society because of his unacceptable responsibility for the creature's actions. Victor's knowledge remains "unspeakable" because no one will believe him, and lacking tangible proof of the creature's existence, will think him mad for exactly the wrong reasons. More importantly, however, Frankenstein *is* mad, and as the creature is proof of his madness, he must ignore its existence or confess his own instability. The violation of the natural order represented by the synthetic creation of a human being, a "blasphemous" fusion of dead human and animal organs, is reflected in the unnatural state of mind required to perform the operation, as well as its subsequent unspeakability.

Though he is unaware of the immense evil that will result from his creation, Frankenstein's motives are still suspect: He seeks personal glory, but above all to conquer death, which took his mother shortly before his departure for the academy. After rushing in horror from the act of creating his monster, Victor collapses on his bed, where he has a classic Freudian nightmare:

I thought I saw Elizabeth, in the bloom of health, walking in the streets of Ingolstadt. Delighted and surprised, I embraced her, but as I imprinted the first kiss on her lips, they became livid with the hue of death; her features appeared to change, and I thought that I held the corpse of my dead mother in my arms; a shroud enveloped her form, and I saw the graveworms crawling in the folds of the flannel. (58)

The prophetic quality is obvious; Victor has indeed planted the kiss of death on Elizabeth, for the vengeful monster strangles her on their wedding night. But more relevant to explaining his motives is the presence of his mother; plainly he associates her with Elizabeth, and the specter of death he so dreads can (and does) steal them both from him. He has sublimated his domestic affections and fears into an act of creation that has produced exactly that from which he flees: death and worse, the dread harbinger of doom, the animated corpse. The creature is a type of living dead, and if in one sense he represents a triumph over death, in another he is the incarnation of Victor's fears and desires, an organic engine of destruction. While one could have monstrous Freudian fun with the phallic worms and the creature as Victor's severed and reanimated organ, the important point is that he has not conquered human mortality as he supposedly set out to do. In fact, he has done quite the opposite, unleashing a terrible destructive force that will take the lives of his family and friends.

An intelligent and sensitive being who keenly feels the human desire for companionship, the creature is, once provoked, also the living embodiment of hatred and destruction, and serves to mirror Frankenstein's own self-imposed isolation from his fellow human beings. Although there is nothing overtly supernatural about the creature or his actions, the pattern of destroying Victor's family is classic Gothic horror, with all of its psychoanalytic love-hate ambivalence, and creature and creator are obviously *doppelgängers*. Frankenstein even remarks, "I considered the being whom I had cast among mankind . . . nearly in the light of my own vampire, my own spirit let loose from the grave, and forced to destroy all that was dear to me" (73). That Victor lacks any real compassion is evidenced by the way he demonizes the creature even while understanding its plight; that he identifies its crimes as his own despite this vilification shows the degree to which he has vivisected his own personality.

However, one should minimize neither Frankenstein's irresponsibility and irrationality nor the creature's capacity for homicidal rage and excessive violence; the two are complementary, neither entirely evil, but each incomplete, seeking but never finding fulfillment of their irrational desires. Frankenstein is appalled that the creature is such a horrifying parody of his conscious intentions, and the creature is unable to claim the love he desires. On the other hand, Victor's narcissistic obsession with his own genius and power to create leads to his voluntary seclusion from a family that has given him everything, by his own admission, and sets the tone for his rejection of his creature. Likewise, if the creature experiences the fear and hatred of humans and performs his first killing unintentionally, he also needlessly incriminates Justine and slaughters Frankenstein's entire family out of an implacable vengefulness that belies his quasi-religious appeals for compassion. His promise to "glut the maw of death" (90) should Frankenstein refuse to aid him reveals a disturbing savagery closer to the biblical character of Cain than to the Adamic heritage he claims.

In fact, one might say, both characters are monsters, the creature a mass-murderer and Frankenstein that most dangerous of all beings, a spoiled child with the creative powers of a god, not unlike those irascible Olympians ironically evoked in the book's full title, *Frankenstein, or, The Modern Prometheus*. Like Prometheus, Frankenstein steals the fire of the gods, and also like him is condemned to torment for his misdeed. There the similarity ends, however, because "forethought" is the one thing Frankenstein lacks, and while Prometheus stole fire as a gift to man (and some myths say, gave him life as well), Frankenstein brings nothing but horror and death to the family that bore him. And in an even more devastating commentary on popular conceptions of religion, like the angry God of Genesis in his dealings with Adam, Frankenstein "promotes" his creature "from darkness" in the Miltonic phrase, only to punish it for behaving according to its own nature. From its conception, then, like the Gothic horror novels from which it arose, sf horror is profoundly ambivalent, in that it critiques not only scientific optimism but also traditional conservative reactions against progress, perceiving the inadequacy of moralized versions of traditional myths to account for the complexity of human motivations and behaviors.

The novel's beginning (also its ending) in the frozen wastes reflects the sterility of Victor's parody of natural creation; having created a being that neither he nor anyone else can duplicate, an evolutionary dead end, he denies his own paternal responsibility to his unnatural offspring. The fall is tragic and complete—tragic because Frankenstein could once have become a great man, whose powers could have benefited humanity; complete because once created, the creature, doomed like Cain to wander, can be neither placated nor destroyed, save by his own hand. Both, like Milton's Satan, carry their own hells within them.

The existential plight of Victor and the creature represents the division of the self into component personalities, the defining characteristic of the (sub)genre, and reflects the theme of the severing of the socialized self from the intellect necessary for clinical detachment, the mad doctor's stance in relation to the rest of the world. The creature's patchwork derivation from odd parts of animals and humans is also significant; in the throes of creative frenzy, Victor fails to recognize the hopelessly parodic and doomed quality of his endeavors, which can never aspire to the greater beauty of naturally evolved life forms. Like the Biblical Satan, the mad doctor can not create independently of preexistent life, and his creations remain mere mockeries of nature. But because he *can* exert power to physically change human nature, he does, to his own destruction.

The implicit caveat is against scientific advancement, which like Pandora's curiosity or Eve's apple leads to the release of all that is evil, in mockery of the creator's supposedly benign intentions. But this is an oversimplification; the ultimate source of horror is the brute irrationality of the flesh, which forever pulls down all flimsily "rational" human attempts to transcend it by revealing that they too are born of desire and not reason. Nature is within us as well as without, and the other, the uncanny, is that side of ourselves and nature which we dare not, *cannot* confront. Frankenstein's real "sin" is selfish hubris, in that he thinks his unexamined motives sufficient cause to unbalance the natural order, an act of childish and yet monstrous egotism. The mad scientist is forever slicing, maiming and killing to create, inflicting torment and degrading in order to realize some supposedly higher good that never materializes. In disrespecting natural forms and natural emotional states, he demonstrates a supreme disregard for any law save his own curiosity, which is inevitably only a partial sublimation of a lust for power.

A similar view of the visionary doctor offered in *Frankenstein* colors *The Island of Dr. Moreau*, which echoes both *Frankenstein* and an earlier book, Jonathan Swift's *Gulliver's Travels*, in fusing the voyage of discovery with the creation/discovery of monsters. The shipwrecked narrator Prendick experiences in various ways the kinship of human beings with animals: from the opening conflict in a lifeboat, where he and his two companions are reduced to contemplating the possibility of devouring one of their number in order to survive, to the island where he must struggle for survival with surgically evolved beastmen who are slowly devolving to real beasts again, to the conclusion where, like Gulliver returned from the land of the Hounyhmmns, he lives out his days in paranoid misanthropy, seeing animal behavior everywhere in humanity, and dreading lest some form of spontaneous devolution occur before his very eyes.

Moreau is subject to a peculiar kind of degeneration; where others are prone to instinctive emotional responses, he aspires to be the equivalent of an automaton. He is indeed a visionary, but one who has succeeded in detaching himself from the "weakness" of human compassion. He sees pain as having no relation to morality, and makes the startling claim that it is Prendick's own compassion, based as it is on *fellow feeling*, that is "materialistic." Moreau, on the other hand, sees himself as a "religious man . . . as every sane man must be," and informs Prendick that "pleasure and pain have nothing to do with heaven or hell. Pleasure and pain—Bah! What is your theologian's ecstasy but Mahomet's houri in the dark? This store men and women set on pleasure and pain, Prendick, is the mark of the beast upon them, the mark of the beast from which they came."[5]

Moreau hopes to "burn out all the animal, . . .[and] make a rational creature of my own" (78–79), revealing the basis of his supposedly objective curiosity—itself an oxymoron—in a similar egotism to Frankenstein's, although Moreau is in a sense more consistent in his commitment to his sadistic scientific practices than Victor, who rationalizes his researches as being for the greater good of society. For Moreau, such social claims are simply invalid: His curiosity is its own justification.

You see, I went on with this research just the way it led me. That is the only way I ever heard of research going. I asked a question, and got—a fresh question. Was this possible, or that possible? You cannot imagine what this means to an investigator, what an intellectual passion grows upon him. You cannot imagine the strange, colorless delight of these intellectual desires. The thing before you is no longer an animal, a fellow-creature, but a problem. Sympathetic pain—all I know of it I remember as a thing I used to suffer from years ago. I wanted—it was the only thing I wanted—to find out the extreme limit of plasticity in a living shape. (75)

Moreau is bitterly disappointed in the tendency of his beast men to revert to animal instincts and desires, and hopes each time that his surgical alterations will "take," and he will have produced an authentically human being, or at least one who will continue on the upward path to true humanity. But what is true humanity to Moreau? He regards compassion as a thing of the brutes, and sees no value in anything save the pursuit of his horrific surgical experiments. He views the ideal "rational" person as one who has left his feelings behind in favor of "intellectual passions," and rejects all claims of conscience in favor of his curiosity. Utterly indifferent to social values of any kind, he is in effect a scientific sociopath.

The beastmen, like Frankenstein's creature, are uncanny because they embody contradictory qualities that threaten the concept of human identity. Just as the creature has a human mind "buried alive" in his horrendously ugly body, so are the demihumans of Moreau animals in human shape. Prendick senses this fact from the moment he first lays eyes on the demihuman M'ling, before he has any notion of Moreau or his surgical feats. "I had never beheld such a repulsive and extraordinary face before, and yet—if the contradiction is credible—I experienced at the same time an odd feeling that in some way I had already encountered exactly the features and gestures that now amazed me" (11). The familiar unfamiliar—the *unheimlich*— is clearly evoked here, for the face of which Prendick is reminded is not human at all, but that of a gorilla. The antinatural masquerades as the natural in the work of the mad scientist, just as his repressed fears and desires are the real source of his "rational" vision.

Once Moreau dies, killed while hunting down one of his creatures that had broken "The Law"—a primitive religion he had instilled, which featured him as Supreme Being—the demihumans rebel, and eventually Prendick is the lone genuine human left on the island, surviving through his enemies' lingering fear of him and his vastly greater intelligence. During the latter part of his stay he witnesses the steady degeneration of the beast folk, their loss of speech and return to instinctive behavior. Part of the purpose of "The Law" was to maintain a religious barrier against such an eventuality; forbidden actions included drinking water without using hands, scratching trees, and of course hunting and killing. With the death of Moreau, the primary religious illusion of immortality is broken; if Moreau was mortal, so are Montgomery and Prendick. Thus the process of disillusionment, begun when Moreau and Montgomery hunted Prendick like an animal, ends with God's death, and the fear to which Prendick still manages to appeal, that Moreau watches from heaven, proves ineffectual in deterring the most aggressive of the beastmen, who are after all good materialists in their own right, like Prendick. The parody of popular religious belief and its use to control the masses is devastatingly accurate; Wells would doubtless savor the irony that certain fundamentalist groups today appeal to science to justify their literalist readings of the Bible.

Throughout the novel the theme of the inner beast in humanity is relentlessly pursued, and the greatest horror is that no model of human nature is presented as desirable or above degeneration. Prendick is the representative of conventional morality, but he can find no arguments to resist Moreau's "scientific" ideals, the brutal cruelty of "pure reason," and is prone to rash, instinctive actions that indirectly result in the destruction of Moreau and his work. Montgomery, Moreau's reluctant assistant, may be the most human of the characters in his desire for companionship, but he is of relatively low intelligence, eventually partying with the beastmen to his undoing. Moreau himself is a monster of false rationality, a cruel and indifferent God who wishes only to play with the forms of his worshippers and is disinterested in their affection. His sterile ideal of a reason surgically detached and antiseptically cleansed of the urges of the flesh is not only undesirable but impossible, as is evident from his own attacks of rage when thwarted and oxymoronic "intellectual passion," revealing that like Frankenstein, he too is in the grip of a creative madness, having lobotomized his conscience for the sake of a delusion of power over natural forces.

In his afterword to the Signet Classics edition of *The Island of Dr. Moreau*, Brian W. Aldiss observes that Wells saw himself as "the candidate for rationality, that rationality by means of which mankind would divest itself of religion in order to advance to far greater things: control of nature, control of itself" (140). Aldiss also remarks that Moreau is "a model for God the cruel experimental scientist" (140) and that Wells would later describe the novel as "an exercise in youthful blasphemy" (144). However, Wells's choice of the hyperrational Moreau as his deity figure is strangely at odds with a didactic critique of Christianity, whose ethos is, "Do unto others as you would have them do unto you," a religion of sympathetic *feeling* rather than cold detachment. Moreau is in many respects the ultimate positivist; Aldiss remarks that "He is reason. He rules by his remorseless logic" (142). But this is an oversimplification at best; while the novel is, like *Frankenstein*, a radical critique of popular Christianity, the positivistic monster who plays God is also an unappealing scientific alternative to religious irrationality.[6] Reason, as Moreau defines it, seems more irrational than most religions.

The problem is that ethical values must be partially based on feelings, the ability to imagine another as oneself, and there is no real basis for compassion in cold equations. When Moreau claims that he is "a religious man," he is not speaking ethically, but rather as a kind of positivistic idealist, in that he believes there must be an ultimate design to things beneath the primordial slime of the flesh. This faith in the ultimate rational explicability of the universe underlies much positivism, at least as it manifests itself in literature, and it is at odds with the traditional Christian view of the value of sympathy, love, and suffering as well as the picture of the universe as presented by science in the early part of the twenty-first century.

It is, however, typical of effective horror fiction that whatever didactic intentions may exist at the start are undercut by the oxymoronic tensions inherent in the horrific effect. Texts have a way of coming to life, of being born as much as written, and all really good stories tend to escape the control of their creators. In horror this tendency is especially pronounced because the emotion of horror itself is a reaction to a cognitive crisis that threatens the foundations of personality and society; the repressed is the logic by which this threat is made plausible, a submerged hole in the reason of and for civilization that the horror writer discovers rather than invents in the process of writing. The best writers allow the story to lead them into this forbidden territory, moral be damned, and we are the richer for their daring.

The early Gothic writers often intended a conservative religious message of some sort, but what they got when they actually succeeded in being disturbing was something else altogether. One thinks, for example, of Ann Radcliffe's ludicrously long-winded "explanations" for the mild supernatural chills in *The Mysteries of Udolpho*, or the absurdity of Christian moralizing in the wake of the horrors of *The Monk* or *Melmoth the Wanderer*. When Mary Shelley describes *Frankenstein* as her "hideous progeny" (xii), she evokes the image of monstrous birth deliberately; the horror writer's imagination *is* the sleep of reason, which breeds the proverbial monster. The unconscious connections between things thought to be mutually exclusive, between the holy and unholy, the *heimlich* and the *unheimlich*, are the stuff of which nightmares are made, and writers give life to these bad dreams through the power of language to create frightening alternative universes, which bear enough resemblance to our own to be plausible and therefore all the more disturbing.

Like the mad doctor, the writer of serious horror fiction is obsessed, compelled to be true to her vision, no matter where it takes her. The text is like the monster in that, although it may be conceived for a specific purpose, it constantly exceeds the boundaries set for it, and like as not turns and rends its creator. Both *Frankenstein* and *The Island of Dr. Moreau* are intended partly as criticisms of the irrationality of popular religion, but they also show the utter sterility of a world without the natural emotional bonding on which the spirit of religion rests. More significantly, both novels call into question the possibility of knowing reality, revealing as they do the patchwork and fragmentary process we term perception, and how deeply dependent that perception is on desire. The doctor's proper office, in this view, is to repair or restore the natural order, not circumvent it, and to attempt a creation of his own is to pretend to a superhuman knowledge of causality, to mistake a part for the whole. There is indeed a method to Nature's madness, the writers of sf horror fiction seem to say, but it is one so vast and complex that we can only dimly glimpse its outlines through the mists of the ages.

For we too are products of Nature's evolutionary agenda, and whether that agenda is purposive or not, it is not our own, and we toy with it at our peril. Aldiss suggests that one of Wells's primary goals in *The Island of Dr. Moreau* was to disabuse Victorians of the popular notion that we are the "lords of creation," the final, best products of evolution, and although, if this was his intention, he certainly succeeds, it is a disillusionment that cuts both ways, for Wells's mad doctor also suggests that the price for "rationality" might be our humanity, just as Shelley suggests that other, less benevolent forces than philanthropy may motivate the researcher, particularly when that research entails repression of the social personality.

In *The World, the Flesh and the Devil*, J. D. Bernal proposes that in order for humans to gain the capacity for interstellar travel, they will probably require a surgical step in evolution where the brain is transplanted into an artificial body which will provide the durability and longevity necessary for survival in the vast distances of outer space. Bernal suspects interstellar voyaging will be necessary for the survival of the human race, and that the brightest of our species will see the reasonableness of such a radical transformation and actually desire it. Those lesser beings who still require a body will remain behind on Earth, which will become only a sort of zoo.

Bernal's title describes "the three enemies of the rational soul," by far the worst of which is "the Devil," or the irrational side of the personality. While he acknowledges that defeating this last adversary will likely prove impossible, Bernal wistfully dreams that it may come to pass that we succeed in gaining our intellectual maturity and becoming synthetic immortals. The idea of the disembodied brain has of course been ripe material for sf horror fiction and films of this century, so Bernal's sense that we humans might have some slight aversion to the surgical disposal of our bodies seems well-founded. What seems astonishing is that a well-educated man living in the first half of the twentieth century, where the necessity of the irrational to human existence had already become virtually self-evident, could seriously make such a proposal. But a contemporary of Bernal's was a fanatical Austrian who believed that the solution to the world's problems was the extermination of the Jews, so perhaps one shouldn't be surprised at the extremes some humans will go to in the interests of evolutionary self-advancement. This is not to equate Bernal with Hitler; on the contrary, what is even more disturbing about Bernal's little treatise is that it was quite probably written with the best of intentions. Monstrosity has a way of cloaking itself in the fairest of guises.

There are a number of fairly self-evident problems with surgical evolution, so rather than enumerating the more obvious already suggested by the writers of sf horror fiction, perhaps we can simply observe that the irrational is not only necessary to human beings, but a part of our mental essence, and to surgically discard it is to excise our humanity. It is significant that Bernal makes Moreau's mistake, essentializing the rational as the only valuable aspect of consciousness. Without the imagination, that ability to project the self into another's place or beyond the stars, much if not all of the progress of civilization would not have occurred. As the Romantics from William Blake to Freud have informed us, the imagination is not simply a rational process, nor can it be bottled and separated from the body, like a cologne. We will never go to the stars until we understand our place on Earth, and the first step is to acknowledge that we are both bodies and minds, and that the two cannot be separated without losing our humanity.

Whatever we may think of its sweeping conclusions with respect to the possibility of knowledge, poststructuralism has shown us that language forms and informs our consciousness to such an extent that it can and does serve to repress psychological phenomena as well as reveal them. In the process of writing speculative fiction, language is used to explore strange new worlds, to exceed through imagination the boundaries of the known. In science fiction, these forays often have considerable predictive value, as in the rockets of Jules Verne or the robots of Isaac Asimov. In the case of sf horror, the "prophecy" is made in the interest of avoiding a dystopic future rather than seeking its realization. Through the process of cognitive estrangement, we gain an "external" perspective on the human condition that allows us to gauge the potential impact of new technology on our lives before it can have irreversible effects. Speculative fiction can therefore serve a useful purpose in the ongoing process of civilization, allowing us to "inhabit" possible future worlds before they become reality.

The relevance of horror as moral corrective to this process is obvious, but as suggested earlier, there is also something in the process of writing horror, its free-form exploration of the repressed of culture, given most direct explication by Freud as the *unheimlich*, which subverts the overt moralizing of the cautionary tale with something more complex, and therefore, more valuable. The idea of text as monster, as allegory for the unspeakable, suggests that much of the process of writing horror involves writing that serves as amanuensis for submerged areas of conflict in the psyche. When these conflicts are located near the heart of a culture, the literature thus produced becomes of immense value in voicing the unsaid, exploring the inconsistencies in idealized notions of truth.[7]

The contemporary view of horror has been to see its primary value as a political corrective, an exposure of the fallacies underlying patriarchal, bourgeois culture. And horror does serve to expose the repressive aspects of traditional cultural discourse, which unquestionably tends to marginalize alternatives to the views of the dominant group. But the danger in contemporary theorists is that they also tend to reify the newly discovered alternative as "The Truth," or as more valuable by virtue of its suppression. Culture is an ongoing dialogue or dialectic, and the vital contribution of the literature of cognitive estrangement to that process, whether science fiction, horror or some other form of fantastic fiction, is that not only does it help us to see where we are going, but who we might become. The case of the mad doctor strongly suggests that there is no shortcut to natural evolution; similarly, horror writers show us that we should not surgically alter the process of thinking by detaching our theory from the ongoing process of culture, the actual human experience, for in so doing we may well create a repressive monster of our own.

Notes

1. Stephen Jay Gould, *Ever Since Darwin: Reflections in Natural History* (New York: W. W. Norton & Co., 1977), 144. The term reflects a typical scientific assessment of religious belief which this chapter will argue is simplistic in a later discussion of the civilized need for human-centeredness.

2. Darko Suvin, *Metamorphoses of Science Fiction: On the Poetics and History of a Literary Genre* (New Haven: Yale University Press, 1979), 4.

3. Sigmund Freud, "The 'Uncanny,' " translated by Alix Strachey, in *Collected Papers*

of Sigmund Freud (Oxford: Oxford University Press, 1957).

4. Mary Shelley, *Frankenstein, or, The Modern Prometheus*, ed. Johanna M. Smith (Boston: Bedford Books, 1992), 52. Later page references in the text are to this edition.

5. H. G. Wells, *The Island of Dr. Moreau*, afterword by Brian W. Aldiss (1896; New York: Signet Books, 1988), 75. All subsequent page references in the text to the novel and Aldiss's afterword are to this edition.

6. Eric S. Rabkin suggested in conversation that *The Island of Dr. Moreau* is not as narrowly didactic as Aldiss implies, and that the text is remarkably subtle in its treatment of evolutionary themes as well as the symbolic uses of names to suggest that Moreau, too, is far from a rational character. I am convinced by his arguments and would only add that this strengthens my case that this supposed critique of religion is also a critique of the scientific mentality that believes any alteration of the natural order can be justified in the name of the advancement of knowledge.

7. Rosemary Jackson's *Fantasy: The Literature of Subversion* (New York: Methuen, 1981) explores this angle, but only to imprison the imaginative freedom of fantasy in the "no exit" psychoanalytic paradigm of Lacan and Freud, which says little or nothing about how the reevaluation of cultural trends can have real predictive value for the future. Much modern criticism makes great claims for the liberating power of such readings without providing a constructive alternative to the society we currently inhabit. Fortunately for us, the writers of speculative fiction are not similarly imaginatively constrained.

8

Sickness unto Death: *Heart of Darkness* and *Journey to the End of the Night*

David K. Danow

At the heart of darkness, at its very core, lies corporeality—the human body, sick, pestilential, moribund, and finally dead. The horror that Kurtz repeatedly intones is the horror of the body, the civilized self in the face of a more powerful primordial call, that self deteriorating in life, decaying already long before the last breath, the final exhalation of the sojourner into a void deprived of spirit but rife with flesh. One need only mine that place, rape the flesh, tear out the tusks from the hide—and get out, as best one can, alive. Ultimately, the triumph, should there be one, is the triumph of physicality, of one's (remaining) health and vigor proving resilient against the odds in what Conrad terms a "fantastic invasion," a reiterated phrase in Joseph Conrad's *Heart of Darkness* (1902). Likewise, Louis-Ferdinand Celine underscores as equally fantastic the several chapters in *Journey to the End of the Night* (1932) detailing a series of unlikely adventures in Africa. The French novelist has his degenerate (anti)hero—a far cry from Conrad's erstwhile Marlow, if not that greatly removed in his essentially defining cynicism from Kurtz—escape from the dark continent toward the end of World War I on board a slave galley, which eventually puts into port in New York. Both works partake of the fantastic, the one through explicit, repeated usage of the term itself (as in the phrase just cited), the other implicitly, as a direct result of the strategic use of that anachronistic galley, which is both significant and unique, since nowhere else in this extensive novel does such a peculiar anachronism find even a remote resonance. The interlude in Africa may thus be seen as isolated and distinct from the rest of the book, and its fantastic effect heightened by this singular circumstance.

In Celine's great existential novel there intrudes, in addition, a repeated speculative element that is equally fantastic in its gross suppositions. "Are there still black people sweltering and pustulating in the caldron? . . . Maybe the whole place is dead and gone, the very name wiped off the maps."[1] So might one wonder when gripped by unrelenting illness, exhaustion, heat, and a resultant compounded, compelling sense of the fantastic. For present purposes, that concept might best be defined in light of Tzvetan Todorov's simplistic but encompassing understanding, as "events which are not likely to occur in everyday life," producing an "impression of irreducible strangeness."[2] This latter impression, of course, is fully exploited in both Conrad's and Celine's novels as central to their respective characters' journey into the depths of the darkness, "made strange" in both physical and metaphysical regards, as Celine puts it, typically cynically: "If you don't want the sun to burn your brains through your eyes, you have to blink like a rat. After five you can indulge in a look around" (127). But might not such "indulgence" yield just that sense of "irreducible strangeness," of astounding *difference*, manifested, simply, as a kind of intrusion of the extraordinary into a world which is more or less ordinary? For as Eric S. Rabkin points out, "the fantastic is important precisely because it is wholly dependent on reality for its existence."[3] In this chapter I seek to point up in these seemingly disparate novelists a respective preoccupation with physical and what may be called "metaphysical well-being"—or lack thereof—in two literary works that might not generally be regarded to partake of the fantastic.

In *Heart of Darkness*, the entire thrust of the work is aimed, with unremitting concentration and no extraneous digression, directly at the heart, a metaphor that refers, among other possibilities, to the deepest recesses of the dark continent as well as to the most secret, hidden innards of man, where lurk a host of psychological realities that resist penetration and analysis no less than the interior of the jungle shuns daylight and the rays of the sun. Celine titles his novel in virtually sympathetic accord, but his "journey to the end of the night" neither projects nor provides, as does Conrad, any real end in sight. Yet both journeys remain indeterminate, left as what Conrad pointedly and repeatedly calls a "mystery," to which are appended an array of synonymous expressions: "incomprehensible," "inconclusive," "unknown," "unreal," "incredible," and "strange." Just as strange is the peculiar foray of Celine's character into and out of the dark continent in a mere sixty-odd pages in a work more than six times as long, and otherwise situated in places that are far more civilized (New York and Paris) and far less remote.

In Conrad's novel, in recognition of what this sort of incursion might mean, the reader is told in the first part of the book: "And outside, the silent wilderness surrounding this cleared speck on the earth struck me as something great and invincible, like evil or truth, waiting patiently for the passing away of this fantastic invasion."[4] Essentially the same sentiment, at least the identical phrase, is reiterated in the second part: "The high stillness confronted these two figures with its ominous patience, waiting for the passing of a fantastic invasion" (55). But all the patience on Earth will not see the "passing" of this "invasion," whether made fleetingly by Celine's misguided war dodger or far more insistently by Conrad's demented ivory seeker. Finally, in the third and last part of Conrad's novel, the same note is struck. "But the wilderness had found him out early, and had taken on him a terrible vengeance for the fantastic invasion" (98). That vengeance is taken in all instances on mind and body, body and mind, in whatever order, by virtue of the absence of civilization, most strikingly manifested (as it always is for the traveler in trouble) by the absence of doctors and medicine, which absence makes, paradoxically, for a felt, unmitigated presence of sickness and death in a variety of ingenious forms dreamt up by a raw and elemental existence from which the jungle only rarely permits escape. Thus if "You stand the climate—you outlast them all" (53). But to what avail? For as Celine notes, "life in the colonies was no great shakes" (113).

With rare luck one gets by, as Conrad puts it, with "a little fever, or a little touch of other things—the playful paw-strokes of the wilderness, the preliminary trifling before the more serious onslaught" (69). Thus Conrad's novel is fairly littered with the dead and dying. "They were dying slowly—it was very clear. They were not enemies, they were not criminals, they were nothing earthly now—nothing but black shadows of disease and starvation, lying confusedly in the greenish gloom" (26), referred to later (more than once) in macabre terms as "the grove of death" (31, 46). The line, ever so thin, between life and death appears so fragile that one "did not know who was dead and who was alive," but nonetheless the reader is treated consistently and even insistently throughout this novel to "a whiff from some corpse" (36–37), either belonging to someone known or (more likely) unknown, but affording in either case an ever-present "taint of death" (44), the sense of "lurking death" (54). But there is a fine line not only between life and death, but also between wellness and illness, as Celine makes eminently clear when his protagonist speaks of his "Diarrhea," "fever," and "chills" (141). Hence the distinction between sickness and health in this "enormous reservation, crawling with animals and diseases" (125) is also a matter of debate and irresolute speculation.

Returning to the problematic distinction between the living and the dead— problematic, for one thing, because under "less fantastic" circumstances no such distinction, or need for one, need arise—we read in Conrad's novel: "It was as though an animated image of death carved out of old ivory had been shaking its hand with menaces at a motionless crowd of men" (101) In the same spirit, one that permeates, even defines, the book (is not Kurtz himself just such "an animated image of death"?), we note that it is precisely such an image that remonstrates menacingly before an even greater crowd of readers. For, in personal, singular terms, in one of the few utterances in the novel directly attributed to him, the moribund figure of Kurtz declares likewise, "Live rightly, die, die" (117), as though there were little difference or distinction between the two missions, as the work itself so often and so disturbingly implies.

Nearly as disturbing, we learn in *Heart of Darkness* that for those coming from the presumably "bright" continent to its so-called dark counterpart, as a kind of grim reciprocation, "the only thing that ever came to them was disease" (39). Worse, concerning these company men come to make their fortune at all costs to the place they rapaciously and fantastically "invade," as well as to their own personal detriment, one charmed soul declares with regard to the others: "All sick. They die so quick, too . . . it's incredible!" (54). He might just as well say "it's fantastic," in the darkest possible sense. On the other hand, but hardly a brighter alternative, one might just as well succumb to "lingering starvation," the slow death that comes from "prolonged hunger" (70). In this novel the chief representative of a slow and lingering death is, of course, Kurtz, that marvel of survival and remarkable endurance, doomed nonetheless never to leave the place he had made his own more than any other he might previously have called home. Kurtz struggles to survive but also, we suspect, prefers to die rather than return to a world ruined by civilized ways. It is thus one thing when, as Marlow intones at the very start of his tale, "this also . . . has been one of the dark places of the earth" (6). But shorn of its "darkness," that place (known as London) is now hopelessly diminished, as Kurtz implies (in another of the very few utterances actually granted him) by referring to his illness figuratively instead of literally. "Sick! Sick! Not so sick as you would like to believe" (104). Yet sick enough to die, in turn, from his ailment's all too concrete effect.

As Celine makes abundantly clear, however, concrete reality, with all of its myriad torments, does not alone bring about "the heart's" rich harvest of untimely death. A disastrous human element compounds the horrific tribulations of the natural environment. "The little energy that hadn't been sapped by malaria, thirst, and the heat was consumed by hatred so fierce and deep seated that it wasn't uncommon for these colonials to drop dead on the spot, poisoned by themselves like scorpions" (107). "The company," which is generically the same in both novels, viciously grasps and pillages, and "consumed quantities of small clerks," which sorry souls Celine refers to with equal doses of irony and contempt as "Pioneers!" (126), "martyrs for twenty-two francs a day" (114). Fair targets for abuse in Celine's equal opportunity novel extend to the indigenous population as well, "a few thinly disseminated tribes stagnated amid their fleas and flies. . . . ravaged by a thousand plagues" (135). Thus the placid observation that "We could just as well have dropped dead" (111) embraces both white and black, exploiter and exploited, in this "heart of darkness," where only the very lucky few survive or manage to get out alive.

The terrain explored in both novels is the same. Primeval and primordial, magnificent and threatening, this "heart of the jungle" (Celine 127) brooks outsiders' visitations reluctantly and far from graciously. Those who penetrate its depths are confronted by a hitherto untapped dimension and a peculiar counter-"invasion": "The great wall of vegetation, an exuberant and entangled mass of trunks, branches, leaves, boughs, festoons, motionless in the moonlight, was like *a rioting invasion* of soundless life, a rolling wave of plants, piled up, crested, ready to topple over the creek, to sweep every little man of us out of his little existence" (Conrad 49; italics added). A clear and evident sense of our own insignificance emerges as our first and basic reality. Yet equally compelling is the complementary sense of the fantastic rendered temporally and spatially as a world as yet unknown.

Going up that river was like travelling back to the earliest beginnings of the world. . . . We were wanderers on a prehistoric earth, on an earth that wore the aspect of an unknown planet. . . . The earth seemed unearthly. [Instead of] the shackled form of a conquered monster . . . there you could look at a thing monstrous and free. It was unearthly. . . . I don't think a single one of them had any clear idea of time. . . . They still belonged to the beginnings of time. (Conrad 55, 58–59, 67–68)

Hence "they" belong while "we" do not. Further, where one sphere appears "shackled" and "conquered," the other is "monstrous and free." But while Conrad acknowledges "remote kinship" (59) between the two otherwise estranged domains, for Celine each in its own way remains simply a monstrosity and little else.

Yet he can rhapsodize at some length on the natural beauty of the dark continent momentarily aglow with the sun's last rays. offering views of "fabulous" sunsets (Celine 145). Nonetheless, shortly thereafter, he undercuts his own vision of beauty: "magnificent . . . for people who love nature. I definitely didn't. The poetry of the tropics turned my stomach. . . . [It is] not for me" (147). Perhaps not for anybody not born to it, for the entire treatise on Celine's African adventure reads like a long litany of sickness and death, punctuated by the all-encompassing sentiment: "I was so sick of all that. . . . I'd have vomited up the whole globe" (149).

Those luckier ones, condemned to interminable illness, Celine depicts in two categories, military and civilian. The "white conscripts" for the most part ended up staying "permanently in the hospital, sleeping off their malaria, riddled with parasites . . . stretched out flat between cigarettes and flies" (123–124). While he speaks with sympathy of the plight of these military men, he is less generous with his country's civil servants, whom he describes as undergoing some "process of devirilization" (109), their wives "menstruating interminably . . . the children, unbearably plump European maggots, wilted by the heat and constant diarrhea" (123), which in and of itself appears in these passages a constant theme.

The final stage of deterioration is gleefully embraced by an all-encompassing taxonomy. "The colonies make these little clerks fat or . . . thin . . . there are only two ways to die under the sun, the fat way and the thin way" (114). Hence the gross understatement: "Survival . . . is quite an achievement" (108), especially in light of such limited options or in recognition of the fleeting passing of life, described thus: "Men, days, things—they passed before you knew it in this hotbed of vegetation, heat, humidity, and mosquitoes. . . . Nothing remained but *shimmering dread*" (126; italics added).

The "sickness unto death" that pervades the heart of darkness thus derives from sources that are both physical and metaphysical. As Shakespeare puts it in a concluding couplet (Sonnet 146):

So shalt thou feed on Death, that feeds on men,
And Death once dead, there's no more dying then.

Yet one gets the sense that in both Conrad's and Celine's novels the *danse macabre*—"the merry dance of death and trade" (Conrad 22)—goes about its business of picking off, indiscriminately, violator and violated, company man and black man, each in turn. Hence the "fantastic invasion," in Shakespeare's vision, linking the physical and metaphysical, may be seen as a rampant incursion into the realm of Death, from which escape is tentative at best. The "sickness unto death" of which Kierkegaard speaks, however, finds its principal source—as do both novels—squarely in the metaphysical domain, what Celine felicitously terms "shimmering dread." That source, defined by the Danish philosopher as despair, refers to the individual's concern for and relation to the self.

In the two novels treated here, this sense of despair extends outward from Kurtz, in particular, to the human condition at large. If Conrad's perspective is based essentially on "realism" (in some broad sense), Celine's is adamantly rooted in cynicism. Yet, in their respective African adventures, both novelists seek to find a definitional core of human being. In Conrad that "core" is essentially primordial, brilliantly reflected in an unwitting, almost compulsive need to respond to "the awakening of forgotten and brutal instincts . . . the memory of gratified and monstrous passions . . . the gleam of fires, the throb of drums, the drone of weird incantations" (112), just as there is the like demanding concession that must be made to the unremitting tolling of one's own (of course) death knell. Further, in both novels, at the core (once more) we find detailed behavior that is both destructive and self-destructive, which conduct is likely an essential source of Kierkegaard's basic, perhaps even primordial, yet ever so human sense of despair, which drives Marlow to say of Kurtz, "But his soul was mad. . . . I tell you, it had gone mad" (Conrad 113), and which puts him beyond the healing ministrations of both physician and metaphysician, healer of the body and healer of the soul.

In close, *comical* proximity to this underlying notion of despair, Celine's demented figure ruminates that "My ambition was to be sick, just plain sick" (121). When viewed in a certain tolerant light, such peculiar sentiments may appear oddly viable in their own limited fashion. Nonetheless, much against the Kierkegaardian grain (which offers a Christian way out), and especially when read against Conrad's novel, it becomes clear that within what Celine's hero terms this "earthly Paradise" (121), this unfathomable heart of darkness, just as outside it, there is neither succor nor solace to be had. Rather, as Kierkegaard puts it, there is "this sickness of the self, perpetually to be dying, to die and yet not die,"[5] signified by that metaphysical cry of despair—"The horror! The horror!" (Conrad 118)—which aptly situates the human being ensnared in the human dilemma, for as long as there is life and breath, or otherwise put, there remains only that sickness unto death.

Notes

1. Louis-Ferdinand Celine, *Journey to the End of the Night*, translated by Ralph Manheim (1932; New York: New Directions, 1983), 139–140. Later page references in the text are to this edition.

2. Tzvetan Todorov, *The Fantastic: A Structural Approach to a Literary Genre* (Ithaca: Cornell University Press, 1975), 34–35.

3. Eric S. Rabkin, *The Fantastic in Literature* (Princeton: Princeton University Press, 1976), 28.

4. Joseph Conrad, *Heart of Darkness*, in *Heart of Darkness and the Secret Sharer* (1902; New York: Bantam, 1989), 37. Later page references in the text are to this edition.

5. Soren Kierkegaard, *The Sickness unto Death: A Christian Psychological Exposition for Upbuilding and Awakening*, edited and translated by Howard V. Hong and Edna H. Hong (Princeton: Princeton University Press, 1980), 18.

9

Big Brother as Doctor:
Curing the Disease of Thoughtcrime in
George Orwell's *Nineteen Eighty-Four*

Robert Van Cleave

When Winston Smith wrote into his diary "*Thoughtcrime does not entail death:
thoughtcrime IS death*" (29; italics in original),[1] he was not referring to a
punishment by the law since we are told that there are no laws in the world of Big
Brother. Thoughtcrime, within the context of the Party, is the symptom of a
sickness. If Winston Smith is a dead man it is because, festering in the alcove
beyond the eyesight of the telescreen, he has let a disease come upon him.

From the very first, we learn that Winston is afflicted with physical ailments.
The protracted coughing and ulcerations along his leg inform us that Winston is not
the picture of health. No effort, however, is made to hide such physical fragilities
from the telescreen. The telescreen has very little interest in such afflictions. The
telescreen's sole function is to probe for thoughtcrime. Against this intrusion,
Winston is continually in search of shelter—whether in his alcove, in Charrington's
loft, or within his own skull. Yet, Big Brother has a means to transgress every
shelter in order to probe for symptoms and eradicate the disease of thoughtcrime.
Since thoughtcrime is naturally a disease of the brain, it is only within the brain—
within the very skull of a person—that the concept of health is manifest for the
Party. It is there, also, that the disease of a "defective" memory can take hold. When
that happens, we are told that it is one's "nervous system" which constantly
threatens to deliver up to the watchful telescreen some "visible symptom" of your
sickness (64). The gazing telescreen in this regard is very much the watchful doctor.

As such, Winston perceives in the mesmerizing face of Big Brother a fearful
power. It seems to him to be a force that quite literally threatens to "penetrate" into
his head in order to break him of all his "sickness" of loyalty, memory, and even the
most basic perceptions (80). Yet, paradoxically, the brain at odds with its own
senses and convictions is considered healthy by the Party. The horrible force that
Winston glimpses from Big Brother's eyes is in fact the very reflection of the curing
process which is manufactured in the bowls of the Ministry of Love. It is within the
Ministry of Love, in the effort to cure party members of their thoughtcrime, that two

plus two can equal five and loyalty, memory and conviction are all incised from the brain like dangerous malignancies.

In the first part of *Nineteen Eighty-Four*, we participate in the various stages of Winston's diagnosis at the hands of the Party. Events unfold, as if by chance, but we know that there are no games of chance in Oceania.[2] The Party seeks to cure the body of the memory of what it means to be human. Of course, Winston understands that humanity is measured by the depth of one's loyalty to others. It is a principle that Winston learns from the Proles. However, Winston has also glimpsed the other side of human nature when he, himself, was a big brother to a starving sister whose meals he pilfered right down to her last wedge of chocolate. This was Winston's first betrayal and it cost him his family.

As a result, for the adult Winston, the concepts of loyalty and betrayal are tantamount to his private thinking. Yet, there is a place, Room 101, which is the ultimate operating room at the Ministry of Love. Its single function is to make one forget one's love and loyalty to others by providing such a shock to the system that one no longer feels connected to the world or human heritage.

However, it is important to note the physical fluctuations of Winston's bouts of sickness and moments of health before his final stop at the Ministry of Love. There is of course the first sickness at the beginning of the novel—the coughing fits, the varicose ulcer and the general fatigue. This unpleasantness in Winston's constitution continues unabated until his hatred for Julia is turned into love. Indeed, the Winston we meet before the introduction of Julia's love seems quite content to be one of the walking dead. Julia's love note reinvigorates Winston's rather morbid soul. For a short time she fills Winston with an urgency to live, and this desire for love and life seems to abate his physical deterioration. Julia, for the moment, is a force to counterbalance Winston's morbidity with a vigorous "We're not dead yet" (137).

Winston's love affair with Julia is, of course, what compels him to take the most decisive act toward his demise. He rents the room over Charrington's shop. Unwittingly, though not by chance, he checks himself into the observation room of the Thought Police. Importantly, a Prole woman at a wash tub begins to sing below the window of that ill-fated room. As such, one cannot overemphasize the importance of rhymes and songs in this story.[3] When one considers the content of this song one realizes that this Prole woman's song, like the musical message of an ancient chorus, is connected in theme and foretells of coming events. With Winston on the verge of apparent destruction, the song of the Prole woman is a haunting refrain. The old woman sings about "an 'opeless fancy" that "passed like an Ipril dye" (139). Similarly, the novel and the love affair between Winston and Julia begins in April. Winston is, no doubt, involved in what he considers a hopeless endeavor. Also, it was little more then a curt glance and a few scribbled words that took hold of Winston's heart.

However, just as there is the Janus-faced aspect of love and hate in *Nineteen Eighty-Four* so, too, not only will this song be sung twice but it is composed of two stanzas. If the first stanza was of the past and present, the second stanza is a portent.

The Prole woman also sings that while people may "sye you can always forget," the memories of the loved one "twist my 'eartstrings yet!" (142). These words about forgetting and remembering will soon find their match within the Ministry of Love and in the final destination of this novel—the Chestnut Tree Café. For instance, with regard to the healing aspect of time, O'Brien tells Winston, "Everyone is cured sooner or later" (277). Indeed, the concept of forgetting is what the process of the cure is all about. As stated, this is what lies at the heart of Winston's disease—his "defective" memory. Of course, our idea of "defective" memory and the Party's idea are two separate things. For the Party, a "defective" memory is one that remembers. This is interesting when one considers the Greek word for truth, *alçtheia*. It is evident that truth has at its root the negation of forgetfulness and loss of memory. The word itself suggests the Greek word *lçthç*, and anyone who knows their underworlds will the know the River of Lethe as the River of Forgetfulness. Truth, to be quite literal in this regard, is what you do not forget.

This is precisely the struggle taking place in *Nineteen Eighty-Four*. It is a struggle between *alçtheia* and *lçthç*—between what one can remember, which is the only real measure of truth left in Oceania, and what one is compelled to forget. Winston, as we have seen throughout, struggles toward the concept of *alçtheia*— toward truth, toward remembering the past and remembering the secret lies in the Office of Records. He struggles, quite hopelessly, as if against some rising river of Lethe that seeks to overwhelm him in its current of oblivion.

It is this struggle toward the truth, toward not forgetting, that has made Winston's memory "defective." Winston confronts O'Brien on this point directly toward the end of the novel. He states, concerning the Party's attempt to control people's memories, "You have not controlled mine!" To which O'Brien responds, "On the contrary, you have not controlled it. . . . You would not make the act of submission which is the price of sanity" (252). This "sanity" is, of course the paradox of the Party. At its core it is the struggle between *alçtheia* is *lçthç*. Truth, for the Party, is forgetting the laws of physics, the history of war, the evidence of one's own senses, and even the most obvious logic of $2 + 2 = 4$. True, also, in the Party's precise book of betrayal, is that it is essential to forget whom one loves in the maddening pain of just surviving.

Yet, before these moments in the Ministry of Love, while Winston is enjoying love with Julia, he is no longer on the verge of just surviving. Winston's body begins to heal. We are told that his drinking, emaciation, coughing, and even the varicose ulcer had all begun to subside (151). His outlook on life had become more optimistic. That is not to say that Winston had forgotten about his disease of thoughtcrime or had disregarded its symptoms. In fact, even at this time, during his temporary elation of spirit and health, he seems to sense that the process is not over.

For Winston, the specter of the Ministry of Love seems to loom like his inexorable destination. Though he has never been there, he can reasonably guess at what happens in that place. He can imagine the "tortures, drugs, delicate instruments that register your nervous reactions" (167). Against such devices, Winston tries to take refugee behind Julia's assertion that, "they can't get inside you" (167).

Winston, no doubt, wishes to believe that this is true and that the thoughts and feelings (indicative of his sickness within the Party) could somehow remain "impregnable" to the devices of Big Brother (168).

However, just as there is only one kind of disease in the Party—thoughtcrime—there is, also, only one manifest branch of scientific endeavor left in Oceania. All the energies of this new "science" work to break down the "impregnable" fortress of the human mind. Indeed, the process of getting inside an individual is the Party's special talent. Goldstein's book tells us that there is no actual science in Oceania (195). In fact, we are told that in Newspeak the word "Science" does not exist (194). What scientific spark may be left in the realm of Oceania works in a twofold manner. First there is the technology to probe individuals for thoughtcrime. In this regard, the telescreens are a technical wonder. In a world where everything else seems to fall apart, one has the sense that the telescreens never break down. Indeed, they are a dream achieved by INGSOC. The other aspect of INGSOC science is brutally manifest inside the Ministry of Love and concerned solely with curing individuals of thoughtcrime.

Curing thoughtcrime seems to be the primary focus of all INGSOC medicine. What we consider to be doctors and hospitals are supplanted by the Ministry of Love and its obscure, white-coated individuals. Very little remains of a medical profession outside those walls. All sickness, it seems, is disregarded in favor of the one principal disease of thoughtcrime. There are, however, some suggestions of other medical endeavors beyond the fantasies of INGSOC to create biological genocide (195). Some work is being done in neuroscience in possible conjunction to eradicating the orgasm. There is also the organization of ARTSEM, which is instituted for the purpose of artificial insemination. Even plastic surgery seems to be a business that thrives in Oceania (174).

True to the spirit of the Party, medical science functions primarily to destroy the bonds between individuals. Interestingly, Goldstein's book tells us that, "the scientist is . . . a mixture of psychologist and inquisitor, studying . . . the meaning of facial expression . . . and testing the truth-producing effects of drugs, shock therapy, hypnosis, and physical torture" (194). This is the doctor in Oceania and his hospital is the Ministry of Love. His operating room can be found down a corridor at Room 101.

However, before Winston can make his trip to Room 101, before the Party can cure him, they must break down his body to such a point that the intellectual notion of thoughtcrime as death becomes a horrid reality. They must make his body reflect what they consider to be his corruption of mind. Further, they must make him believe that his indulgence in thoughtcrime is the sole instigator of his emaciated and broken body. It is here that Winston experiences his second and worst lapse of sickness.

Yet, the point of all the subsequent physical abuse in the Ministry of Love is not to exact a confession, nor is it done from sadistic pleasures or with the intent to kill. The beatings are, in fact, precise and monitored by ambiguous doctors who, along with the beatings, prescribe the necessary time required for "recovery" (244). At these times for Winston in the Ministry of Love, we are told there were "unsympathetic men in white coats feeling his pulse, tapping his reflexes, turning up his eyelids, running harsh fingers over him in search of broken bones, and shooting needles into his arm to make him sleep" (244).

In the manuscript of *Nineteen Eighty-Four*, it is clear who these men in white coats are. The same passage is written as "efficient, unsympathetic *doctors* re-set the plaster on his nose, disinfected his wounds, smeared ointment on his bruises" (Manu. 243; italics added). Another page of the manuscript describes it as, "unsympathetic *surgeons* testing his pulse & reflexes" (Manu. 243; italics added).

One may wonder why Orwell removed from the final text most of the overt references to doctors found in the manuscript. One hypothesis, perhaps, may pertain to the creation of O'Brien himself. While Orwell wanted the process that was taking place in the Ministry of Love to be seen as a medical process of being cured, he knew such a process was beyond the grasp of a mere doctor. As such, he did not want O'Brien to be portrayed only in medical terms. Likewise, he did not want those who worked with O'Brien, the unspeaking men in white coats, to be elevated to the prestige or power of doctors. Indeed, the men in white coats are consecutively demoted in the manuscript in order to decrease their status, from surgeons to doctors, till they become the nondescript men in white coats we find in the final text.

In the world of Oceania, the true doctor is elevated far beyond what we would consider to be a physician's responsibilities. Likewise, his talents lie far beyond the constraints of any medical discipline. The true doctor in Oceania is an amalgamation of disciplines. Those who flitter about in their white coats have been deftly made obscured by Orwell so as not to directly incur any of the connotations a reader might ascribe to doctors. In the same way, O'Brien, who is the main "physician" attending to Winston's cure, is elevated by Orwell beyond the mere status of a doctor.

In the novel, O'Brien becomes the tripartite of teacher, priest, and doctor. This is precisely how he is described in the novel. He is a man who has the apparent "air" of these three professions (249). As such, it is only the ambiguous "air of a doctor" which Orwell wishes to place upon O'Brien. Hence, O'Brien is not constrained to a doctor's power. Interestingly, just as Orwell removed the term "doctor" or "surgeon" from the men in white coats, so too, one can find in the manuscript where O'Brien's specific connection to being a doctor is made more emphatic. As it states in the manuscript, O'Brien, "had less the air of an inquisitor examining a suspect than of a doctor explaining something to a difficult patient" (Manu. 248).

Such overt references to "doctor" are eliminated from the final text so as to allow O'Brien to more fully grow into that ambiguous triple practitioner. O'Brien becomes a practitioner over the three basic elements of human nature. He is a doctor for the body, a teacher for the mind, and a priest for the metaphysical. Of course, what he does to the body, soul, and mind is a perversion in our eyes—he breaks the body, empties the intellect, and replaces God with an indifferent power. Though he only possesses the mere "air" of his many professions, he possesses the power of all things Big Brother. Only as an amalgamation of doctor, teacher, and priest can one so totally cure the individual from his own humanity.

The reality of this situation manifests itself in the voice of O'Brien. Winston soon realizes that O'Brien is in charge of the cure. Winston recognizes that O'Brien is both his sanctuary from those who would desire to kill him, and also the minister of excruciating pain. O'Brien, we are told, "decided when Winston should scream with pain, when he should have a respite . . . when the drugs should be pumped into his arm" (247). O'Brien's message, amongst the horror, is simple "I shall save you, I shall make you perfect" (247).

Of course, pain is part of Winston's prescription. In this regard, O'Brien holds all the power to send Winston into horrible agony. Nevertheless, the triple practitioner that is O'Brien manages to accompany the pain with a voice that is "gentle and patient" (249). Interestingly, in the manuscript O'Brien talks specifically about "the treatment" for Winston's sickness. He says, "We have had your confession . . . that part is finished. Now there is the treatment" (Manu. 248). O'Brien's diagnosis for Winston's sickness, as I have stated, is simple, "You suffer from a defective memory" (249). Further, with regard to Winston's "defective" memory he states, "I am well aware, you are clinging to your disease" (249). Yet, O'Brien is quite optimistic about his patient's condition. He says, "Fortunately it is curable" (249). As such, the treatment begins. Pain is mixed with physical deprivation and coupled with countless lessons on doublethink. One must be willing to intellectually submit to an almost brain-damaged state where amnesia, disorientation, and lack of logical and perceptual skills become the very "price" of Party sanity. It is as O'Brien tells Winston, "Shall I tell you why we have brought you here? To cure you! To make you sane! . . . [N]o one whom we bring to this place ever leaves our hands uncured" (256). O'Brien then tells Winston the important fact, that the Party does not care about actual illness or "overt" actions or crimes (256). All the Party cares about is diseased thought.

To cure the thoughtcriminal O'Brien speaks quite graphically, "we capture his inner mind, we reshape him. We burn . . . all illusion out of him" (258). This fits nicely with the Party's notion of power, which is the "tearing of human minds to pieces" and the subsequent reordering of mental processes (270). In fact, something like this actually does occur in the Ministry of Love. Winston suddenly feels, as he is hooked up to an apparatus, a sudden shock within his head. He describes the feeling as if "a piece had been taken out of his brain" (260). The subsequent void in Winston's mental processes is fertile ground for O'Brien to instill the principle cure for thoughtcrime. That cure is, of course, doublethink.

Ultimately, however, Winston's most important, though tragic lesson, is when he is brought before a mirror and shown the terrible ravages that his disease of a "defective" memory has created in his body. Winston sees himself in the mirror and sees all the manifest signs of physical illness that started the novel blatantly and grossly magnified by the Party (274). Seeing his body so close to death, of course, has the desired impact upon Winston. Staring at the "creature" in the mirror, he notes that his body looks as if it had been ravaged by some "malignant disease"

(275). O'Brien taunts Winston in this state by saying, "Look at the condition you are in!" Then, pulling out one of Winston's teeth, he exclaims, "You are rotting away" (275). In the manuscript, O'Brien goes even further and says to Winston, "What are you? A bundle of diseased bones" (Manu. 276).

No doubt, O'Brien has made his crucial point. He says, "You have seen what your body is like. Your mind is in the same state" (276). Obviously, it was necessary to force Winston's body to conform to the Party's imaginary disease. In essence, the Party wants Winston's body to be an outward manifestation of his inner corruption. It is for that reason that O'Brien takes no responsibility for the horrid state of Winston's physical demeanor. Winston exclaims, "You reduced me to this" (276). However, O'Brien only states, "No, Winston, you reduced yourself to it" (276).

Winston is laid bare at the Ministry of Love. His body and mind are connected in a sort of mutual corruption. He is made to realize that doublethink could have stopped this disease before it started. Now, stronger measures are necessary to return Winston to health. Once again love becomes the instrument. Crucially, O'Brien asks Winston whether he has succumbed to total "degradation" to which Winston responds, "I have not betrayed Julia" (276).

Once Winston reveals his deepest secret to the Party, he is allowed to get better. He grows fatter and stronger every day while treatment is provided for his various wounds (277). It is at this point also that Winston begins deliberately trying to reeducate himself in doublethink so as not to relapse into the sickness of thoughtcrime. Naturally, while Winston re-educates himself, his body is allowed to continue to thrive. He notes how his "body was healthy and strong" (282). Indeed, all seems almost perfect in him except that he is not totally transparent. His love of Julia and his hatred of Big Brother have taken refuge in his brain like that rare and delicate piece of coral within the glass paperweight from Mr. Charrington. Winston is determined to lock away both his love and his hate into what he calls "a kind of cyst" (284).

However, the Party has special surgeons to get at the "cysts" and secret places in one's head. They are two hungry creatures who know the exact anatomy of the brain to reach that place of betrayal. Now, despite his contention to hold all that is dear to him bottled up inside, horrible devices in the form of rats materialize before his eyes with the actual intent of getting inside him. Against this threat, the sanctity of one's spirit must truly shatter. Pain is a horrid capitulator. In the panic of death, our bodies betray us. But the nightmare of Room 101 is beyond even what we nominally call the threshold of pain. As O'Brien tells Winston, "for everyone there is something unendurable" (287). The Party knows that, in the recesses of one's most primitive instincts, one is only obedient to one's own self-preservation.

In Room 101, one is faced with the singular proposition. If you want the rats gone, it can be done. However, the Party, like the Pied Piper of old, has a price. Like the Piper, too, the means by which one leads the most horrible things in the world away will also lead away the things most precious in your life. Yet, only one thought fills Winston's mind when he is faced with O'Brien's proposition of rats burrowing into his face (288). We are told that Winston discovers one idea in all this horror to abate the rats. He must put the "body" of another person "between himself and the rats" (289). Just as he had, as a young boy, put the starving body of his sister between himself and hunger, now with the hunger of rats before him, he cannot help but face the process of another betrayal.

For Winston this event, like the entire scope of his seven years of examination, has been a no-win situation. Falling through this nightmare into the very bowels of the Ministry of Love, Winston is like a drowning man who has expired his last bubble of breath wherein all that he loved has been compressed like the tiny universe of that glass paperweight. It rises and shatters. The mouth comes up to breathe, and willingly breathes the breath of rats and the air of Big Brother. Winston exclaims, "Do it to Julia! Not me!" (289). It is only then that, in a Dantesque way, Winston is allowed to pass from this, the most compressed circle of Hell.

When we meet Winston again at the Chestnut Tree Café, we see a healthy, cured individual. He is quite content to stay in the shelter of this café, hovering over a chess game and a bottle of gin. The Chorus of the Prole women has long since finished. The Proles no longer sing to Winston. Though the Prole woman's song had foretold this moment of smiles and tears, now a new chorus takes its place. The chorus of the telescreen sings a familiar song, the song of betrayal. "Under the spreading chestnut tree / I sold you and you sold me" (296). For Winston there is no longer any danger. The disease of a "defective" memory is cured. As such, the "doctors" at the Ministry of Love turn their attention away from Winston. Having been cured of his disease, he is no longer under observation.

It cannot be denied that despite the fact that we as readers leave this novel feeling miserable, we leave Winston a happier man than when we found him. Perhaps this is what unnerves us the most. In the end, we are asked to accept the new Winston and to accept his love of Big Brother. Cured of his loyalties and cured of his humanity, he has been brought back full circle to the child who only lives at the expense of others. He is reconciled under the smile of Big Brother. He sits, as if in a trance, content in the revelry of the imaginary victory of Big Brother over the Eurasian army. Indeed, Winston realizes how the love of Big Brother washes in like gin to fill all the empty places in his mind. And as Winston tells us, "everything was all right" (300).

The disease of a "defective" memory that leads to thoughtcrime, in the end, was little more than an innocuous cyst and it disappeared without complication. Sitting in the Chestnut Tree Café, Winston pushes away thoughts of loyalty and betrayal. He pushes away, also, his fondest childhood memories. Pushed away is anything that leads to the disease of thoughtcrime, and the gaze and smile of Big Brother are there to fill the void. The most noxious love we can imagine rushes in to fill Winston's cured mentality. As such, he is suddenly overcome by all the health and tranquility that is offered by Big Brother. At that moment, Winston receives his "final indispensable, healing change" (300).

Notes

1. A number in parentheses alone denotes a page from a standard edition, George Orwell, *Nineteen Eighty-Four* (1947; New York: Harcourt, 1977). When a passage is quoted from the manuscript (Peter Davison, editor, *Nineteen Eighty-Four: The Facsimile of the Extant Manuscript* [New York: Harcourt; MA: M&S Press, 1984)], the abbreviation "Manu." will precede the page number.

2. This point is exemplified by the Party's own indulgence in the game of chess. Chess is, indeed, an important game to the Party. It is a game not left to chance. In particular, the Party indulges in endgames in which it is always white's move to win. So, even the element of possibility is eliminated from INGSOC's chess. This is juxtaposed to the fond memory Winston has at the very end of the novel about a childhood game of Snakes and Ladders—a game of pure chance. The memory of this game, which is the only good memory Winston has of his immediate family, is the last hold Winston has to a world outside the Party. When this recollection is pushed from his mind as a "false" almost immediately we are told he returns to his chess game (299).

3. The principal song and/or nursery rhyme of the novel is, of course, the rhyme "Oranges and Lemons." Winston is continually putting together bell after bell of each stanza. Indeed this rhyme has some very ominous implications, not merely for the last line "Here comes a chopper to chop off your head," but for the childhood game associated with the song. Played with a group of children, the *Oxford Dictionary of Nursery Rhymes* tells us two larger players form an arch having decided separately who will be an orange and who will be a lemon. The song proceeds as the children pass under the arch until the climax of "here comes a candle to light you to bed / here comes a chopper to chop off your head." At which point someone is caught and must decide if he or she is an orange or a lemon. It is something of the same struggle between Big Brother and the Brotherhood. The tug of war that is the culmination of the game is meaningless. The object of the game is to get caught. The game itself is essentially narrated to Winston by Mr. Charrington, who has also given to Winston the first stanza of the rhyme (98). However, even more disturbing is the aspect suggested by the *Oxford Dictionary of Nursery Rhymes* that the song derives its origins from the spirit of executions—the bells ring out for the man about to die as he walks the street. Appropriately enough, as Winston struggles to put this rhyme together, first Mr. Charrington tolls a bell in providing a stanza, then Julia, then O'Brien. All toll the bells of his demise.

10

Doctors' Ordeals: The Sector General Stories of James White

Gary Westfahl

No discussion of medicine in science fiction can neglect James White, creator of what is unquestionably the genre's longest and most significant series of medical adventures, the Sector General stories. In twelve volumes published over the course of four decades, White described how human and alien doctors in the distant future worked together at a huge space station, Sector Twelve General Hospital, confronting baffling medical mysteries and curing patients from all over the cosmos. Unlike other science fiction series, the Sector General stories remained consistently fresh and involving, and they grew in prominence as the series progressed, as indicated by White's selection as the Guest of Honor of the 1996 World Science Fiction Convention.

Seeking to explain the series' popularity, commentators have generally discussed the appealing kindness and altruism displayed by White's heroic physicians, and they have particularly focused on White's loathing of war and advocacy of pacifism. Brian Stableford observes in his "Introduction to the First Sector General Omnibus" that "White always saw the future in terms of a highly problematic but desperately necessary quest for lasting peace, whose establishment would require a respectful tolerance for all differences of form and faith" and refers to both White's "personal development as an exceptionally tolerant and compassionate human being" and his "pacifist sympathies."[1] Certainly, there is textual support for the notion that pacifism is a recurring theme in the series: in a "prequel" later added to the series and included in *Sector General*, "Accident," it is explained that Sector Twelve General Hospital was originally founded primarily as a way to help the alien civilizations of the galaxy interact and bond with each other; the second book in the series, *Star Surgeon*, features a large amount of antiwar rhetoric as the space station comes under attack by a misguided alien race; and other stories in the series, including the final novel *Double Contact*, condemn armed conflict as a method of resolving disputes.

Still, even granting that White's doctors are consistently altruistic and at times vocally pacifistic, one finds it difficult to view this as a dominant theme in the

Sector General stories. After careful examination of the language throughout the stories, another, quite different subject seems to be brought up more frequently, and that is *madness*. Everyone at White's space hospital is constantly, almost obsessively, concerned with the possibility of either themselves or the people around them going insane.

This preoccupation with incipient madness can virtually be quantified. While reading through several Sector General novels, I attempted to jot down every single word or phrase that referred to mental problems of some kind. For example, these are all the words or phrases I recorded in the novel *Star Healer*:[2]

mental distress (3, 64, 69, 97)
phobia (15)
mental well-being (20)
xenophobia (21, 151)
mental stability (21)
neurosis (21)
serious mental distress (22, 130)
your overworked brain (27)
an extreme form of multiple schizophrenia (28)
inferiority complex (37)
racial psychosis (37, 74)
untold psychological damage (57)
phobic individualism (57)
mental or physical distress (61)
doctor, you're mad (68)
maddening confusion (76)
mind-destroying conditioning (77)
severe mental trauma (80)
sanity (85, 148)
serious psychological discomfort (90)
madhouse like this (92)
mental confusion (97, 151, 193, 213)
psychologically disturbed patients (98)
last few hours of sanity (100)
mental havoc (104)
overly distressed mind (104)
physical or mental trauma (110)
mass psychosis called war (112)
going out of its supercooled, crystalline mind (117)
insane (148)
madhouse (149)
peace and calm which your mind requires so badly (150)
multiple schizophrenic (156)
permanent psychological damage (156)
mental quirk (171)
mind went off on a tangent (177)
mental overcrowding (188)
psychoses (190)

psychologically distressed (193)
sadistic (213)

To be sure, some of these phrases occur in routine language repeated elsewhere in the series, such as the descriptions of war as a "psychosis" and of the use of Educator tapes as a form of "multiple schizophrenia," and other phrases occur when someone is *denying* the existence or possibility of mental illness (as on page 193, where the full reference is to someone who is "not psychologically distressed"). Still, it can hardly be denied that worries about mental stability are regularly expressed throughout this and other books in the series. To provide some statistics, in all the Sector General books where I attempted to count such phrases, these were the approximate results:

Final Diagnosis	50 references
The Galactic Gourmet	24 references
The Genocidal Healer	49 references
Hospital Station	30 references
Major Operation	17 references
Mind Changer	90 references
Sector General	20 references
Star Healer (as listed above)	50 references
Star Surgeon	36 references

The mean number of references per novel is 40.7, with a standard deviation of 21.3, suggesting that a typical Sector General book has from 20 to 60 references to madness or mental health.

From one perspective, there is nothing surprising about this pattern. In my study of space stations in science fiction, *Islands in the Sky*, I noted that residents of space stations "display an alarming tendency to go mad" and that "almost every conceivable type of specific mental problem has afflicted at least one station inhabitant in science fiction."[3] Another similarity between the Sector General books and other space station stories is that White employs, as a method to alleviate this tendency to insanity, a strategy observed in series ranging from E. C. Eliott's Kemlo novels of the 1950s to the television program *Star Trek: Deep Space Nine* in the 1990s: arranging for residents to leave the station as often and for as long as possible. Thus, much of the action of the second and third books in the series, *Star Surgeon* and *Major Operation*, takes place away from Sector General, and the fourth book introduces the titular *Ambulance Ship*, called the *Rhabwar*, which in later adventures regularly takes White's heroes to remote regions of space to deal with medical emergencies. And generally, the references to madness or mental problems tend to diminish when the story moves away from the Sector General space station.

Still, the situation of White's hospital personnel is unique. Residents of other space stations are driven to the brink of madness by certain recurring problems; they complain about cramped quarters, barren steel walls, constant fears of sudden death, and monotonous routines, and they long to return to a comfortable life on a planetary surface. None of these things, however, pertains to the people at Sector General: their space station is large and spacious, filled with variegated environments replicating conditions on many different worlds; despite occasional incidents, their station seems secure from danger, and they express no concerns about their safety; a constant stream of medical puzzles involving aliens of various species, and often unknown species, means that their lives are never boring;[4] and staff members uniformly profess that they are thrilled and delighted to be working at the galaxy's most advanced medical facility and reluctantly return to planetary homes only upon their mandatory retirement. In other words, none of the problems that lead to madness on other space stations are present at Sector Twelve General Hospital, so their obsessive concerns about insanity demand a special explanation.

As it happens, upon close examination, Sector General strangely is a place that seems *designed* to drive doctors insane; in three respects, the problem of incipient madness is a result of deliberate policy decisions.

In the first place, Sector General is bizarrely a medical facility without any specialists. It is true that the alien Thornnastor and his assistant, the former nurse Murchison (clumsily elevated in her status as a response to the rise of feminism), are called "pathologists," but there is nothing about their medical activities to suggest any special focus on the study of infectious diseases. Every other staff person is simply a "doctor" or a "nurse." While we are informed that alien species often have nervous systems, circulatory systems, and reproductive systems similar to those in humans, Sector General has no neurologists, no cardiologists, and no gynecologists. Further, given routine attention to diverse alien species that live underwater, resemble large insects, or absorb radiant energy directly from their environments, one would imagine that new fields of medical specialization would emerge to treat the specialized organs of such beings—but apparently they have not. Thus, all doctors at Sector General must be ready to deal with all medical problems involving all species at all times, a situation that would surely generate a considerable amount of tension.

As a further complication, one would expect that, at the very least, an effort would be made to pair doctors and patients of the same species, so a human doctor would deal mainly with human patients, a furry Kelgian would deal mainly with Kelgian patients, and so on. Quite the contrary; as we are told more than once in the series, Sector General follows the policy of *preventing* doctors from working with patients of their own species—ostensibly as one facet of its overall mission to improve relationships between different races in the galaxy. Thus, while a human doctor facing a human patient with any number of possible problems would be stressful enough, that doctor will more likely be required to put on a suit and mask and enter a room filled with a poisonous chlorine atmosphere to minister to a patient resembling a large houseplant.

Second, in order to remedy the obvious problem of physicians who are unqualified to treat their patients, Sector General employs "Educator tapes": the mind patterns of famed physicians from various worlds are recorded and then temporarily implanted into doctors' minds, so that they are instantly equipped with the knowledge and experience they need to deal with a patient of that physician's species. The problem is that the entire personality of the alien physician, not simply its medical information, is transferred into the recipient's mind, leading to obvious perils; in *Hospital Station*, for example, when an inexperienced Dr. Conway takes on the mental patterns of an alien that lives by absorbing energy, he almost burns himself up as he compulsively seeks to be close to sources of heat. For the senior physicians known as "Diagnosticians," who retain tapes from several different aliens in their mind at one time, they are obliged to endure what White repeatedly describes as "an extreme form of multiple schizophrenia,"[5] leading to another of the series's frequently repeated observations: "anyone sane enough to be a Diagnostician was mad."[6]

Third, given all the dangers to mental health caused by stress and the Educator tapes, Sector General clearly requires, and does have, a supervising official with the title of "Chief Psychologist" who is assigned to assist physicians with their personal problems. Unfortunately, the person holding this position happens to be both completely unqualified and rather sadistic.

Chief Psychologist O'Mara is unquestionably the series's most striking and most peculiar character. Originally he was merely a construction worker helping to assemble Sector General, universally disliked because of his unrelenting taunting of an injured coworker and assigned as a punishment to care for a monstrous infant left by alien parents killed in an accident. However, he figures out how to handle his charge—in large part by building a machine to mercilessly pummel the creature, an experience it regards as affectionate petting—and when he reveals that his cruel insults were deliberately designed to counteract the excessive kindness shown by other workers and to allow the man to return to normalcy, it is decided on the spot that O'Mara would be the ideal man to serve as the hospital's Chief Psychologist. Yet a disturbing pattern has been established: O'Mara treats patients by torturing them, and his brutality toward the alien baby and ruthless berating of a colleague constitute behaviors rendered no less disturbing by their apparent efficacy.

In subsequent stories, O'Mara consistently figures as the station's despised, domineering overseer, ready with a harsh comment or humiliating order for anyone who seems to be stepping out of line. Repeatedly, it is said that he is like "a latter-day Torquemada"[7] and that his office "resembled . . . a medieval torture chamber."[8] Physicians are scared to death of O'Mara and approach him with problems only reluctantly, sure that he will respond with anger and, perhaps, with a determination to exile the complainant from the station. To be sure, we are repeatedly told that O'Mara is a highly intelligent man, that he is cruel only for excellent reasons, and that his brutal strategies for coping with problems invariably turn out to be well-chosen. Still, there remains an inescapable incongruity in having an obnoxious bully assigned to serve as the hospital's psychologist, and his brusk and tyrannical supervision of Sector General surely contributes to its unrelenting atmosphere of incipient insanity.

As the series progressed, White visibly endeavored to address the disquieting questions raised by O'Mara's oppressive presence. Characters seem to grow a little less frightened of him, and he seems to speak a little less harshly. He is provided with some assistants, who are infinitely nicer and more approachable, to better assist the troubled residents of Sector General, and one of them, Braithwaite, eventually emerges as his successor. Finally, in the eleventh book of the series, *Mind Changer*, O'Mara is removed from office in a story that looks back on his entire tenure, as he approaches retirement, and offers new insight into his character. We learn that early in his career, O'Mara took on the Educator tape of a Kelgian physician and found her thoughts so attractive that he illegally retained her personality in his mind, sought her out on her home world during occasional vacations, and established a platonic relationship with her. Given that Kelgians are famous for their bluntness, the presence of this mind partner does serve to explain O'Mara's cold, brusk character. More to the point, we learn what we might have suspected from the very beginning: that Sector General's Chief Psychologist, charged with preventing insanity on the station, was himself totally insane, a willing victim of a multiple personality disorder.

We will never know how Sector Twelve General Hospital might have changed for the better—or worse—in the absence of O'Mara, because the novel immediately after *Mind Changer, Double Contact,* takes place entirely away from the station, and White died before he could begin another Sector General adventure. The question we can attempt to answer would be *why* White's futuristic, technological-advanced hospital became, as it is twice described in *The Galactic Gourmet,* "this medical madhouse."[9] Two explanations come to mind.

First, considering the Sector General novels as representative works of science fiction, produced by a writer who was intimately familiar with the genre first as a fan and later as a writer, one might draw upon ideas in previous chapters, particularly those by Kirk Hampton and Carol MacKay and by Frank McConnell, to suggest the following. As a form of literature essentially hostile to the body, science fiction feels a powerful impulse to marginalize and suppress those future citizens who remain stubbornly dedicated to the preservation of the body. Despite their astounding scientific resources and potentially godlike power to draw upon the minds of the galaxy's greatest intelligences and effect miraculous cures, the physicians of Sector General must be kept constantly on the verge of a nervous breakdown and firmly under the thumb of a bellowing nincompoop in order to control them and to punish them for their misguided priorities. Even placing these doctors in a huge, isolated space station, instead of leaving them with compatriots on their homeworlds, could be viewed as a device to isolate and imprison these threats to ultimate human progress by means of renunciation of the body. And White, even while attempting to employ doctors as the heroes of straightforward medical mysteries and adventures, might have felt the influence of these generic tendencies in rendering their lives so maddening.

Second, and in a more down-to-earth fashion, one might regard the Sector General stories only as the works of a distinctive individual author who casually drifted into writing a series of medical science fiction without any real knowledge of medicine. In this respect, White might have been far more ignorant of his subject than anyone has ever imagined. He certainly never troubled to get his basic terminology straight: I have already suggested that White demonstrates little awareness of the special meaning of the term "pathologist" to refer to a physician who treats diseases; since his "Diagnosticians" in fact treat patients, and do not simply diagnose them, that term is inappropriate as well; and White commits a common layman's mistake in referring to the problems caused by Educator tapes as "schizophrenia" when they would actually be cases of split personality, or multiple personality disorder. As he built upon vague images of emergency-room medicine in constructing his early stories, it may not have occurred to White that the doctors staffing a vast space hospital would logically be specialists, not general practitioners, or that supervising their work and dealing with their personal problems would require someone with professional medical training, not merely a domineering martinet with a knack for ingenious if sometimes sadistic solutions.

Then, as its popularity kept the series going far beyond White's original expectations, White for the sake of continuity had to carry on with his makeshift creation, unable to correct his blunders, even as he was obliged to acknowledge that the space hospital he had hastily devised was causing severe problems for its personnel. Far from supporting any grand thesis about the central themes of science fiction, then, White's Sector General stories might be regarded only as illustrations of a simple principle: when you ask someone who doesn't know anything about medicine to set up a system of medical care, you will get a system that does not make sense, a system that drives doctors to the brink of insanity.

And, as a concluding conceit, I might suggest that White's Sector Twelve General Hospital therefore has some relevance to today's American health care system.

Increasingly dominated by bureaucratic HMOs, modern American medicine has manifestly been reorganized by people who, like White, lack medical training or knowledge. In the name of cutting costs, the HMOs often pressure general practitioners and family physicians to avoid referring patients to specialists and to instead treat their varied illnesses themselves, effectively forcing doctors to confront a wide range of problems beyond their formal training or expertise and reducing the role of specialists. While there is nothing precisely analogous to the Educator tapes to provide these overwhelmed doctors with up-to-date information, they do confront a bewildering number of research studies and journal articles that frequently reach contradictory conclusions about the value of a given medicine or treatment due to the conflicting agendas of the groups sponsoring the research—so that doctors are receiving information that, like the data placed into the brains of the Sector General physicians, contains personal biases. And the decisions of the HMO bureaucrats regarding proposed medical treatments, frequently criticized as arbitrary, dictatorial, and ignorant, do intriguingly recall the approach and mindset of Chief Psychologist O'Mara. It further cannot be denied that, as a result of this system, doctors today are under more stress and are more frequently subject to mental disorders—yet because doctors paradoxically often do not have good medical insurance, they often lack access to the expert psychological care they need, just like the doctors of Sector General.

So in life as in science fiction, when you have people without a medical background set up a structure for health care, the result will be a system that drives doctors crazy.

If there is a silver lining to this cloudy analogy, it lies in James White's oft-cited optimism: Despite all the problems they face, his dedicated and capable physicians somehow manage to carry on with their work, to treat all the patients they minister to compassionately and effectively, and to maintain their sanity and good humor in the process. As the physicians of twenty-first century America confront a similar array of challenges, we will have to hope that they will be able to carry on just as well.

Notes

1. Brian Stableford, "Introduction to the First Sector General Omnibus," in James White, *Beginning Operations: A Sector General Omnibus* (New York: Tor Books, 2001), 10, 11, 8.

2. James White, *Star Healer* (New York: Del Rey/Ballantine Books, 1984). All page references in the text are to this edition.

3. Gary Westfahl, *Islands in the Sky: The Space Station Theme in Science Fiction Literature* (San Bernardino, CA: Borgo Press, 1996), 70.

4. While there is some monotony in their lives, to be sure, they seem to relish their monotony; thus, whenever the doctors of Sector General have a dinner, Conway is sure to order a big, juicy synthetic steak while the insect-like alien Prilicla will always be hovering above him enjoying his favorite food, spaghetti, contentedly knitting the noodles into a rope that he then swallows.

5. James White, *The Genocidal Healer* (1991; New York: Del Rey/Ballantine Books, 1992), 79.

6. James White, *Sector General* (New York: Del Rey/Ballantine Books, 1983), 53.

7. James White, *Hospital Station*, 1962, in White, *Beginning Operations: A Sector General Omnibus* (New York: Tor Books, 2001), 93.

8. White, *Star Healer*, 20.

9. James White, *The Galactic Gourmet* (New York: Tor Books, 1994), 67, 109.

11

Doctors of the Mind: Effective
Mental Therapy and Its Implications

Greg Bear

Science fiction has often been regarded as a literature that appeals to adolescents. And the adolescents' view of their bodies is typically that they are immortal and they don't really need doctors; they can do anything that they want to themselves and will not suffer damage for it. Correspondingly, science fiction has displayed this attitude in its more adventurous forms: Whatever society does to itself in the future will not burn it. Fortunately or unfortunately, what I have tended to do in my fiction is to show that everything you do can burn, and can burn badly—that all of the changes you will undergo have consequences, sometimes positive, sometimes negative, usually both.

Bodily change is a very disturbing thing for most people who read science fiction. The reactions I have gotten from people who have read *Blood Music*—which has physicians in it, dealing with an uncontrollable force, because again they've gone too far—is that the change at the end is just too much. And the reason it's too much, it seems to me, is that we're dealing with a transition from an adolescent image of the body as something immortal to a mature image of the body as something which will eventually dissolve and go away. It represents the realization that you are, in fact, playing an endgame after your middle years, and that if change is going to happen, it's going to be disturbing. A lot of readers reacted negatively to this, regarding *Blood Music* as a horror story. In fact, only one person I know of actually responded in a totally positive way to this book, and that was Bruce Sterling, who said, "I can't wait for it to happen!" (If you know Bruce, that's perfectly appropriate.)

But originally, I personally viewed the novel with a kind of sublime ignorance of the implications of what I was talking about. I had danced blithely into these disquieting territories, written about them with great glee, and enjoyed the reactions they had gotten. Then I said to myself "Well, that's good—now I've taught people a lesson!" And I still maintained that adolescent feeling of, basically, being untouchable. I subsequently wrote another novel, *Queen of Angels*, in which I dealt with the notion of mental therapy, of effective doctors of the mind. And the fact that they were really effective was a genuine stretch for some science fiction thinkers: not only did they believe that the mind didn't really need doctors because of their adolescent vision of the permanent near-perfection of their mental/mechanical abilities, but they weren't positive, actually, that a doctor could ever do anything for somebody's mind if it *did* go wrong, because they were locked into the notion that psychiatry was a "soft" science, not at all like engineering.

In *Queen of Angels*, what I tried to show was that, in fact, the doctors of my near-future world were good at what they did, and that they could effectively change or correct mental problems. However, there was a problem of definition that I skirted over in the book, namely: What is a mental problem? Here, we begin to suspect that the "last frontier" of social acceptance is the notion of mental variation and disease. If you have extreme mental variety (meaning that you vary from the norm), it's not socially acceptable; neither is extreme mental disease. You are ostracized for both of these conditions. And we tend to classify both of these things as being diseases when, in fact, they may not be. You may have extreme mental variety that could be called creativity—although in certain social circles, *that* will not necessarily be considered desirable. And then, of course, we have the common belief, which I tended to deny through most of my career, that there is a connection between creativity and madness. Nonsense! Geniuses don't have to end up mad; sometimes they do, but then again, so do many "normal" people. And statistics demonstrate that one usually finds higher levels of mental illness among the less intelligent people.

So I finished *Queen of Angels*, again with this kind of blithe illusion that I was going to shock people, while still maintaining my adolescent vision of not really disturbing myself too much. Then something happened that showed me that not only was *Queen of Angels* ahead of its time, but it was, in fact, *behind* its time. Effective mental therapy exists now, and it is a matter of great controversy, though I was for some reason ignorant of this, except on a theoretical level. When one enters into what I would sublimely call a "midlife crisis," suddenly you start to experience fluctuations in your mental state, and they are not controllable. And when you go to the doctor, you are told, "Yes, there are now treatments for these things," and you start taking those treatments. Pretty soon, like Philip K. Dick, you are watching the fluctuation of your mind from day to day and you suddenly recognize the deep issue that *Queen of Angels* and even *Blood Music* were really dealing with. And the issue is: What does it mean to be a thinking being, and to what extent are you merely a mechanism, and at what extent are you a spiritual entity? And when you experience mental changes, are you maturing, or are you simply going crazy?

All these questions came into play in the novel I went on to write, / (or *Slant*), which begins about four years after *Queen of Angels* leaves off and deals with a society where therapy is not only manifest all over the place, but is absolutely essential. When I was writing this book, I heard a doctor describing a paper he had delivered to a conservative think-tank, on the uses of mental therapy in society, in which he said, "mental therapy is there because we need it." Our social structure is such that we are now putting what doctors call "allostatic load" on every individual to such a great extent that, even though they can balance out and maintain an active mental life and economic existence, they are in fact wearing down their mental pathways, their mental abilities. They are putting a tremendous amount of pressure on the machine. Now, we envision allostatic load in terms of a balance beam on which you have stress of whatever sort on one side, and compensation of a chemical nature on the other side, since the body reacts chemically to stress. The allostatic load is the balance beam, which *looks* like it's balanced, bending on both ends—too much stress, too much chemical response. And you cannot bring it back to its previous condition without extreme physical intervention, such as deep-level neurological intervention, neuronal fix-ups, chemical adjustments,and so on.

What I was thinking about when I was writing *Queen of Angels* was that there are going to be many different kinds of therapies required for different cultures, because every culture will exert stress on different portions of a person's total mentality. Therefore, doctors will need different skills in different cultures; and, of course, it occurred to me at this point that, "Gee, Freud might have been right—for Victorian England!" Not necessarily in his metaphysical overview, that is, but when the doctor was describing the social conditions of Victorian England—these weird manifestations of hysteria, paralysis, and so on—that was, perhaps, perfectly true at the time, and his theories would apply to that. But in *our* culture, they don't, because the stresses have changed. However, the science has also changed.

What Freud and Jung were looking for back in those days was neurological explanations for what they were seeing; they were looking for deep structure and they had no way of finding it. And so, ultimately frustrated, they started going off onto what we would today call mystical tangents. Jung is more famous for this, but Freud also created an approach to psychiatry as an expression of Law—of which he was the Moses—and any deviation from this must be punished in some way or another. He also began to ignore basic social things that were outside his personal ability to respond to; for example, he ignored instances of sexual abuse in families, believing that they were simply imagined. So Doctor Freud was ultimately unable to help his patients. Jung always backed up his theories with the proviso that someday a science would come along that would explain these things. And we have, in a sense, begun to lay down the foundations for that science, and it is chemistry—and that is quite amazing.

So, suddenly, within my own life and within my own mind, as well as within my own fiction, I found myself going through the midlife crisis of realizing that our adolescent beliefs about our immortality and our physical resistance to stress are dead wrong. Throughout our lives, we are dealt—depending upon our culture, social situation, genetic background, family origins, and other factors—a variety of stresses which give us allostatic load; that is, we are warped by our life. As we continue on in our lives, sometimes those things erupt into what we call mental disease. Genetic factors predominating early may lead children to be depressed; extreme social or environmental factors may also lead to childhood depression. Doctors are now finding out that children can be treated by chemical means as well, to relieve most of the symptoms of these depressions, as long as the chemistry is maintained. But lo and behold, the chemistry has consequences; and lo and behold, the pharmaceutical establishment and the doctors—almost as if in a science fiction story—don't always want us to know about these things.

So we are dealing with a very complex system, and in treating this in science fiction, and in medicine, we have to look upon it as an opportunity for things to go wrong—because, of course, every story has to have something horrible go wrong within it. And what goes wrong, horribly, in mental treatment is this: For every adjustment you make that brings relief in one area, you bring on distress in another area. There are very few people who make use of the chemical therapies now available—such as Prozac, other antidepressants, and treatments for obsessive-compulsive disorders—who don't experience consequences. The major consequence of Prozac, usually not terribly well publicized, is that it results in a reduction or alteration of libido. There appears to be some connection between having enough serotonin in your brain to feel contented, and finding that your sexual desires are reduced. Nobody can be quite sure what this is, but it occurs; my guess is that it happens with something like 70 or 75 percent of people using Prozac (the pharmaceutical company's estimate is 2 percent). Of course, the doctors do not want you to know this because you probably won't take the drug, and you probably will remain depressed. In fact, Prozac can be very effective as an antidepressant, and it is also effective against obsessive-compulsive disorder.

Now, for readers who have never had obsessive thoughts—or have never had a creative moment in their lives—an obsessive thought is one that doesn't seem to have any relevance to what you're doing now but, like a well-remembered ditty, keeps coming back to you, again and again and again. And it circulates through your mind, as if someone has walked a pathway around your particular mental garden until all the grass has gone, forming a rut, and that is where you keep going. Something happens as a result of chemical therapy that makes the rut no longer important; it goes away.

Now, what does that mean about obsession? What do obsessive people have to do with our society? What do depressed people have to do with our society? If you have a society well supplied with therapies, whom do you choose to apply therapy to, and on what basis? What if you have a Christian therapist, or a Moslem therapist, who decides that by applying a certain chemical change to people's minds that they can bring people spiritually into line? And what if they feel compelled to take action so that those people will have a greater chance, not only of fitting into their social and religious structure, but of literally getting into heaven? How do you do that—is it possible? Can you find a chemical that will give you the experience of having a deep connection with the godhead? Some people have already; and I don't just mean alcohol, LSD, or anything else. There are a variety of treatments that can provide you with a feeling of deep, spiritual peace. Is that false or true? It is artificial, quite often, but what about the real thing? Is that also artificially induced by changes in your own chemistry which are chemically analogous to the changes induced by drugs? Serotonin is chemically related to LSD; no surprise.

Nicotine tends to act much like various other neurotransmitters in your bloodstream: When applied in sudden, huge doses, it gives you an immense feeling of change, positive change. Caffeine replaces an energizing molecule and tends to make your neurons "believe" that there is more of this energizing molecule in your cells than you would otherwise have; caffeine is absolutely accepted in our society, but its long-term effects are absolutely unknown.

And what I discovered, not only by writing these books but also by going through the midlife crisis and trying out some of these treatments, is that everything having to do with personality and creativity and what we would call the soul also has to do with some rather mysterious chemical balances which have consequences. I also learned during this midlife crisis that in going through the crisis you are in fact maturing because your brain chemistry is changing naturally. What we are trying to do by going through therapy is essentially to take some aspirin for the headache that results from this change.

Now, since I haven't had long episodes of deep depression in my life, I couldn't be considered clinically depressed, or bipolar, or anything like that; basically, I was just having the thinking equivalent of a headache, and Prozac treated that very nicely, though with side effects that were uncomfortable. But what also happened to me—since I am a writer and a Philip K. Dick type in my head, self-consciously examining all these things—is that I began to experience many different kinds of characters. This blew my experience of writing fiction wide open, because suddenly I realized, yes, perhaps creativity *is* in fact connected to madness; perhaps it *is* connected to obsession; perhaps it *is* connected in the way that any insight is an extreme variation of your mental state. Bang! Everything in society, the positives and the negatives from genius to sociopathy, therefore becomes a function of brain chemistry, the structure of your neurons, and the way you process information— how you take it in, what you ignore, what you absorb— every aspect of character and personality.

As it happens, I was not undergoing extreme changes, but for some reason— perhaps because I am a novelist and like to look at different characters—I could extrapolate. I found that when I came down with a cold or virus of some sort and chemical changes happen which wouldn't have happened when I was a teenager, I went into a state of anhedonia that was absolutely awful; it was like being in hell, because everything's going right, yet you have no appreciation for it. Suddenly I knew how Hannibal Lecter feels—I knew how a real sociopath feels! Because if you're flatline all of your life, and all you can do to get a rise—to raise that level of serotonin in the back of your brain to a comfortable level of simply being around as a contented, thinking being—is to do something really extreme, then you're a sociopath.

That insight into character led me to announce this fact to friends like Gregory Benford and David Brin. Gregory responded, "Hey, this might be a good idea, maybe I should try this out, get some tips on being a writer." And I informed him, "No, it'll just make you more arrogant." Of course, offering that medical judgment without having the proper training was rather arrogant in itself—thus proving my point! For me, there is no embarrassment in any of these things simply because I've been weird all my life in one way or another, but outwardly socially acceptable; now the outward social acceptability was getting a little weirder and the inner stuff was starting to change.

So the book I started to write, /, talked about what happens when society becomes so capable of changing itself and so powerful that conservative elements within the society cannot comfortably exist. When you start getting sociopathic manifestations of entire cultures, we get terrorists. Of course, we've had those for generations, since it is just a part of any kind of major cultural change or political change. But what happens when, say, Christian fundamentalists can no longer fit into the financially powerful world of the Western paradigm—what do they do? Where do they go? Where do devout people go when they are being told that everything they believe is demonstrably, chemically, false? What do they do? Where do they go? Do they "gafiate," do they "get away from it all"? Do they go someplace to a desert island and establish a commune? That's been tried in periods of cultural stress. However, the cultural stress on our planet is so great now that there is no place you can hide. So in this book I postulated that someone gets really ticked off and sets up a way to remove all therapy from the world, so that everyone who ever had any kind of illness—mental illness, headache, extreme depression, bipolar manic/depression, whatever you want to call it—all the varieties which I, in my science fiction universe, term as "pathic or thymic disturbances or imbalances"—finds all these things coming back to them within a week because all of their underpinnings have been pulled out. And of course, the therapy of the future consists not just of neuronal changes, but of putting in monitors to keep your chemistry balanced within your brain, little nanotechnological devices, which made all of this reasonably convincing as a prognostication of what's going to happen in the future.

As I modeled this society, I suddenly realized that this wasn't simply going to happen in the future—*it was happening now.* Our entire culture is going through an adolescent change, toward a kind of mature realization of our physical limitations as human beings. So personal experience mimics science fiction experience, and fictional experience mimics cultural experience. Maybe this was the time for this book to be written, right before the millennium, right before some really interesting changes come on. There have already been many reactions in society to Prozac— among them, interestingly enough, the reactions of a group established by science fiction writer L. Ron Hubbard back in the 1950s, the Scientologists. They had an explosive, deep, and negative reaction to the notion of therapy for mental illness. Perhaps this reflected their realization that if Prozac were spread widely among the Scientologists, there wouldn't be as many donations coming in, there wouldn't be as much seeking to get "clear," and so on—all these mental "headaches" that besiege us when we search for metaphysical solutions would basically go away. As one comedian expressed it, suddenly people are going to find themselves at a temperature of 72 degrees "in your head" all year long! That's interesting, because that's sort of what it is like to be on Prozac. What are the natural reasons and functions of mentally varied people? Let's not call them mentally diseased people or creative people or anything; just what are the varieties and functions of extreme mental variety, and why are they there—what are the purposes of these things?

I don't know for sure, but I can tell you a number of theories that have been presented and are going into my fiction as I puzzle them out. The reason that doctors treat some illnesses and don't treat others is that some illnesses are within natural variation; until the culture decides that these are, in fact, illnesses, real illnesses, negative illnesses, they won't be treated. To wit, Alan Turing, a brilliant man who probably saved England during World War II and may have saved much of our culture by creating ways of cracking German codes and essentially burned his brain out doing so, was a homosexual; the British medical establishment and the law at the time deemed that an admitted homosexual must be treated as being psychopathic; so they put him on hormone therapy, which they did not understand at all, which gave him female characteristics and led him eventually to commit suicide. He was an extreme mental variant in two ways—in his sexual variation and his mental variation: He was brilliant, he was a genius. He was an outsider, he was an alien, and we treated him like shit. So how do we atone for that? We don't do it again! But what if your moral imperative says that culture must be shaped in a certain way, and what if you have the tools to shape it that way? What if the culture comes along and is suddenly able to make you 72 degrees in your head all year long; churchgoing, calm, deliberate, tithing regularly, a good member of society? We suddenly end up with, perhaps, "the body snatchers," where all of the people are very much alike except that they look like us.

That is a fear that science fiction has always expressed, that adolescents have always expressed—the fear of the negative consequences of growing up. What I try to do in my books, what I tried to do in *Queen of Angels*, is to show that the consequences are, of course, both positive and negative. I very seldom go into the dystopian mode, but in writing /, I found myself getting really mad, really ticked off, because I saw forces coming down the road that were having a severe cultural allergenic reaction to the changes in society. What they are going to do is not going to be pleasant, and there is a lot of money and political power behind them. I wasn't exactly sure where it was going to lead while I was writing that book, and I'm still not exactly sure now.

My concluding observation is that social control of thought and behavior is a feedback system. You cannot have a *Nineteen Eighty-Four* because, economically, it's going to fall apart. Everyone will be so deeply depressed that they finally just won't do any work at all—and Big Brother up there and the fellows below him with all their jackboots on, grinding into the face of humanity forever, eventually will starve to death. Then, some social outcasts will eventually be able to reestablish a functional economy. Nightmares are not realistic visions; they are, however, hormonal urges to correct—and that's what fiction does. Fiction provides a therapy of its own kind, both social and psychological; it allows us to compare ourselves to the experiences of others.

How then will fiction change, when the type of fiction that is being done is changing? For example, I have offered very few literary allusions in this chapter, and one hears absolutely no literary allusions on CNN. All texts are now being discriminated against—not by a great conspiracy, but by a financial need for new experience, new things like motion pictures, television, video games, and multimedia experiences. Reading has been declining for seventy years now, and I'm starting to be afraid that the cultural means and the cultural needs served by text are going to be changed. What happens when text no longer is important as a communication medium in society, when everything is visual? Our minds will change; our culture will change; and, of course, our psychological illnesses and variations will change. We will become a different culture; and perhaps, just as Freud's theories engendered by Victorian England have little meaning today, all of the theories that I am relating to you now will have no meaning at all in our transformed future. It's the sort of idea that could drive a person crazy.

12

1950s Science Fiction Film Doctors and the Battle between Individualism and Conformity

Susan A. George

In *The Youngest Science*, Lewis Thomas has documented how the role of the doctor changed in the twentieth century. In the past, the doctor's tasks had been primarily to diagnose patients and to comfort them when (as was usually the case) there was no real treatment available to cure them. Doctors served as friends, confidants, and counselors. After World War II brought new treatments and techniques to the forefront, however, the doctor emerged as a miracle worker, employing strange new medicines and machines to cure previously fatal diseases. Moving from the homey offices of a Norman Rockwell painting, doctors were now aligned with the cold, distant bureaucracies of hospitals, universities, corporations, and governments.

Of course, this was only one of many developments that affected the U.S. during in the 1950s, which was, as historians such as David Halberstam and John Patrick Diggins have noted, a turbulent time. Changes were touching every aspect of people's lives and raised concerns regarding issues such as "the much publicized increase in divorce"[1] to larger political issues including "the Korean war and the return of the brainwashed . . . the spiraling arms race, loyalty oaths, fallout and the rising fear of cancer, the fluoridation controversy, flying saucers and a rising interest in science fiction, cloning and the spiritual supermarket."[2] Of special interest, perhaps, was the assault upon the archetypal image of the frontier hunter or rugged individualist that had been a staple of the U.S. narrative tradition as far back as the novels of James Fenimore Cooper and the tales that grew out of the exploits of historical figures like Daniel Boone and Davy Crockett.[3] People were questioning the notion, made popular by Adam Smith and John Locke, "that there is a natural and harmonious relationship between the desires of individuals and the demands of social necessity, that individuals who act out of self-interest will automatically move the society as a whole in the direction of natural perfection."[4] By the 1950s there was a great deal of tension and uncertainty regarding the values of the rugged individualist and where they would lead the nation in the modern era.

The notion of the individual leading the nation to a natural harmony, indeed the notion of individualism itself, had become suspect. There was a strong new desire for a conformity that would lead to a stable, united American community that could repel the threat of communist infiltration as well as withstand domestic turmoil. Conformity, maintaining the status quo and the norm, was the new standard of the decade: "During the 1950s a concern for respectability, a need for security and compliance with the system became necessary prerequisites for participation in the reward structure of an increasingly affluent society. Conformism had replaced individuality as the principle ingredient for success."[5] As maintaining the status quo and staying within a predetermined "norm" became the new standard of success in 1950s, the team player threatened to replace the individualist as the key figure in literature and films.

This new conformity and conservatism started to take over Hollywood after the House Un-American Activities Committee (HUAC) trial of the Hollywood Ten and the McCarthy blacklists ended many promising Hollywood careers. The new Hollywood project was to support the status quo and cold war ideologies, make sure the nuclear family was safe and strong, and promote the new archetypal character— the team player or "organization man." Peter Biskind notes that one segment of 1950s society valued experts especially "experts who would join the team and play ball.[6] He also notes that "the individualist that was sentimentalized in Chandler and Hammett is now sleazy and selfish. Living on the edge of the law is no longer romantic; it's dangerous to society.[7] However, it would be an overstatement to say that the conformist completely replaced the archetypal individualist. There was just as much concern and anxiety surrounding conformity as there was surrounding the values of individualism. The primary concern was that excessive conformity would turn U.S. citizens into mindless followers who would not be that much different from the Soviet-style communists so feared in the decade.

In the battle between individualism and conformity that raged in the 1950s, then, which side would be taken by representatives of the medical profession? In their older role as companions and caretakers, doctors might be expected to stand up for individualism; in their newer role as scientific technicians, they might better serve as avatars of conformity. If one examines the science fiction films of the 1950s, the surprising answer seems to be that doctors can be observed on both sides of the battle, with some doctors fighting for individualism and others fighting for conformity—sometimes within the same film.

For instance, in *Invasion of the Body Snatchers* (1956), Dr. Miles Bennell, a small-town general practitioner, becomes the unwilling individualist hero of the film while Dr. Danny Kaufman, the town psychiatrist, becomes the spokesperson for the conforming pods. As a way to place this film in context, Patrick Lucanio's *Them or Us: Archetypal Interpretations of Fifties Alien Invasion Films* suggests that there were two types of invasion films in the 1950s: the classic text, in which the threat of invasion comes from an external source, such as life forms beyond the Earth; and the Prometheus variation, in which the threat comes from an internal source.

Invasion of the Body Snatchers is a classic text in which seeds traveling through space (as Danny Kaufman tells Miles and his love interest Becky), take root and start to duplicate and replace the inhabitants of the sleepy town of Santa Mira. Kaufman goes on to tell Miles and Becky that the pods offer a world without pain, tears, struggle and suffering, but also a world without love and autonomy. In the world of the pods "there's no need for love. . . . Love. Desire. Ambition. Faith. Without them life's so simple."[8] The world offered by the pods not only runs counter to the ideology of the rugged individualists which Miles eventually embodies, it also runs against the tenets of (early) capitalism, where an individual's ambition and hard work can lead not only to financial security but to personal happiness.

However, in a sense, this release from fear, desire, and ambition was exactly what many American citizens where searching for in the 1950s. As Samuels notes, "concern with conformity grew out of a need to escape from confusion, fear, worry, tension and a growing sense of insecurity."[9] Some of those who could afford it were turning to psychiatrists, psychologists, sociologists, and a variety of other "specialists" who were offering advice that might help them solve personal as well as social problems. When that did not work, some turned to tranquilizers. As Elaine Tyler May writes, "These experts advocated coping strategies to enable people to adapt to the institutional and technological changes taking place. The therapeutic approach that gained momentum during these years was geared toward helping people feel better about their place in the world, rather than changing it. It offered personal solutions to social problems."[10] The pods offer the ideal conformity quickly and easily without repeated trips to the psychiatrist or refilling prescriptions. All you have to do is go to sleep. When you wake up you are a member of a society that may be without love but is also without pain and fear. The social problems are eliminated through the pods' solution—change the person. *Invasion of the Body Snatchers* critiques the notion that conformity will solve the ills of 1950s society as the hero remains not only a general practitioner concerned with the aliments of his patients, whom he all knows by name, but an individualist in a world of specialists trying to solve social problems by convincing people to be happy with their lot in life.

Other science fiction films of the 1950s portray individualistic medical figures as opponents of alien-induced or science-induced conformity. For example, in *Invaders from Mars* (1953), when Martians are taking over adults' minds, it is the school psychologist who believes a boy's reports about his parents' odd behavior and instigates action. Also worth noting is that in *I Married a Monster from Outer Space* (1958), when the distraught wife seeks out reliable allies to battle the sinister aliens that have replaced her husband, she runs to the maternity ward of a local hospital, and in that comforting medical setting she obtains the assistance she needs.

However, while doctors and related figures are frequently the heroes in 1950s science fiction films, they are not always represented as rugged individualists; they can be team players as well. In Prometheus variation invasion films, where the threat is "the direct result of man's intervention in the natural order of the cosmos," the individualistic and reclusive scientist or doctor, who has the best intentions and wants to improve the human condition, becomes dangerous to society because of his individualist values and social isolation.[11] The contrast between insidiously individualistic scientists and benevolently conformist physicians can be clearly seen in Jack Arnold's *Tarantula*—which, as Lucanio notes, is a fine example of the Prometheus variation invasion film.[12] In *Tarantula* two reclusive scientists, Dr. Jacobs and Dr. Deemer, with their assistant Paul, work secretly in their desert lab. They are developing an inexpensive synthetic nutrient that will supplement the world's food supply ending hunger now and in the future as the world's population increases. The binding and triggering agent is a radioactive isotope. They have used it on various animals and a tarantula. Those that survive show increased size and an accelerated growth rate. Although the nutrient has proven to be unstable, Jacobs and Paul, who become impatient with the scientific process, decide to inject themselves with the nutrient before it is stable or properly tested. It causes a rare and slowly progressing disease, acromegaly, to develop quickly resulting in the death of both men. Before Paul dies he wrecks the lab and injects Deemer with the nutrient. Though the ensuing lab fire destroys most of the experimental animals, the tarantula escapes and begins its desert rampage.

When Jacobs's malformed body is found in the desert another character is introduced, the town's medical doctor, Matthew Hastings, who is, like Miles, a general practitioner and an active member of the desert community. Hastings is unsatisfied with Deemer's explanation regarding the cause of Jacobs' death. Hastings tries to get the sheriff to question Deemer further but the sheriff refuses to question the authority of such a prestigious scientist. Hastings then voices the opinion that some segments of American society held toward specialists as he tells the sheriff, "There's nothing like the safety of prestige."[13] In the turbulence of the postwar period, while some Americans were turning to specialists for advice on a wide range of subjects, there were others, like Hastings in *Tarantula*, who looked upon them with suspicion. After all, reclusive scientists had developed the atomic bomb and many people, including some of the scientists themselves, had ambivalent feeling regarding this new technology. The sheriff dismisses Hastings's objections as professional jealousy, replying, "Do you want me to charge him with confusing a country doctor?" Hastings, however, persists: "Have you ever asked yourself what Deemer and Jacobs were working on in their lab? . . . Deemer's specialty is nutrient biology. Jacobs is a leader in the same field. Now when two big shots like that get together and hole up in the desert, 20 miles from civilization, I'd say they might be working on something they're not to anxious to talk about." Hastings's skepticism about Deemer and his work gives a voice to the concerns that many at that time had about scientists. As it turns out, Hastings's doubts are well founded. Deemer and his colleagues' experimentation has indeed gone too far, too fast, and it leads to disaster. Deemer does his best to help rectify the situation, but it is too late for him.

Hastings emerges as the "hero, who is often an authority figure" to counterbalance the isolated specialist.[14] Such authority figures are also, necessarily, team players. Society turns to them for leadership because they represent the new values and ideologies of the big organization. And medical doctors may be ideal avatars of these values, since they both match the scientists' educational credentials and typically remain (unlike the scientists) in close contact with human communities, treating and interacting with patients on a daily basis and working cooperatively with other doctors and hospital staff members. Thus after the brilliant scientists Jacobs and Deemer, working in isolation, threaten society with disaster, it is only fitting that a medical doctor, Hastings, should emerge as their adversary.

Hastings keeps finding a strange white foamy substance at the sites of the killings. After analyzing the substance, he starts to put things together. When the failing Deemer eventually tells Hastings that one of the experimental creatures was a tarantula, he decides to confirm his findings. For verification, instead of turning to Deemer who works in isolation, he turns to part of the big organization outside of Desert Rock, the Arizona Agricultural Institute. A doctor at the institute verifies that the substance is tarantula venom. It is of little consequence that the doctor at the institute does not believe Hastings' story about a huge tarantula, as Hastings is now sure of the truth and returns to Desert Rock to launch an assault against the arachnid.

After several failed attempts to destroy the ever-advancing spider themselves, the group (minus the individualist Deemer), decide to call in reinforcements. Ultimately, the hero and the small group of people left in Desert Rock (which has been evacuated) must depend on the larger organization, in this case the United States Air Force, to protect and keep the community intact. The small group cheer as they see the four fighters flying in tight formation to their rescue. Though Hastings cannot mount an effective defense by himself, his plan turns out to be the final solution. When the military's "rockets" also prove ineffective, Hastings's idea, napalm, finally does the trick as the huge tarantula goes up in flames. Therefore, the film supports the team and team players over the isolated, obsessed individualist. Here the reclusive egghead doctors, though trying to help humanity, become dangerous to society. Hastings, again a regular M.D., represents the intelligent person who is connected to and committed to the community. In the end, this film is critical of the individualist and models the effectiveness of the individual when channeled through the group.

Hastings is not the only 1950s film doctor who embodies the values of a conformist society battling isolated, individualistic antagonists. *Creature with the Atom Brain* (1955), for example, is another example of the Prometheus variation invasion film in which a doctor working for the police department, Chet Walker, successfully opposes the efforts of a mad scientist to create an army of atomic-powered zombies.

Overall, then, the science fiction films of the 1950s seem to suggest that the general practitioner, the country doctor, is always to be trusted, whether he is a team player or an individualist. The town doctor's close ties with the community make it less likely that he will fall prey to either excessive conformity, as represented in films like *Invasion of the Body Snatchers*, or to the temptations of scientific hubris, as represented in *Tarantula*. It might seem strange that medical doctors, at least general practitioners, should consistently emerge as heroic figures in the science fiction films of the 1950s, employed as champions both in those films that assailed conformity and those films that endorsed conformity. Perhaps, however, this is not really surprising. At a time when so many divisive controversies embroiled U.S. society, when so many traditional values were being challenged, one of the few things that everyone could celebrate was the astounding advances in modern medicine. Dr. Jonas Salk, the conqueror of polio, was a universally admired figure who combined the personality of a maverick with an up-to-date knowledge of vaccines to develop a treatment for what was then the world's most-feared disease. Recalling that sick people will always wish to regard their doctors as caring and capable heroes, one might characterize the U.S. in the 1950s as a sick society, seeking a similar sort of reassurance from the representation of good doctors that they could find in the science fiction films of the 1950s.

Notes

1. Glen M. Johnson, " 'We'd Fight. . . . We Had To': *The Body Snatchers* as Novel and Film," *Journal of Popular Culture*, 8 (Summer, 1979), 8.
2. Arthur Le Gacy, "*Invasion of the Body Snatchers*: A Metaphor for the Fifties," *Literature\Film Quarterly* (Summer, 1978), 290.
3. Richard Slotkin, *Gunfighter Nation; The Myth of the Frontier in Twentieth-Century America* (New York: HarperPerennial, 1992), 25.
4. Stuart Samuels, "The Age of Conspiracy and Conformity: *Invasion of the Body Snatchers*," in John E. O'Connor and Martin A. Jackson, editors, *American History/American Film: Interpreting the Hollywood Image* (New York: Ungar Publishing Company, 1979), 210.
5. Samuels, 207.
6. Peter Biskind, *Seeing Is Believing: How Hollywood Taught Us to Stop Worrying and Love the Fifties* (New York: Pantheon Books, 1983), 54.
7. Biskind, 55–56.
8. Daniel Mainwaring, *Invasion of the Body Snatchers*, edited by Al La Valley, Rutgers Films in Print Series (New Brunswick: Rutgers University Press, 1989), 88.
9. Samuels, 207–208.
10. Elaine Tyler May, *Homeward Bound: American Families in the Cold War Era* (New York: Basic Books, 1988), 14.
11. Patrick Lucanio, *Them or Us: Archetypal Interpretations of Fifties Alien Invasion Films* (Bloomington: Indiana University Press, 1987), 46.
12. Lucanio, 50.
13. *Tarantula* (Universal, 1955). All quotations in the text are taken from a videotape of the film, not the film's script.
14. Lucanio, 49.

13

Synthetics, Humanity, and the Life Force in the *Alien* Quartet

Mary Pharr

For twenty years now, Ellen Ripley has journeyed the cinematic universe as the hero of the *Alien* quartet, films depicting her struggle against the fearsome procreation of a xenomorph species and the heedless cupidity of our own *Homo sapiens*. Hovering between horror and science fiction, the quartet's segments vary in quality; the *Alien* series as a whole, however, is a legitimate epic, a sweeping dissertation on the ontological extremes possible in both existence and behavior. While the series titles and effects privilege the aliens, the film narratives present not an exclusive opposition between alien and human but rather a tripartite structure, unevenly balanced among (1) the xenomorphs as predators, (2) Ripley and whatever pack she leads as prey, and (3) the remaining humans serving a military-industrial trap that forces predator and prey together. These three sides continually collapse into chaos: the xenomorphs destroying both prey and trap, only to be themselves destroyed by the absolute valor of Ripley. The series' manifest message may not be profound, but it is unambiguous: bugs from beyond are bad, but people who exploit other beings—human or alien—endanger everyone through their greed.

Understandably, then, most of the critical attention focused on the quartet has concentrated either on the H. R. Giger-inspired monsters or on Ripley's complex female strength. What has not been examined closely is the equally complicated role of synthetics in the series, robots who do not so much bridge the gap between human and alien as move beyond it. Criticism of contemporary cinematic synthetics has instead focused on either the Tyrell replicants of Ridley Scott's *Blade Runner* (1982) or the Skynet hunters in James Cameron's two *Terminator* films (1984, 1991). Considering these films, Forest Pyle has observed that "deconstruction opens a critical questioning" of the ways by which cinematic "sounds and visions get tangled up with our notions of the human."[1] Though its questions are not as distinct as those of the films Pyle considers, this tangling is also evident in the *Alien* discourse. If the synthetics are privileged above the xenomorphs or above either group of humans, then the series takes on a different character.

Making no distinction between androids and robots, the quartet has three "fabricated beings" essential to the narrative: Ash, the science officer on the *Nostromo*; Bishop, the executive officer aboard the *Sulaco*; and Call, the pirate/spy on the *Auriga*. Viewed separately from a humanist perspective, the three synthetics are recognizable types: Ash the Frankenstein monster gone amok in Ridley Scott's *Alien* (1979), Bishop the sympathetic android doomed by his decency in both James Cameron's *Aliens* (1986) and David Fincher's *Alien3* (1992), and Call the Second Generation fembot serving as Ripley's sidekick in Jean-Pierre Jeunet's *Alien Resurrection* (1997). Taken together, the three robots ironically highlight the inhumanity within *Homo sapiens*; that is, they become pawns in the relentless misery human beings inflict upon one another.

More than pawns, however, they are also *döppelgangers*, not so much inhuman as ahuman, doubles that signify the mystery of existence. Something that Joseph Francavilla observes about the replicants in *Blade Runner* applies to the synthetics in the Alien series as well: "scientifically manufactured," these entities "function as mirrors for people, by allowing examination and moral scrutiny of ourselves, our technology, and our treatment of other beings."[2] Repositioned, postmodern synthetics like Roy Batty and Rachael Tyrell—or like Ash, Bishop, and Call— suggest the inevitable dissolution of the line between natural and unnatural or artificial life, a line that has thinned out not just in film but in—everything.

The first *Alien* film is a replay of the classic contention between humanity and science, but as in all Frankenstein stories, something unspoken lurks beneath the surface. Within the deep- space freighter *Nostromo*, a crew is caught between the luminous blue-white sterility of their highly technological habitat and the dark womb of some strobe-lit horror hiding in the bowels of their ship. Though a master of pacing, Scott borrows many of his movie's *mise-en-scene* elements from Howard Hawks's *The Thing*, Mario Bava's *Planet of the Vampires*, Stanley Kubrick's *2001: A Space Odyssey*, and John Carpenter's *Halloween*. Beyond the inherited visuals, however, Scott has several advantages over his predecessors: a plausible if spare script, exceptional actors embodying memorable characters with minimal melodrama, and the remarkable biomechanical designs of H. R. Giger. Thus empowered, Scott takes his film past run-of-the-mill "old dark house" movies, suggesting instead something both postmodern and Dantesque.

Giger's primary creation is the xenomorph, fearsome in its organic polymorphism and in its unwitting link to corporate rapacity. For it's the Company that owns the *Nostromo* that has deliberately sent an unprepared and ignorant crew directly in the path of an alien species that has potential as a bio-weapon. Thus, the plot sets the essential oppositions of crew versus alien versus the military-industrial trap. Science officer Ash is part of that trap. No one—characters or audience— knows that he is a robot until he goes berserk and batters Ripley. Until that moment, he has seemed merely the cold scientist added to the crew just before the trip began and with no discernible reason to be "buddies" with his mates. Descended from a thousand mad doctors, Ash is fascinated by the alien as "perfect organism," one whose "structural perfection is matched only by its hostility."[3] He's what we expect from humanity corrupted by knowledge, but he's set in opposition to the truly human Ripley from the start.

When Ripley refuses a near-hysterical command from Dallas, her captain, that she open the *Nostromo*'s hatch and potentially infect the entire ship with an unknown life form, Ash blandly releases the hatch and explains that he was merely "obeying a direct order" (*Alien*). And when she complains to Dallas about Ash's deviation from standard safety procedure, the captain's response is a profane version of Ash's own rationale for putting everyone in jeopardy: "Standard procedure is to do what the hell the Company tells you to do" (*Alien*). Pliant Dallas is doomed, but so, too, is the equally obedient Ash. Only Ripley, privileged by her rebellious skepticism, will survive.

If, however, we privilege the robot instead of the human, we find that Ash is neither a madman nor an absolute machine. Aware that he is Company merchandise, Ash is content in his programming, which simply instructs him to bring this "perfect organism" to Earth, all else being expendable. "You do your job. Let me do mine" (*Alien*), he tells Ripley; and so he goes on, confident and purposeful. For more than anyone else, Ash recognizes the import of the alien. He's shown repeatedly sitting in the lab studying the thing and its traces. Like space itself, Ash cares neither for the humans on the ship nor for the Company men on Earth (these latter will, after all, get a most unpleasant surprise when he lets them have their alien). What he does care about is "collating," to use his term of choice. And what he collates is not just information but sentience, awareness of a universe far wider than either aliens or people understand. The alien wants to propagate and the crew wants to escape; Ash wants to know.

Ripley also wants to know but only enough to allow escape. After a computer informs her of the Company's directive, she shoves Ash against a wall, thus precipitating the cranial injury that drives him berserk and forces the crew to tear his head off. Revealed as a "goddamned robot," Ash—or at least his mutilated head—is brought back to momentary life by a Ripley desperate to know how to kill the alien. He tells her what he believes to be the truth—that she can't kill it—and confesses that he admires the alien for being "A survivor unclouded by conscience, remorse, or delusions of morality" (*Alien*). He's describing himself, of course—or the self he would have been had Ripley not interrupted his study. That interruption merits the ironic little joke of his last words: "I can't lie to you about your chances, but you have my sympathies" (*Alien*). And so Ash dies again, this time sane and smiling even as Ripley kicks his head away in disgust. A paradox, Ash perceived himself as both Company tool and sentient being. And looked at from his perspective, he was right.

In James Cameron's *Aliens*, Bishop is the anti-Ash, the android who is not only benign to humans but also protective of them—all this goodness the product of new and improved technology in the form of factory-installed "behavioral inhibitors." Technology is as much a hallmark of this sequel as is its vaunted maternalism. Cameron's set designs have a graphic-novel quality, gleaming and toy-like and studded with bric-a-brac machinery. Through such crowded sets race a band of stock characters: mostly standard movie marines, with Ripley, a Company representative, and a small child thrown in to give the hero a focus for her maternal instincts. Wrapped in fancy armor, riding shining transports, and clutching powerful weapons, these characters depend far more on techno-good things than on their intelligence. None of their nifty technology looks very futuristic, but in the context of Cameron's crowd-pleasing vision, that's just fine. Rather than repeat the slow, somber elegance of the first film, he reverses it, making his movie a democratic celebration of mankind's simple love of action. And by ultimately focusing that love on the maternal combat between Ripley and the Alien Queen, Cameron has his glossy violence and political correctness, too.

Bishop's just one cog in the machinery Ripley uses to rescue her adopted child; if privileged, however, he functions as a kind of double döppelganger, not just the inverse of Ash but also a mirror of the humane side of humanity. The first clear words we hear him say are "Trust me"[4]—more the plea of an old retainer than the command of a military officer. Open about his origin, Bishop prefers to be called an "artificial person" rather than a synthetic, yet he continually displays a sense of resigned obedience to the "real" persons. Despite his assurances that Ash was a defective model and that he, Bishop, can neither "harm [n]or by omission of action allow to be harmed a human being" (*Aliens*), Ripley detests him on sight. Only when Bishop guilelessly reveals the evil plans of the Company man and quietly volunteers for a dangerous rescue mission does Ripley come round, telling him upon the apparent success of his mission, "Bishop, you did okay" (*Aliens*). This being the case, she doesn't kick his head off. Unfortunately, the hidden Alien Queen does—or at least she truncates this fellow who is, presumably, no use to her as food or incubator. Horribly wounded, Bishop yet lives and saves Ripley's child from the winds of decompression while the hero is busy knocking the Queen into space. Like Ash, Bishop is last seen smiling, but this time with praise for Ripley: "Not bad for a human" (*Aliens*). For a moment, they're equals.

Mark Jancovich believes that in both Cameron's *Terminator* and his *Aliens*, woman "comes to stand for that which is truly human, not man."[5] But Bishop's quiet assistance suggests something more complex. Like all living things, he's interested in self-preservation, to the point that he'd prefer not to expose himself to danger: "I may be synthetic, but I'm not stupid" (*Aliens*). This line amused any number of reviewers, but beneath its surface naivete is paradox: no *Homo sapiens* believes any robot to be stupid, but even the stupidest of humans presumes superiority to robots; for a synth to assert his intelligence is not to state the obvious so much as the unacknowledged. When no one challenges his assertion, the newly acknowledged Bishop can volunteer for the rescue mission, not apparently because of his programming (nobody orders him to go) but because of both practical necessity (he's best qualified for the job) and genuine affinity with the endangered humans. Part of what makes the entire *Alien* quartet resonate with audiences is its unstated but emphatic awareness of the struggle between the urge to live and the urge to help others live. In his understated sense of self and sacrifice, Bishop models humanism just as surely as does Ripley.

And they both survive to *Alien3*. David Fincher's consciously profane exercise in existential gloom and glory is set on Fury 161, a prison/mining planet so bleak that it makes one long for the creepy quiet of the first film and the crammed sets of the second. But that's precisely Fincher's point: Nature howls on the outside of this storm-soaked world, and man howls within its yellowish-brown bowels. Figuratively as well as literally, everybody's trapped on Fury, with no escape pods available this time. Except for Ripley, alive by blind chance, and an alien embryo, the *Sulaco*'s human survivors die in the crash that welcomes them to this windy hell. Bishop's eviscerated remains are simply thrown in the trash. Bereft of human kinship, Ripley seeks out and repowers the robot—what's left of him, at least. A marginally restored head and torso, Bishop cracks a joke, complains of pain in his missing legs, and calls himself "a glorified toaster."[6] Ironically reduced to that which he fought so hard to avoid, Bishop sadly admits, "I'm not what I used to be" (*Alien3*). He also informs Ripley that the Company has again betrayed humanity and then begs her for final death. In a scene that J. Hoberman believes to have "intimations of mythological grandeur,"[7] Ripley lets the android die, "be nothing," in his own words.

It's a reversal of the guarded optimism of Cameron's film, a reversal widened when a human duplicate of Bishop demands Ripley's unborn alien offspring. At first, she's not sure if this new Bishop is even human, but he identifies himself as the android Bishop's designer, the creator who made life in his own image. Now this Company father offers to kill the alien embryo and return a normal life to Ripley. Approaching the wavering woman, Bishop the man repeats Bishop the robot's first words: "trust me" (*Alien3*). But there's a difference: The robot couldn't and didn't want to harm people; the man could and will. Sensing this, Ripley plunges to her death, while the Company Bishop screams frantically that she's throwing away not a human life but "the chance of a lifetime" and "a magnificent specimen" (*Alien3*). He can't understand her sacrifice any more than he would understand her feeling for his creation. With a postmodern irony discernible to even the slowest members of the audience, Bishop the man has created Bishop the android as his double, but the creation is far more humane than the creator.

Nonetheless, Bishop's fate is similar to that of Ash, with both the bad robot and the good one lost in the human battle for control of non-humans. In Jean-Pierre Jeunet's *Alien Resurrection*, however, the question of human control becomes irrelevant. All the important characters in this fourth film are non-human: Ripley, now a clone generated from old blood samples; Call, a robot made by robots; about a dozen aliens hatched from the eggs laid by the Ripley clone's new Queen daughter; and the Newborn, a particularly nasty genetic hybrid. As for everyone else, the human pirates, soldiers, and scientists of the space lab *Auriga*, they are petty beings who foist themselves on the others. Actress Sigourney Weaver says that to the transformed Ripley, humans now "seem ridiculous" because "they're always squabbling."[8] And certainly the humans on the *Auriga*—and by implication on Earth—don't seem to have the learning curve of other life forms. They are, perhaps, the alpha but surely no omega.

Nor does the film feel like a fitting omega to the series. It's no more futuristic looking than _Aliens_, despite being set 200 years later. Except for an underwater sequence, Jeunet's conception is itself a nasty hybrid of his predecessors: the film's dominant colors are gleaming white, combat blue-black, and sticky brown; its main sets reflect the medic-lab and the endless corridors of Scott's movie; its sporadic low lighting reminds one of Fincher's trademark gloom; and its graphic violence is simply Cameron's action taken into the extremis of the 1990s. To top it off, scriptwriter Joss Whedon has admitted lifting the watery stuff and the escape plot from that cinematic classic, _The Poseidon Adventure_.[9] More than anything else, _Alien Resurrection_ feels like a bridge movie, a way to get Ripley back on screen for some unseen grand finale.

Nonetheless, the movie is the only one of the series that explicitly privileges its humanoid ahumans. Call, the Second Generation auton, is part of a synthetic series withdrawn by the government because in Ripley's words, "They were too good,"[10] that is, too ethical and emotional to obey blindly, and so able to kill on their own recognizance for the greater good of mankind. This not-quite Asimovian conceit is readily apparent in Call, who dons the persona of a pirate as a means of getting close to the resurrected (and thus still alien-impregnated) Ripley, whom Call intends to destroy for the sake of the humans who massacred her fellow robots. But the auton's timing is off; the new aliens are already on the loose and headed toward Earth, a planet no one but Call cares enough about to save. Characteristically, the true humans on board express their gratitude for her concern by labeling her a "toaster oven" (_Alien Resurrection_). This inadvertent reference to Bishop's final self-mockery is echoed in Call's own lack of esteem: She describes her inorganic insides as "disgusting." Shadowing the humans, Call is prejudiced against robots.

Not so Ripley—not after Bishop and resurrection. As a clone, Ripley is herself synthetic, discounted by humans as a "meat byproduct" but really a new life form given extraordinary strength, acidic blood, and heightened senses by her genetic ties to the Alien Queen. Transformed, Ripley understands Call. On first realizing that Call is an auton, Ripley muses, "I should have known. No human being is that humane" (_Alien Resurrection_). Now primarily interested in her own survival, the clone yet cooperates with Call in the destruction of the aliens and their hybrid. In so doing, she gives Call a measure of self-respect, of equality with a superior being. After Ripley destroys the seven mutated clones whose imperfections led to her own exalted existence, Call punches out the human scientist who created these monstrosities, leading one male pirate to muse, "Must be a chick thing" (_Alien Resurrection_). It's really a synthetic thing, a bonding beyond gender.

Ripley never explains why she helps Call save Earth, though at one point she does note that the aliens are in her way. So, too, of course, are the humans. A more complete answer may lie in the film's latent discourse. As the movie ends, Call asks Ripley what they'll do on Earth, and Ripley can only respond, "I don't know. . . . I'm a stranger here myself" (_Alien Resurrection_). Like Call, Ripley is a combination of what is best though least familiar among the species that created her. Synthesis enkindles both heroes, allowing Call to communicate with the inanimate _Auriga_ and the absurdly animated pirates, allowing Ripley to communicate with humans, robots, and xenomorphs. For both clone and Second Gen, the cost of such communication is the loss of an intimate feeling of enclosure within a species, but the reward is a mutual receptivity to existence itself—to humanness and strangeness alike. This receptivity may be the reason that Call and Ripley can afford to save an undeserving planet. In them, the word *synthetic* attests to the fusion of scientific possibility and organic empathy, inspired by the Conradian life force that the *Alien* epic suggests is universal.

Notes

1. Forest Pyle, "Making Cyborgs, Making Humans: Of Terminators and Blade Runners," in Jim Collins, Hilary Radner, and Ava Preacher Collins, editors, *Film Theory Goes to the Movies* (New York: Routledge, 1993), 240.
2. Joseph Francavilla, "The Android as Döppelganger," in Judith B. Kernan, editor, *Retrofitting Blade Runner*, Second Edition (Bowling Green, OH: Bowling Green State University Popular Press, 1997), 14.
3. *Alien* (Twentieth-Century Fox, 1979). All quotations in the text are from a videotape of the film, not the film script.
4. *Aliens* (Twentieth-Century Fox, 1986). All quotations in the text are from a videotape of the film, not the film script.
5. Mark Jancovich, "*Terminator*: The Machine as Monster in Contemporary American Culture," *The Velvet Light Trap*, 30 (Fall, 1992), 16.
6. *Alien3* (Twentieth-Century Fox, 1992). All quotations in the text are from a videotape of the film, not the film script.
7. J. Hoberman, Review of *Alien3*, *The Village Voice Film Special*, 2 (June, 1992), 20.
8. Rachel Abramowitz, "Leave It to Weaver," *Premiere: Women in Hollywood* (1998), 59.
9. Edward Gross, "Clone Encounters," *Cinescape Insider*, 3.9 (1997), 74.
10. *Alien Resurrection* (Twentieth-Century Fox, 1997). All quotations in the text are from a videotape of the film, not the film script.

14

The Body Apocalyptic:
Theology and Technology in Films
and Fictions of the MIME Era

Howard V. Hendrix

Despite erosion from 1970 onward in numerous global markets such as automobiles and consumer electronics, American companies throughout the 1980s maintained a dominant market position in at least three fields: weapons manufacture, biomedical research, and entertainment "software" (including movies and TV). Nowhere was dominance in these industries more important than in President Ronald Reagan's adopted home state of California, particularly Southern California, home of Hollywood, UCLA Medical Center, the Rand Corporation, the Salk Institute—and the final resting place of one out of every four dollars spent by the Pentagon.

Dwight Eisenhower, in his final major statement as President in 1960, warned against the development of a "military-industrial complex." What developed in Southern California in the 1980s, however, was something much more interesting. A curious coevolution began to take place. Computer algorithms, originally designed to enable cruise missiles to find their targets by terrain-mapping, were soon spun off to the task of recognizing biomedically important molecular shapes. Industrial robotic arm programs were, with only a little rewriting, able to describe the spatial orientation and motion of biological molecules. Morphing programs, originally designed for movie special effects, were soon being used for everything from advertising to military and industrial design. Even the ghost of the long-lost fighter jet in military-derived simulation space lingered on as the joystick of computer games.

All the pieces—military, industrial, medical, entertainment—swapped back and forth so easily perhaps because they were all part of the same technorationalist worldview, the same total system of meaning responding to fear of Bolsheviks, fear of bacteria, fear of boredom. Eisenhower's Military Industrial Complex had evolved into MIME, the Military Industrial Medical Entertainment complex.

Like most technological changes, these were thoroughly enmeshed in cultural change, functioning neither totally autonomously nor in a totally determining fashion—neither free of social constraints and value frameworks on one hand, nor serving as the sole shaper of social destiny on the other.[1] Hollywood, for instance, grew as part of the MIME complex in a number of ways, most obviously in the rise of military-tech themed movies like *Top Gun*, *Red Dawn*, and *The Hunt for Red October*. More intriguing, though, were Hollywood's projections of the future of its own global/local world, particularly as that world was depicted in films such as *Blade Runner* (set in Los Angeles in 2017) and *The Terminator* (set in Los Angeles in both 1984 and 2024).

In both films, Los Angeles is the arena in which the crucial question of "What does it mean to be human?" is addressed, if not necessarily settled. That question is largely a biomedical issue in these films. Harrison Ford's Deckard, in *Blade Runner* (1982), is at least as much diagnostician as detective. Deckard's Voigt-Kampff empathy test measures "capillary dilation of the so-called blush response, fluctuation of the pupil, involuntary dilation of the iris," as the creator of the Nexus 6 Replicants, Dr. Tyrell, remarks.[2] All the members of the team of Replicants who have made it to Earth are military-connected. All these replicants (referred to in cop-slang as "skin jobs") are stronger and more agile than the genetic engineers who created them, and very nearly as intelligent. All have been given very short (four year) life spans in order to prevent them from developing memories crucial to an emotional awareness—emotions being the single criterion most clearly separating the android slaves from their human masters.

The implication is that, if these manufactured humanoids lived long enough to develop emotions, they would be virtually indistinguishable from their human creators, perhaps becoming more human than human, and therefore entitled to rights they are currently denied because of their status as manufactured products.

The renegade team of Nexus 6 replicants comes to Earth to demand of their creator, Dr. Tyrell, what Americans generally demand of their white lab-coated Doctor Gods: in the words of the replicant team's leader, Roy Batty, to Dr. Tyrell, "I want more life." The issue is longevity, the prolonging of biological life against mortality, and the linkage between the replicants' situation and all of ours is made specific when Deckard, who has fallen in love with the replicant Rachel, is taunted with the words "Too bad she won't live—but then again, who does?" Dr. Tyrell, however, with his imposition of four-year life spans on the Nexus 6s, is a creator who has hidden the Tree of Eternal Life even more completely than the Creator in Eden once did.

Nor is the comparison to God overblown. Dr. Tyrell speaks of himself in consciously "divine" terms, and the filmmakers (screenwriters Hampton Fancher and David Peoples, and director Ridley Scott) have played quite a bit with Masonic symbols of mystical power, particularly the incomplete pyramid topped with the image of the eye found on the back side of American $1 bills (surrounded by the Latin motto "Annuit Coeptis Novus Ordo Seclorum" citing 1776 as the incept date for a "new order of the world"). The Tyrell corporation is headquartered (and Dr. Tyrell resides) in a flat-topped pyramid like that on the $1 bill. The filmmakers are constantly juxtaposing images of the eye with this flat-topped corporate pyramid, suggesting the linkage of money, biomedicine, and almost mystical power in the corporate "New World Order" that Dr. Tyrell has helped establish. As a *Blade Runner*, Deckard too is in some ways a "private eye," though mainly he function as both diagnostician and executioner—"good doctor" and "good terminator."

He has some cause to kill. The replicants we meet can be nasty folks. The favored unarmed killing technique of replicants Leon and Roy involves gouging into the brain through the eyes, and it is through the specialized eye-designer biotechnician at Eye World that the replicants learn how to gain access to their Creator. Eyes and access recall the Renaissance notion that "the eyes are the windows of the soul" and that through them one can access the truth about someone's humanity.

In seeking out their creator, the replicants are not asking for more life merely for more life's sake; they are asking for more life so that they might more readily be able to pass for human and be seen as human—so that their eyes will not betray them in the eyes of others. The replicant Roy Batty to some degree dies for humanity's sins and in his dying is depicted in obviously Christological terms—pierced through the hand by a nail, and clutching a white dove (traditional representation of the Holy Spirit) which flies free when he dies, giving up his "ghost." True, when this prodigal Son of God asks "My God, my God, why have you forsaken me?" and doesn't get an answer he likes, he gouges out God the Father's eyes—but nonetheless, like the case of Christ in the Incarnation, Roy Batty is more than human passing for human.

This trope of "passing" and "being seen for" human also figures prominently in another MIME-complex movie of the 1980s, *The Terminator* (1984).[3] The cyborg super-soldier from the future (played with convincing robotic stiffness by Arnold Schwarzenegger) is a literal "skin job": human dermis and externals over a robot chassis. The eye as gateway to the soul also figures prominently here. When, after various ballistic encounters, the cyborg is so damaged that he loses the use of his biological eye-facade, he takes a scalpel and removes the dead flesh. This necessitates his wearing a large pair of Gargoyle sunglasses, however, so that his true redly glowing robotic eye will not be noted or remarked upon.

Overall, though, the medical specialty field in *The Terminator* is not so much ophthalmology as anatomy and physiology. Both the Terminator and human rebel-soldier Kyle Reese arrive naked in 1984 because the time-travel field generator can only transport living matter. At one point in the film, we see the Terminator wounded in the forearm, revealing the mechanical workings beneath the skin, the glowing red robotic eyes and, eventually, after all the flesh facade is burned away by a tanker-truck explosion, the hulking robot that lurks underneath.

The master-slave and Godhead tropes are played out in this film as well, only this time the creations of humanity are not the persecuted slaves (as was the case in the *Blade Runner* future), but rather humanity itself is pursued and enslaved in the 2024 of *The Terminator*. In the past of that Terminator future, a defense super-computer achieved a sort of sentience, came to view all of humanity (not just the designated cold war opponent) as the enemy, and started nuclear armageddon to eliminate the human vermin from the planet. The defense super-computer, SkyNet, then created automated factories to build robots to hunt down the remaining humans, who are captured, put in concentration camps, and worked to death as slaves or killed outright—humanity as the Jews to the robot Nazis.

Humanity is on the brink of extinction until the appearance of John Connor, the military-savior of humanity, who rallies the remaining humans to resist the robot master race. Human soldier Kyle Reese has been sent back from the future to protect Sarah Connor, mother of John, from the Terminator, the cyborg sent back to kill Sarah before she can give birth to the father of the resistance. Kyle Reese ends up making love (once) with Sarah, and in Hollywood one-shot sure-shot almost-immaculate conception fashion the man from the future ends up becoming the father of the father of the resistance. That the military messiah of the future has the initials J.C. should not be surprising, nor the idea of Sarah as a sort of paramilitary Blessed Virgin Mary.

The Terminator, gone from nude man to naked uncontrolled robot, is finally destroyed in an industrial, factory-line setting. This setting is, curiously enough, replete with contemporary industrial robots which, in a remarkable case of nostalgia for the present, are seen here as an older, more comprehensible, and therefore more subservient technology.

This theme is further elaborated in *Terminator 2: Judgment Day* (1991), which is in many ways a big-budget retelling of *The Terminator*, only this time robot T-100 series Arnold returns as the protective good-cyborg.[4] Just as the T-100s in *The Terminator* made humans "obsolete," so too have the T-100s themselves been made obsolete in turn by the creation of the new bad-guy morphing T-1000 series. The message linking the two films is that, if humans are obsolete, then obsolescence is somehow humanizing.

Terminator 2, though made a dozen years after *Blade Runner*, parallels the latter more closely in its ending than does *The Terminator*. In *The Terminator*, it is human soldier Kyle Reese who dies for humanity's sins and thereby helps assure its future survival. In *Terminator 2*, however, as in *Blade Runner*, it is the manufactured humanoid Other who dies for humanity's sins and in so doing assures humanity's future survival. Despite the fact that Arnold as T-100 retains much more of his human skin surface in *Terminator 2*, the "good Terminator" in his "death" is essentially Christ in chrome. Just as Christ, miraculous healer and Doctor God, cures future humanity of the Sin of Genesis through his sacrifice, so too does T-100 Arnold, an old god passing, through his sacrifice cure future humanity of the Sin of Apocalypse, the Sin the physicists have known and which so shaped the Cold War period.

A synergistic and coevolutionary relationship exists not only among the four primary components of the MIME, but even between and among subunits of those individual component parts. The feedback relationship between print and film in the Entertainment sector is an important example of this coevolution. Both *Blade Runner* and *The Terminator* owe considerable (and acknowledged) debt to the print works of science fiction authors of a previous generation—Philip K. Dick and Harlan Ellison, respectively.[5] (*Blade Runner* also owes a glancing debt to the experimentalist William Burroughs and the medical doctor/sf writer Alan E. Nourse.)

Many sf authors who came to prominence in the 1980s—particularly those whose names pop up in Bruce Sterling's 1986 *Mirrorshades* anthology—similarly owed a debt to films such as *Blade Runner*, *Videodrome* (1982), and *The Terminator*. Though he has in numerous interviews listed his primary literary influences as Thomas Pynchon and William Burroughs, William Gibson was perhaps even more influenced by *Blade Runner*, which, upon seeing it in 1982, he felt had already accomplished on screen what he was trying to accomplish in prose.[6]

Though the works of many of the so-called cyberpunks of the 1980s shared much of the same fascination with the gritty, apocalyptically violent MIME future expressed in the works of their film counterparts, the workers in print tended to associate the notion of human obsolescence with the idea of the obsolescence of the physical body per se. In works as diverse as Greg Bear's *Blood Music*, Walter Jon Williams's *Hardwired*, and William Gibson's *Mona Lisa Overdrive*, the other side of the apocalypse coin comes up.

The "armageddonic" and the "rending of this vale of tears in end-time catastrophe" associations of the word "apocalypse" were what film speculation in the 1980s tended to emphasize. Many in the print sf community, however, were alternatively emphasizing the "Rapturous," the "ecstatic" (as in ekstasis, or out-of-body), the Millennial, the transcendent, the mystical, the meaning of apocalypse as "revelatory," a lifting of the veil of this world rather than its rending.

A *New York Times* poll taken in 1985 indicated that Americans considered the atom bomb and the computer the two most important inventions of the twentieth century. Film and politics may have still been hooked on the bomb, borscht and big missiles of the Cold War, but the work of many sf writers during the 1980s tacitly assumed the obsolescence of that worldview and focused instead on what had also been developing throughout the postwar period: namely, the dawning of the Age of Code, characterized by both the initial decryption of the DNA code for organic life following on the work of Watson, Crick and Wilkins, and the initial encryption of the digital code for electronic life following particularly on the work of Turing and Von Neumann.

Undeniably, the military and industrial components of the MIME complex remain abundant in the futures created by 1980s cyberian sf writers, but the emphasis has shifted. Their gritty futures are less "military-industrial" than they are "army-surplused" and "post-industrial." Large standing armies have given way to the mix of combat and commerce, policing and profit embodied in cyberpunk's mercenaries and private security forces, while the movements of the revolution have morphed into gangs and criminal organizations—theft as politically unconscious social protest.

Realization that all aspects of the MIME—military, industrial, medical, and entertainment—are underlain by the control and manipulation of information as the great unifying factor allows for the shift in emphasis from "MI" to "ME"—from a national mass-production society of bombs, Buicks, and Berlin Walls to a transnational de-massified information society of designer DNA, designer drugs, and the real-life drama of designer downsizing.

This shift in emphasis within the MIME complex from production to information, from military industrial to medical-entertainment is clearly exemplified in Gibson's *Mona Lisa Overdrive*. Limited nuclear war and the coming to full sentience of an AI are both historical events in the world of the novel but, of the two, limited nuclear war in MLO is presented as much less important to the world than the "When It Changed" brought about by the AI Wintermute's coming to consciousness.

The movement from product society to information society in *Mona Lisa Overdrive* is specifically reflected in the etherealization of human beings, their transformation to pure information downloaded to machine systems as they leave their bodies behind them. This sublimation and etherealization is medically framed. A major figure in Gibson's Sprawl trilogy, Bobby Newmark—the console cowboy whose handle was "Count Zero" in the book of the same name—spends his time in MLO strapped into a gurney, pretty much comatose, furiously remming and dreaming cyberspace through "a mother-huge chunk of biosoft" called the aleph, while tended by Cherry Chesterfield, who once had "an aborted career as a paramedical technician Grade 6."[7]

Bobby's ex-beloved, entertainment simstim star Angie Mitchell, has been having her problems since the days of Count Zero as well—mainly drugs and superstar drug rehab, though it turns out that the "drugs" are actually psychotropics laced with "subcellular nanomechanisms programmed to restructure the synaptic alterations [the v_v_s] effected by [her father] Christopher Mitchell."[8] These v_v_s were originally implanted in her by her father in his "hostage exchange" deal with the AI forms inhabiting the matrix. As a result of the deal, the AIs have a human who can dream them, and Christopher Mitchell obtains from the AIs the information needed to perfect the biochip that lies at the heart of the Maas-Neotek biosoft technology.

The upshot of all this is that, after much shooting and detective work in worlds both real and virtual, Bobby and Angie leave their bodies behind and load off into the cyberspace matrix, rapturing out into the gnostic apocalypse, the Neon New Jerusalem and millennial Heavenly Kingdom where their—what? souls? personality data constructs? whatever—are joined in a mystical union, a Sacred Marriage of human and AI, tech and flesh, silicon and biosoft that would no doubt have made Carl Jung himself ecstatic.

Gibson's virtual worlds, which began as combat data spheres but have long since expanded into the worldwide (and mostly nonmilitary) matrix, have a parallel in our own world, of course: namely the Internet, originally designed by the Defense Advanced Research Projects Agency (DARPA) as an information network intended to be capable of surviving a nuclear war but now growing to support a majority of extra-military uses and users. The history of the Net in fact perfectly illustrates the shift from the national production economy of the MI-dominated MIME to the transnational information economies of the ME-dominated MIME.

Many more factual, fictional, and filmic examples of the important growth of the MIME (and its entire technorationalist worldview) during the 1980s and beyond could be given here, but a few will suffice to indicate the MIME's persistence. In 1996 alone, MIME films like *Independence Day* and *Escape from L.A.* played to large audiences.

Largely a remake of H. G. Wells's textual, Orson Welles's audio, and George Pal's filmic versions of *The War of the Worlds*, *Independence Day* gives that tradition a twist of MIME: foregrounded high-tech military and information heroes and situations (Bill Pullman's fighter-jock President, Will Smith's fighter-pilot giant killer, Jeff Goldblum's telecommunications and computing nerd); industrial destruction (obliteration of buildings and automobiles); medical scenes and themes (the secret Area 51 facility in Nevada, which turns out to be predominantly a medical research facility with preserved aliens from the Roswell crash, an "alien autopsy" sequence, and the failure of medicine there in its attempt to save the first lady); and entertainment industry linkages (the info-nerd hero who works in cable TV, the fighter pilot's super-heroine girlfriend who works as a stripper).

Most interesting of all is the overlap between the medical and the informational in the final defeat of the aliens. In previous versions of the *War of the Worlds* story, the alien invasion was defeated not by human actions but by Terran viruses and microbes which the invaders' immune systems had no defense against. In *Independence Day*, human action plays a part, this time administering the fatal blow by injecting into the alien computer system a computer virus (a term that is in itself a wonderful example of the convergence of the medical and information spheres).

A virus also figures prominently in *Escape from L.A.*, for Kurt Russell's Snake Pliskin character is conned into accepting a military mission after supposedly being infected with a supervirus that only his military handlers can cure. Like *Independence Day* (which also spends much of its film time either in Los Angeles or on military bases in the American southwest), *Escape* rings all the MIME changes: foregrounded military technology (from the one-man atomic mini-sub that takes Snake into L.A., to the garrison-state crowd-control tech of the L.A. superprison, to the orbiting superweapons system known as the Sword of Damocles); industrial decay (the collapse of the L.A. infrastructure and the city/prison's general state of disarray); medical themes and situations (not only Pliskin's viral infection but also the organ-legging and corpse-collecting Beverly Hills plastic surgery ghouls); and entertainment industry linkages (barbaric bloodsports, even a major character whose is a former entertainment agent, Steve Buscemi's "Map to the Stars" Eddie).

Independence Day, *Escape from L.A.*, and their audience appeal demonstrate some powerfully negative audience feelings toward the command, control, communications, and intelligence structures of our MIME society, coupled to a yearning for a less complex world. This yearning manifests itself in these films in the large-scale destruction of industrial society. This MIME society is ultimately vindicated in *Independence Day*, where the day after Independence Day is presumably characterized by a more unified humanity living in a smaller-scale, more intimate world. In *Escape from L.A.*, however, MIME society is conclusively rejected when Snake Pliskin makes the decision to send the signal that causes the Sword of Damocles system to generate a global electromagnetic pulse and thereby eradicate all higher-level technology from the face of the Earth. The day after in this film is presumably a return to a new (and supposedly somehow more honest and less superficial) dark age.

These films inevitably lead to this question: What, then, is the future of the Future? As Yogi Berra once noted, "It's always hard to predict, especially about the future." The "smaller scale" world, alluded to in these 1996 films, is more likely to work out this way, if trends of the recent past have any predictive force: The things of the mass—mass culture, mass production, mass consumption, mass destruction, mass leisure, mass literacy, massed armies, mass political movements, mass religion—are all likely to go through a process of demassification, moving more into the background as the emphasis within the MIME complex, under the impact of information speed-up, shifts toward splinter culture, pinpointed or individualized production and consumption, so-called low-intensity conflict, designer leisure, specialized literacies, private security, factions and pseudo-anarchic movements, personal Jesuses and personal saviors of every stripe.

This of course brings us back to the theological patterns underlying both the practice of medicine and the practice of science fiction. One might say that both medicine and science fiction involve a specific type of reification, the turning of theological abstractions into physical objects. Certainly in science fiction the statement "Everything happens twice, first as theology, then as technology" would seem to have some applicability—as we have seen in the salvific and apocalyptic yearnings noted in the films and books discussed here.

Of all the scientific fields, medicine as the science of the healer most clearly partakes of mystical and metaphysical powers associated with figures like Christ and, much more deeply and anciently, the entire tradition of shamanic healing older than civilization itself. The medical doctor has long since taken over many of the traditional functions of the shaman, prophet, and priest: healer, explainer, reader of the entrails, and guardian against the ravages of mortality. The fear of death is fundamentally a fear of meaninglessness and indeed undergirds much of the reason of, and reason for, the technorationalist worldview. Whether medicine or the sciences can provide that fundamental meaning or assuage that fundamental fear—religious faith's traditional prerogative—remains to be seen. In a technologically-oriented world increasingly shifting from the mass market to the individualized market—where yet the individual's power will more likely remain far more "virtual" than real—those questions of fear and meaning becomes all the more important.

Two final theological concepts—those of eschatology and teleology, of the end and ends of time and the future itself—are also involved in this reifying theology-to-technology shift. This is where the science fiction writer has traditionally been a "doctor," inoculating the mundane present with bits of the "what if?" and "if this goes on . . . " of speculative futures. In science fiction during the 1980s, the shift from mass culture to splinter culture was already being seen. Massed endings of time, whether nuclear armageddon or socialist utopia, no longer seemed to work well as scenarios, in genre sf or in the world at large, by the end of that decade.

Yet the future offered by cyberpunk—transnational corporate feudalism from which the individual escapes into the too-easy transcendence of a virtual Heavenly Kingdom—does that work? Even hard sf writers like Poul Anderson, in a note to *The New York Review of Science Fiction*, remarks that reading Antonio Damasio's *Descartes' Error* "makes me question whether we'll ever be able to download human personalities into machines, as happens in a few yarns of mine."[9] If computer resurrection and digital salvation and other such technological wards against death fail, what then?

Too bad we won't live, but then again, who does? Death is part of what makes us human, the ultimate planned obsolescence, and perhaps obsolescence is itself humanizing. Human beings are in fact becoming increasingly obsolete: industrial technology made more and more human and animal muscle power obsolete for work purposes in the nineteenth and twentieth centuries, and information technology seems likely to make more and more human mental effort obsolete during the twenty-first.

If science fiction is, in its endings, to be more than bad religion in techno-drag, I submit that it must focus more fully not only on the beauties and ecstasies but also on the pain and suffering of this human life as it is lived through and died out of—essentially, the question of the meaning and meaningfulness of human life faced with the loss of what formerly made for meaningful life. Science fiction must address the question "What are human beings for?"—and then move beyond that question too.

Speculation and diagnosis become one in a MIME society. The future of this genre of futures could do worse than to diagnose the present by speculating on what may yet come. Perhaps in the direction of the expanded present we may come upon the other meaning of apocalypse: the revelation of lasting meaning, through the lifting of the veil of this world.

Notes

1. For these thoughts on the non-autonomy and non-globally deterministic aspects of technological changes I am indebted to Robert E. McGinn's *Science, Technology, and Society* (Englewood Cliffs, NJ: Prentice-Hall, 1991).

2. *Blade Runner* (Ladd Co., 1982), directed by Ridley Scott. Director's Cut released in 1992. Later references in the text are to the director's cut.

3. *The Terminator* (Cinema 84/Pacific Western Productions, 1984), directed by James Cameron. Later references in the text are to the original theatrical release.

4. *Terminator 2: Judgment Day* (1991), directed by James Cameron. All references are to the theatrical release version.

5. *Blade Runner* is dedicated to the memory of Philip K. Dick, and Harlan Ellison is given an on-screen acknowledgment (albeit following a lawsuit) in the credits for *The Terminator*.

6. Gibson has stated this in numerous interviews. See for instance the *Spin* interview (October, 1993, 91–93) or the *Details* interview (October, 1993, 152–154).

7. William Gibson, *Mona Lisa Overdrive* (1988; New York: Bantam Spectra, 1989). 286.

8. Gibson, 258.

9. Poul Anderson, "Read This," *The New York Review of Science Fiction* (March, 1996), 8.

Bibliography of Science Fiction
Works Involving Disease and Medicine

Since no one to our knowledge has yet attempted to compile a comprehensive bibliography of science fiction and fantasy works involving disease and medicine, we have endeavored, within the parameters of our limited time and space, to list as many relevant texts as possible, a total of 687 items, to aid future researchers. In the first two sections, devoted to novels and short stories and to films and television programs, we focused primarily on science fiction works that involve physicians as characters, while also including some works that more generally deal with disease or body transformation as well as scattered works of fantasy. In the third section, devoted to works of nonfiction, we sought to include all published studies of medical science fiction, with more selective references to works focused on future medicine or on topics of special interest, such as Mary Shelley's *Frankenstein* or images of the cyborg in contemporary culture. For stories in anthologies, complete bibliographical data for the anthology is omitted if there is a separate entry for the book under the first editor's name or if the data are available in an entry immediately preceding the entry.

I. Novels and Short Stories

Abé, Kobo. *Inter Ice Age 4*. Translated by E. Dale Saunders. New York: Alfred A. Knopf, 1970.

Adams, Douglas. *The Hitchhiker's Guide to the Galaxy*. 1979. In Adams, *The More Than Complete Hitchhiker's Guide*. Stamford, CT: Longmeadow Press, 1986, 5–143.

Aldiss, Brian W. *Frankenstein Unbound*. 1973. New York: Fawcett Crest, 1975.

———. *Greybeard*. 1964. New York: Signet, 1965.

———. *An Island Called Moreau*. New York: Pocket Books, 1981.

Amosov, Nikolai Mikhailovich. *Notes from the Future*. Translated by George St. George. New York: Simon & Schuster, 1970.

Anderson, Kevin J. *Resurrection, Inc.* New York: New American Library, 1988.

Anderson, Poul. *Mirkheim*. New York: Berkley, 1977.

Anthony, Piers. *Prostho Plus*. London: Gollancz, 1971.

Ash, Constance, editor. *Not of Woman Born*. New York: Roc, 1999.

Asimov, Isaac. *Fantastic Voyage*. New York: Bantam, 1966.

———. *Fantastic Voyage II: Destination Brain*. Garden City, NY: Doubleday, 1987.

————. *Foundation and Empire*. 1952. New York: Avon, 1966.

Atwood, Margaret. *The Handmaid's Tale*. 1985. New York: Ballantine, 1987.

Ballard, J. G. *The Crystal World*. New York: Farrar, Straus & Giroux, 1966.

————. *The Drowned World*. New York: Berkley, 1962.

Balzac, Honoré de. *The Wild Ass's Skin*. 1831. New York: E. P. Dutton, 1954.

Bear, Greg. *Blood Music*. 1985. New York: Ace, 1986.

————. *Darwin's Radio*. New York: Ballantine, 1999.

————. *Queen of Angels*. New York: Warner, 1990.

————. "Shrodinger's Plague." In Ursula K. Le Guin and Brian Attebery, editors, *The Norton Book of Science Fiction*. New York: W. W. Norton, 1993, 477–484. Story first published in 1982.

————. /. [*Slant*] New York: Tor, 1997.

Bell, Neil. [as by Paul Martens] *Death Rocks the Cradle*. London: Collins, 1933.

Bellamy, Edward. *Dr. Heidenhoff's Process*. New York: Appleton, 1880.

————. *Looking Backward, 2000–1887*. 1888. New York: Signet, 1960.

Benford, Gregory. [as by Sterling Blake] *Chiller*. New York: Bantam, 1993.

Bester, Alfred. *The Demolished Man*. 1953. New York: Random House, 1996.

Blish, James. "The Oath." In Blish, *The Best of James Blish*, edited by Robert A. W. Lowndes. New York: Ballantine, 1979, 281–302. Story first published in 1960.

Bloch, Robert. "I Do Not Love Thee, Doctor Fell." In David G. Hartwell, editor, *The World Treasury of Science Fiction*. Boston: Little, Brown, 1989, 876–884. Story first published in 1955.

Blum, Ralph. *The Simultaneous Man*. New York: Little, Brown, 1970.

Blumlein, Michael. *The Brains of Rats*. Los Angeles: Scream/Press, 1989.

————. "The Brains of Rats." In Blumlein, *The Brains of Rats*, 1–20.

————. "Shed His Grace." In Blumlein, *The Brains of Rats*, 77–87.

————. "Tissue Ablation and Variant Regeneration: A Case Report." In Blumlein, *The Brains of Rats*, 21–37.

Borges, Jorge Luis. "The Immortal." Translated by James E. Irby. In Borges, *Labyrinths: Selected Stories and Other Writings*, edited by Donald A. Yates and Irby. New York: New Directions, 1964, 105–118.

Bova, Ben. "Foeman, Where Do You Flee?" In Bova, *Maxwell's Demons*. New York: Baronet, 1978, 62–126. Story first published in 1968.

Bradbury, Ray. "A Medicine for Melancholy." In Bradbury, *A Medicine for Melancholy*. 1959. New York: Bantam, 1960, 11–20.

Bretnor, Reginald. "Dr. Birdmouse." In Thomas M. Scortia, editor, *Strange Bedfellows: Sex and Science Fiction*. New York: Random House, 1972, 147–164. Story first published in 1962.

Brown, Eric. "The Frankenberg Process." *Interzone*, No. 171 (September, 2001), 6–16.

Brunner, John. *The Shockwave Rider*. New York: Ballantine, 1975.

Budrys, Algis. "The Distant Sound of Engines." In Budrys, *The Unexpected Dimension*. New York: Ballantine, 1960, 34–38.

————. *Who?* New York: Pyramid, 1958.

Bujold, Lois McMaster. *Ethan of Athos*. New York: Baen, 1986.

Bulgakov, Mikhail. *The Heart of a Dog*. 1925. Translated by Michael Glenny. New York: Harcourt, 1968.

Bulwer-Lytton, Edward. *A Strange Story*. Leipzig: Tauchnitz, 1861.

Burgess, Anthony. *A Clockwork Orange*. 1962. New York: Ballantine, 1965.

Burns, Stephen L. *Flesh and Silver*. New York: Roc, 1999.

Burroughs, Edgar Rice. *The Master Mind of Mars*. Chicago: A. C. McClurg & Co., 1928. Barsoom #6. First published in magazine form in 1927.

———. *Synthetic Men of Mars*. Tarzana, CA: Edgar Rice Burroughs, Inc., 1940. Barsoom #9. First published in magazine form in 1939.

Busby, F. M. *The Breeds of Man*. New York: Bantam, 1988.

Butler, Octavia E. *Adulthood Rites*. New York: Warner, 1988. Xenogenesis #2.

———. *Clay's Ark*. New York: St. Martin's Press, 1984.

———. *Dawn*. New York: Warner, 1987. Xenogenesis #1.

———. *Imago*. New York: Warner, 1989. Xenogenesis #3.

———. *Parable of the Sower*. 1993. New York: Warner, 1995.

Butler, Samuel. *Erewhon, or, Over the Range*. 1872. New York: Signet, 1960.

Caidin, Martin. *Cyborg: A Novel*. New York: Arbor House, 1972.

Card, Orson Scott. *Alvin Journeyman*. New York: Tor, 1996. Alvin Maker #4.

———. *Heartfire*. New York: Tor, 1998. Alvin Maker #5.

———. *Prentice Alvin*. New York: Tor, 1989. Alvin Maker #3.

———. *Red Prophet*. New York: Tor, 1988. Alvin Maker #2.

———. *Seventh Son*. New York: Tor, 1987. Alvin Maker #1.

Carey, Peter. *The Unusual Life of Tristan Smith*. Brisbane, Australia: University of Queensland Press, 1994.

Castell, Daphne. "The Patent Medicine Man." In Roger Elwood, editor, *The Berserkers*. New York: Trident Press, 1973, 132–149.

Celine, Louis-Ferdinand. *Journey to the End of the Night*. 1932. Translated by Ralph Manheim. New York: New Directions, 1983.

Chapman, Samuel. *Doctor Jones' Picnic*. New York: Whitaker & Ray, 1908.

Clarke, Arthur C. *Childhood's End*. New York: Harcourt, Brace & World, 1953.

———. "Death and the Senator." In Clarke, *Tales of Ten Worlds*. New York: Harcourt Brace Jovanovich, 1962, 115–140. Story first published in 1961.

———. *2001: A Space Odyssey*. New York: Signet, 1968.

Compton, D. G. *Synthajoy*. New York: Ace, 1968.

Conklin, Groff, and Noah D. Fabricant, M.D., editors. *Great Science Fiction about Doctors: Eighteen Choice Tales of the Outermost Worlds of Medicine*. New York: Crowell-Collier, 1963.

Conrad, Earl. *The Da Vinci Machine: Tales of the Population Explosion*. New York: Modern Literary Editions, 1968.

———. "Medical Chart of Stephen Payne." In Conrad, *The Da Vinci Machine*, 103–105.

Conrad, Joseph. *Heart of Darkness*. New York: Modern Literary Editions, 1968. Also in Conrad, *Heart of Darkness and The Secret Sharer*. New York: Bantam, 1989.

Cook, Glen. *The Black Company*. New York: Tor, 1984. Black Company #1.

———. *Shadows Linger*. New York: Tor, 1984. Black Company #2.

———. *The White Rose*. New York: Tor, 1985. Black Company #3.

Cook, Robin. *Abduction*. New York: Putnam, 2000.

———. *Acceptable Risk*. 1995. New York: Berkley, 1996.

———. *Blindsight*. New York: Putnam, 1992.

———. *Brain*. New York: Putnam, 1981.

———. *Chromosome 6*. New York: Putnam, 1997.

———. *Coma*. New York: Signet, 1977.

———. *Contagion*. New York: Putnam, 1995.

———. *Fatal Cure*. New York: Putnam, 1994.

———. *Fever*. New York: Putnam, 1982.

————. *Godplayer*. New York: Putnam, 1983.

————. *Harmful Intent*. New York: Putnam, 1990.

————. *Invasion*. New York: Berkley, 1997.

————. *Mindbend*. New York: Putnam, 1985.

————. *Mortal Fear*. New York: Putnam, 1988.

————. *Mutation*. New York: Putnam, 1989.

————. *Outbreak*. New York: Putnam, 1987.

————. *Shock*. New York: Putnam, 2001.

————. *Terminal*. New York: Putnam, 1993.

————. *Toxin*. New York: Putnam, 1998.

————. *Vector*. New York: Putnam, 1999.

————. *Vital Signs*. New York: Putnam, 1991.

Cooper, Edmund. *All Fool's Day*. 1966. New York: Berkley, 1967.

Correy, Lee. *Space Doctor*. New York: Ballantine, 1981.

Counselman, Mary Elizabeth. "Healer." In Lin Carter, editor, *Weird Tales #1*. New York: Zebra, 1980, 194–218.

Cowper, Richard. *The Twilight of Briareus*. 1974. New York: DAW, 1975.

Crichton, Michael. *The Andromeda Strain*. 1969. New York: Dell, 1970.

————. *The Terminal Man*. New York: Alfred A. Knopf, 1972.

Dahl, Roald. *George's Marvelous Medicine*. New York: Alfred A. Knopf, 1991.

D'Alpuget, Blanche. *White Eye*. New York: Simon & Schuster, 1994.

Davidson, Avram. "Help! I Am Dr. Morris Goldpepper." In Davidson, *The Avram Davidson Treasury: A Tribute Collection*, edited by Robert Silverberg and Grania Davis. New York: Tor, 1998, 47–59. Story first published in 1957.

————. "Dr. Morris Goldpepper Returns." *Galaxy*, 21 (December, 1962), 55–69.

del Rey, Lester. *Nerves*. New York: Ballantine, 1956. Based on a novelette first published in 1942.

Dick, Philip K. *Do Androids Dream of Electric Sheep?* Garden City, NY: Doubleday, 1968.

————. "The Preserving Machine." In Dick, *The Preserving Machine*. New York: Ace, 9–18. Story first published in 1953.

Disch, Thomas M. *The MD: A Horror Story*. New York: Alfred A. Knopf, 1991.

Donovan, Rita. *The Plague Saint*. Edmunton: Tesseract, 1997.

Doyle, Arthur Conan. *The Poison Belt*. 1913. New York: Berkley, 1966.

Drachman, Theodore S. *Cry Plague!* New York: Ace, 1953.

Duane, Diane. *Dark Mirror*. New York: Pocket Books, 1993. A *Star Trek: The Next Generation* novel.

————. *Doctor's Orders*. New York: Pocket Books, 1991. *Star Trek* Novel #50.

————. *The Romulan Way*. New York: Pocket Books, 1987. *Star Trek* Novel #35.

du Maurier, Daphne. "The Breakthrough." In du Maurier, *Don't Look Now*. Garden City, NY: Doubleday, 1966, 59–106.

Ellison, Harlan. "Adrift Just Off the Islets of Langerhans: Latitude 38° 54', Longitude 77° 00' 13" W." In Ellison, *Deathbird Stories: A Pantheon of Modern Gods*. New York: Harper & Row, 1975, 262–300. Story first published in 1974.

————. "The Diagnosis of Dr. D'arqueAngel." In Ellison, *Strange Wine: Fifteen New Stories from the Nightside of the World*. New York: Harper & Row, 1978, 247–262.

Engling, Richard. *Body Mortgage*. New York: New American Library/Penguin, 1989.

Faddis, C. R. "Caduceus." In Cynthia Manson and Charles Ardai, editors, *Aliens and UFOs: Extraterrestrial Tales from Asimov's Science Fiction and Analog Science Fiction and Fact*. New York: Smithmark Publishers, 1993, 225–265.

Fairbairns, Zoe. *Benefits*. London: Virago, 1979.

Finney, Jack. *Invasion of the Body Snatchers*. Revised Edition. New York: Dell, 1978. First published as *The Body Snatchers* in 1955.

Forster, E. M. "The Machine Stops." In Ben Bova, editor, *The Science Fiction Hall of Fame, Volume IIB*. 1973. New York: Avon, 1974, 248–279. Story first published in 1909.

Frank, Pat. [Harry Hart Frank] *Alas, Babylon*. Philadelphia: Lippincott, 1959.

Friesner, Esther. *Warchild*. New York: Pocket Books, 1994. *Star Trek: Deep Space Nine* Novel #7.

Gayton, Bertram. *The Gland Stealers*. Philadelphia: Lippincott, 1922.

Ghosh, Amitav. *The Calcutta Chromosome: A Novel of Fevers, Delirium, and Discovery*. New York: Avon, 1997.

Gibson, William. *Count Zero*. New York: Arbor House, 1986. Sprawl Trilogy #2.

———. *Mona Lisa Overdrive*. New York: Bantam, 1988. Sprawl Trilogy #3.

———. *Neuromancer*. New York: Ace, 1984. Sprawl Trilogy #1.

Goldberg, Marshall, and Kenneth Kay. *Disposable People*. New York: Tower, 1980.

Goulart, Ron. "Calling Dr. Clockwork." In Donald A. Wollheim and Terry Carr, editors, *World's Best Science Fiction: 1966*. New York: Ace, 1966, 31–41. Story first published in 1965.

Griffith, Mary. *Three Hundred Years Hence*. 1836. Philadelphia: Prime Press, 1950.

Griffith, Nicola. *Ammonite*. New York: Ballantine/Del Rey, 1993.

Gunn, James. *The Immortals*. New York: Bantam, 1962.

Haldeman, Joe. *Buying Time*. New York: Morrow, 1989.

Hambly, Barbra. *Crossroad*. New York: Pocket Books, 1994. *Star Trek* Novel #71.

———. *Ghost Walker*. New York: Pocket Books, 1991. *Star Trek* Novel #53.

Hamilton, Edmund. "The Man Who Evolved." In Isaac Asimov, editor, *Before the Golden Age: A Science Fiction Anthology of the 1930s*. Garden City, NY: Doubleday, 1974, 23–38. Story first published in 1931.

Harness, Charles L. *The Catalyst*. New York: Pocket Books, 1980.

———. *The Rose*. New York: Berkley, 1953.

Harrison, Harry. *Plague from Space*. 1965. New York: Bantam, 1968.

———. *Spaceship Medic*. London: Faber & Faber, 1970.

Hawkey, Raymond. *Side-Effect*. London: Jonathan Cape, 1979.

Hawthorne, Nathaniel. "The Birthmark." In Hawthorne, *Young Goodman Brown and Other Tales*, edited by Brian Harding. New York: Oxford University Press, 1987, 175–192. Story first published in 1843.

———. "Dr. Heidegger's Experiment." In Hawthorne, *Young Goodman Brown and Other Tales*, 158–168. Story first published in 1837.

———. "Rappaccini's Daughter." In Hawthorne, *Young Goodman Brown and Other Tales*, 285–316. Story first published in 1844.

Heinlein, Robert A. *I Will Fear No Evil*. 1970. New York: Berkley, 1971.

———. "Successful Operation." In Heinlein, *Expanded Universe*. New York: Ace, 1980, 28–33. Story first published in 1940.

———. "Waldo." In Heinlein, *Waldo and Magic, Inc.* 1950. New York: Pyramid, 1963, 9–103. Story first published in 1942.

Herbert, Frank. *Dune*. Philadelphia: Chilton, 1965.

Hubbard, L. Ron. *Ole Doc Methuselah*. New York: DAW, 1970.

Huxley, Aldous. *After Many a Summer Dies the Swan*. New York: Harper, 1939.

———. *Brave New World*. London: Chatto & Windus, 1932.

———. *Island*. 1962. New York: Bantam, 1963.

Huxley, Julian. "The Tissue-Culture King." In Robert Silverberg, editor, *Great Tales of Science Fiction*. 1983. New York: Galahad, 1994, 144–159. Story first published in 1926.

Isherwood, Christopher, and Don Bachardy. *Frankenstein: The True Story.* New York: Avon, 1973.

James, P. D. *The Children of Men*. London: Faber and Faber, 1992.

Jeter, K. W. *Blade Runner: Replicant Night*. New York: Bantam Spectra, 1996.

———. *Blade Runner 2: The Edge of Human*. New York: Bantam Spectra, 1995.

———. *Dr. Adder*. New York: Bluejay, 1984.

Jones, Raymond F. "A Bowl of Biskies Makes a Growing Boy." In Roger Elwood, editor, *The Other Side of Tomorrow: Original Science Fiction Stories about Young People in the Future*. New York: Random House, 1973, 106–133.

Kagan, Janet. *Uhura's Song*. New York: Pocket Books, 1985. *Star Trek* Novel #21.

Kahn, Bernard I. "For the Public." In Andre Norton, editor, *Space Service*. Cleveland: World Publishing Co., 1953, 175–206. Story first published in 1946.

Katz, Robert I. *Edward Maret: A Novel of the Future*. Holliston, MA: Willowgate, 2001.

Keller, David H. "The Psychophonic Nurse." In Conklin and Fabricant, editors, *Great Science Fiction about Doctors*, 143–162. Story first published in 1928.

———. "Stenographer's Hands." *Amazing Stories Quarterly*, 1 (Fall, 1928), 522–529, 569.

Kelly, James Patrick. "Death Therapy." In Terry Carr, editor, *The Best Science Fiction of the Year #8*. New York: Ballantine, 1979, 281–303. Story first published in 1978.

Keyes, Daniel. *Flowers for Algernon*. 1966. New York: Bantam, 1967. Based on a story first published in 1959.

King, Stephen. *Firestarter*. New York: Viking, 1980.

Knight, Damon. "Masks." In Donald A. Wollheim and Terry Carr, editors, *World's Best Science Fiction 1969*. New York: Ace, 1969, 76–86. Story first published in 1968.

Koontz, Dean. *Mr. Murder*. New York: Putnam, 1993.

———. *Phantoms*. New York: Putnam, 1983.

———. *Strangers*. New York: Putnam, 1986.

Kornbluth, C. M. "The Little Black Bag." In Robert Silverberg, editor, *The Science Fiction Hall of Fame, Volume I*. New York: Avon, 1971, 410–439. Story first published in 1950.

Lackey, Mercedes, and Mark Shepherd. "Medic." In David Drake and Bill Fawcett, editors, *Battlestation, Book Two: Vanguard*. New York: Ace, 1993, 85–114.

Langelaan, George. "The Other Hand." *The Magazine of Fantasy and Science Fiction*, 21 (October, 1961), 56–69.

Le Guin, Ursula K. "The Diary of the Rose." In Le Guin, *The Compass Rose: Short Stories*. New York: Harper & Row, 1982, 88–111. Story first published in 1976.

———. *The Left Hand of Darkness*. New York: Ace, 1969.

———. "Nine Lives." In James Blish, editor, *Nebula Award Stories Number Five*. 1970. New York: Pocket Books, 1972, 56–82. Story first published in 1969.

Leinster, Murray. [Will Jenkins] *Doctor to the Stars: Three Novelettes of the Interstellar Medical Service*. New York: Pyramid, 1964. A Med Service Book.

———. *Med Service*. New York: Ace, 1959. Also published as *The Mutant Weapon*. A Med Service Book.

———. "Ribbon in the Sky." In Conklin and Fabricant, *Great Science Fiction about Doctors*, 199–242. Story first published in 1957. Also in *S.O.S. from Three Worlds*.

———. *S.O.S. from Three Worlds*. New York: Ace, 1966. A Med Service Book.

———. *This World Is Taboo*. New York: Ace, 1961. Also published as *Pariah Planet*. A

Med Service Book.

Lem, Stanislaw. "Doctor Diagoras." In Lem, *Memoirs of a Space Traveler: Further Reminiscences of Ijon Tichy*. 1971. Translated by Joel Stern and Maria Swiecicka-Ziemianek. New York: Harcourt Brace Jovanovich, 1982, 111–137.

―――. *Solaris*. 1961. Translated by Joanna Kilmartin and Steve Cox. New York: Walker, 1970.

Lever, Charles. "Post-Mortem Recollections of a Medical Lecturer." In Robert Morrison and Chris Baldick, editors, *The Vampyre and Other Tales of the Macabre*. Oxford: Oxford University Press, 1997, 165–174. Story first published in 1836.

Levin, Ira. *The Boys from Brazil*. New York: Random House, 1976.

Lewis, C. S. *The Lion, the Witch, and the Wardrobe*. London: Macmillan, 1950.

Lewis, Sinclair. *Arrowsmith*. New York: Harcourt, Brace, & Co., 1925.

Llewellyn, Edward. *The Bright Companion*. New York: DAW, 1980. Douglas Convolution #2.

―――. *The Douglas Convolution*. New York: DAW, 1979. Douglas Convolution #1.

―――. *Prelude to Chaos*. New York: DAW, 1983. Douglas Convolution #3.

London, Jack. *The Scarlet Plague*. 1915. In Richard Gid Powers, editor, *The Science Fiction of Jack London*. Boston: Gregg Press, 1975, 285–455.

―――. "A Thousand Deaths." In H. Bruce Franklin, editor, *Future Perfect: American Science Fiction of the Nineteenth Century*. Revised Edition. London: Oxford University Press, 1978, 230–239. Story first published in 1899.

Lovecraft, H. P. "Herbert West, Reanimator." In Michael Parry, editor, *The Rivals of Frankenstein*, 126–157. Story first published in 1922.

MacLean, Alistair. [as by Ian Stuart] *The Satan Bug*. 1962. New York: Popular Library, 1963.

MacLean, Katherine. "Contagion." In Pamela Sargent, editor, *Women of Wonder: Science Fiction by Women about Women*. 1974. New York: Vintage, 1975, 18–58. Story first published in 1950.

―――. "Syndrome Johnny." In Harry Harrison, editor, *SF: Author's Choice*. New York: Berkley, 1968, 183–200. Story first published in 1951.

Maine, Charles Eric. *The Darkest of Nights*. 1962. London: Panther, 1965.

Malzberg, Barry N. "The Men Inside." In Robert Silverberg, editor, *New Dimensions II*. Garden City, NY: Doubleday, 1972, 193–229.

Marley, Louise. *The Terrorists of Irustan*. New York: Ace, 1999.

Matheson, Richard. *I Am Legend*. New York: Fawcett Gold Medal, 1954.

Matthews, Susan R. *An Exchange of Hostages*. New York: Avon, 1997. Andrej Kosciusko #1.

―――. *Hour of Judgment*. New York: Avon, 1999. Andrej Kosciusko #3.

―――. *Prisoner of Conscience*. New York: Avon, 1998. Andrej Kosciusko #2.

Maupassant, Guy de. "Le Horla." In Maupassant, *Le Horla et Autres Contes Cruels et Fantastiques*, edited by M.-C. Bancquart. Paris: Classiques Garnier, 1976, 411–420.

―――. "Le Horla (seconde version)." In Maupassant, *Le Horla et Autres Contes Cruels et Fantastiques*, 421–449.

McCaffrey, Anne. *The Ship Who Sang*. New York: Ballantine, 1970.

McClure, Ken. *Crisis*. London: Simon & Schuster, 1993.

―――. *Donor*. London: Simon & Schuster, 1998.

―――. *Fenton's Winter*. 1989. London: Pocket Books, 1997.

―――. *Pandora's Helix*. London: Simon & Schuster, 1997.

―――. *Resurrection*. London: Simon & Schuster, 1999.

———. *The Scorpion's Advance*. 1986. London: Pocket Books, 1998.

———. *Tangled Web*. London: Simon & Schuster, 2000.

———. *Trauma*. London: Simon & Schuster, 1995.

McIntosh, J. T. "Hallucination Orbit." *Galaxy*, 3 (January, 1952), 132–158.

McIntyre, Vonda N. *Dreamsnake*. Boston: Houghton Mifflin, 1978.

———. "Of Mist, and Grass, and Sand." In Pamela Sargent, editor, *Women of Wonder: Science Fiction by Women about Women*. 1974. New York: Vintage, 1975, 257–285. Story first published in 1973.

Miller, Walter M., Jr. "Blood Bank." In Miller, *The Best of Walter M. Miller, Jr.* New York: Pocket Books, 1980, 120–169. Story first published in 1952.

———. "Dark Benediction." In Miller, *The Best of Walter M. Miller, Jr.*, 322–387. Story first published in 1951.

Moon, Elizabeth. "ABCs in Zero-G." *Analog Science Fiction/Science Fact*, 106 (August, 1986), 82–107.

———. *Divided Allegiance*. New York: Baen, 1988. Deed of Paksenarrion #2.

———. *Oath of Gold*. New York: Baen, 1989. Deed of Paksenarrion #3.

———. *Sheepfarmer's Daughter*. New York: Baen, 1988. Deed of Paksenarrion #1.

Moore, C. L. "No Woman Born." In Groff Conklin, editor, *Treasury of Science Fiction*. 1948. New York: Bonanza, 1980, 164–201. Story first published in 1944.

Moore, Ward, with Robert Bradford. *Caduceus Wild*. Los Angeles: Pinnacle, 1978. First published in magazine form in 1959.

Morrison, William. "Bedside Manner." In Groff Conklin and Noah D. Fabricant, editors, *Great Science Fiction about Doctors*, 271–292.

Morrow, William C. "The Monster-Maker." In Christopher Lee and Michael Parry, editors, *From the Archives of Evil*. New York: Warner, 1976, 161–181. Story first published in 1887.

Murphy, Pat. "His Vegetable Wife." *Interzone*, No. 16 (Summer, 1986), 33–35.

Nesvadba, Josef. "Doctor Moreau's Other Island." In Nesvadba, *Vampires Ltd.*, translated by Iris Urwin. Prague: ARTIA, 1964, 109–121.

Niven, Larry. "The Ethics of Madness." In Niven, *Neutron Star*. New York: Ballantine, 1968, 173–208.

———. "The Jigsaw Man." In Harlan Ellison, editor, *Dangerous Visions #2*. 1967. New York: Berkley, 1969, 72–85.

———. "The Organleggers." *Galaxy*, 27 (January, 1969), 116–175.

———. *Ringworld*. New York: Ballantine, 1970.

Noto, Cosimo. *The Ideal City*. 1903. New York: Arno Press, 1971.

Nourse, Alan E. *The Bladerunner*. New York: D. McKay, 1974.

———. *The Fourth Horseman*. New York: Harper & Row, 1983.

———. *The Mercy Men*. New York: D. McKay, 1968.

———. *Rx for Tomorrow: Tales of Science Fiction, Fantasy, and Medicine*. New York: D. McKay, 1971.

———. *Star Surgeon*. 1959. New York: D. McKay, 1967.

Nye, Jody Lynne. *Medicine Show*. New York: Ace, 1994. Taylor's Ark #2.

———. *Taylor's Ark*. New York: Ace, 1993. Taylor's Ark #1.

Offutt, Andrew J. "For Value Received." In Harlan Ellison, editor, *Again Dangerous Visions 1*. 1972. New York: Signet, 1973, 135–143.

Orwell, George. *Nineteen Eighty-Four*. 1947. New York: Harcourt, 1977.

Parry, Michael, editor. *The Rivals of Frankenstein: A Gallery of Monsters*. 1979. New York: Barnes & Noble, 1980.

Peel, Jesse. "Heal the Sick, Raise the Dead." In George Scithers, editor, *Isaac Asimov's Masters of Science Fiction*. New York: Davis Publications, 1978, 112–119.

Piercy, Marge. *Woman on the Edge of Time*. New York: Alfred A. Knopf, 1976.

Poe, Edgar Allan. "The Facts in the Case of M. Valdemar." In Poe, *The Complete Tales and Poems of Edgar Allan Poe*. New York: Barnes & Noble, 1992, 656–663. Story first published in 1845.

———. "The Imp of the Perverse." In Poe, *The Complete Tales and Poems of Edgar Allan Poe*, 637–641. Story first published in 1845.

Porges, Arthur. "Emergency Operation." In Conklin and Fabricant, editors, *Great Science Fiction about Doctors*, 333–344.

Preston, Robert. *The Cobra Event*. New York: Random House, 1997.

Rand, Ayn. *Anthem*. New York: Caxton, 1946.

Renard, Maurice. *The Hands of Orlac*. 1920. Translated and adapted by Florence Crewe-Jones. New York: E. P. Dutton, 1929.

———. *New Bodies for Old*. 1908. New York: The Macaulay Company, 1923.

Richter, Conrad. "Doctor Hanray's Second Chance." In editors of *The Saturday Evening Post, The Post Reader of Fantasy and Science Fiction*. New York: Popular Library, 1963, 7–18.

Robinson, Kim Stanley. *Blue Mars*. 1997. New York: Bantam, 1997. Mars #3.

———. *Green Mars*. 1994. New York: Bantam, 1995. Mars #2.

———. *Red Mars*. New York: Bantam, 1993. Mars #1.

Robson, Justina. *Mappa Mundi*. London: Macmillan, 2001.

Ross, Ronald. "The Vivisector Vivisected." In John Gawsworth, editor, *Strange Assembly*. London: Unicorn Press, 1932, 53–78.

Roszak, Theodore. *The Memoirs of Elizabeth Frankenstein*. New York: Random House, 1995.

Rucker, Rudy. *Freeware*. New York: Avon, 1997. Software #3.

———. *Software*. New York: Ace, 1982. Software #1.

———. *Wetware*. New York: Avon, 1988. Software #2.

Russ, Joanna. *The Female Man*. New York: Bantam, 1975.

———. "When It Changed." In Harlan Ellison, editor, *Again, Dangerous Visions I*. 1972. New York: Signet, 1973, 271–279.

Ryman, Geoff. *The Child Garden*. London: Unwin Hyman, 1989.

Saul, John. *Brainchild*. New York: Bantam, 1985.

———. *Darkness*. New York: Bantam, 1992.

———. *The God Project*. New York: Bantam, 1983.

———. *Shadows*. New York: Bantam, 1993.

———. *Sleepwalk*. New York: Bantam, 1990.

Scortia, Thomas M. and George Zebrowski, editors. *Human Machines: An Anthology of Stories about Cyborgs*. New York: Vintage, 1975.

Shango, J. R. "A Matter of Ethics." In Groff Conklin and Noah D. Fabricant, editors, *Great Science Fiction about Doctors*, 345–366.

Sheckley, Robert. "Bad Medicine." In Sheckley, *Pilgrimage to Earth*. New York: Bantam, 1957, 77–93. Story first published in 1956.

Shelley, Mary. *Frankenstein, or, The Modern Prometheus*. 1818 Edition. Edited by James Rieger. Indianapolis: Bobbs-Merrill, 1974.

———. *Frankenstein, or, The Modern Prometheus*. 1831 Edition. Edited by Johanna M. Smith. Boston: Bedford, 1992.

———. *The Last Man*. 1826. Edited by Hugh J. Luke, Jr. Lincoln: University of Nebraska

Press, 1965.

———. "The Mortal Immortal." In Shelley, *The Mortal Immortal: The Complete Supernatural Short Fiction*. San Francisco: Tachyon Publications, 1996, 1–11. Story first published in 1831.

Silverberg, Robert. "Blindsight." In Jerry Pournelle with John F. Carr, editors, *Cities in Space: The Endless Frontier, Volume III*. New York: Ace, 1991, 131–152. Story first published in 1986.

———. "Caught in the Organ Draft." In Isaac Asimov, Martin H. Greenberg, and Charles G. Waugh, editors, *Caught in the Organ Draft: Biology in Science Fiction*. New York: Farrar, Straus & Giroux, 1983, 141–156.

Simak, Clifford D. "Eternity Lost." In Everett F. Bleiler and T. E. Dikty, editors, *The Best Science Fiction Stories 1950*. New York: Frederick Fell, 1950, 96–131. Story first published in 1949.

———. "Huddling Place." In Robert Silverberg, editor, *The Science Fiction Hall of Fame, Volume I*. New York: Avon, 1971, 261–280. Story first published in 1944.

———. *Why Call Them Back from Heaven?* New York: Ace, 1967.

Simmons, Dan. *Children of the Night*. New York: Putnam, 1992.

———. "The River Styx Runs Upstream." In Simmons, *Prayers to Broken Stones*. Arlington Heights, IL: Dark Harvest, 1990, 15–26. Story first published in 1982.

Siodmak, Curt. *Donovan's Brain*. New York: Alfred A. Knopf, 1943.

Sladek, John. "The Happy Breed." In Harlan Ellison, editor, *Dangerous Visions #3*. 1967. New York: Berkley, 1969, 81–99.

Slee, Richard, and Cornelia Atwood Pratt. *Dr. Berkeley's Discovery*. New York: Putnam, 1899.

Slonczewski, Joan. *The Wall Around Eden*. New York: Morrow, 1989.

Smith, Cordwainer. [Paul Linebarger] "A Planet Named Shayol." In Smith, *The Best of Cordwainer Smith*, edited by J. J. Pierce. New York: Ballantine, 1975, 338–377. Story first published in 1961.

Smith, E. E. "Doc." *Second Stage Lensman*. 1953. New York: Pyramid, 1975.

Snell, Edmund. *Kontrol*. Philadelphia: Lippincott, 1928.

Spinrad, Norman. *Bug Jack Barron*. New York: Avon, 1969.

———. *Journals of the Plague Years*. New York: Bantam, 1995. First published as a novella in 1988.

Stableford, Brian. "The Magic Bullet." In Stableford, *Sexual Chemistry: Sardonic Tales of the Genetic Revolution*. New York: Simon & Schuster, 1991, 59–80. Story first published in 1989.

Stapledon, Olaf. *Star Maker*. 1937. In Stapledon, *Last and First Men and Star Maker*. New York: Dover, 1968, 247–438.

Sterling, Bruce. "Spider Rose." In Sterling, *Crystal Express*. Sauk City, WI: Arkham House Publishers, 1989, 27–44. Story first published in 1982.

Stevenson, Robert Louis. *The Strange Case of Dr. Jekyll and Mr. Hyde*. 1886. Lincoln: University of Nebraska Press, 1990.

Stewart, George R. *Earth Abides*. 1949. New York: Fawcett Crest, 1971.

Swayne, Martin. *The Blue Germ*. London: Doran, 1918.

Taine, John. [Eric Temple Bell] *G.O.G. 666*. Reading, PA: Fantasy Press, 1954.

———. "The Ultimate Catalyst." In Groff Conklin, editor, *Great Science Fiction by Scientists*. New York: Collier, 1962, 35–59. Story first published in 1939.

Tenn, William. "Down Among the Dead Men." In Tenn, *Of All Possible Worlds*. New York: Ballantine, 1955, 13–39. Story first published in 1954.

Tepper, Sheri S. *The Gate to Women's Country*. New York: Foundation, 1988.

Thayer, Tiffany. *Doctor Arnoldi*. New York: J. Messner, Inc., 1934.

Thomas, Thomas T. *Crygender*. New York: Baen, 1992.

Tiptree, James P., Jr. [Alice Sheldon] "The Girl Who Was Plugged In." In Tiptree, *Warm Worlds and Otherwise*. New York: Ballantine, 1975, 79–121. Story first published in 1973.

———. "Houston, Houston, Do You Read?" In Isaac Asimov, Martin Greenberg, and Joseph Olander, editors, *Isaac Asimov's Science Fiction Treasury*. New York: Bonanza, 1980, 116–173. Story first published in 1977.

———. "The Last Flight of Dr. Ain." In Tiptree, *Warm Worlds and Otherwise*. New York: Ballantine, 1975, 61–68. Story first published in 1969.

———. "Painwise." In Robert Silverberg and Martin H. Greenberg, editors, *Great Tales of Science Fiction*. 1983. New York: Galahad, 1994, 455–469. Story first published in 1972.

———. "The Screwfly Solution." In Tiptree, *Out of the Everywhere and Other Extraordinary Visions*. New York: Ballantine, 1981, 53–75. Story first published as by Raccoona Sheldon in 1977.

———. "Your Haploid Heart." In Donald A. Wollheim and Terry Carr, editors, *World's Best Science Fiction 1970*. New York: Ace, 1970, 138–170. Story first published in 1969.

Tolkien, J. R. R. *The Fellowship of the Ring*. 1954. New York: Ballantine, 1965. The Lord of the Rings #1.

———. *The Return of the King*. 1955. New York: Ballantine, 1965. The Lord of the Rings #3.

———. *The Two Towers*. 1954. New York: Ballantine, 1965. The Lord of the Rings #2.

Turner, George. *Drowning Towers*. [*The Sea and Summer*] 1987. New York: Arbor House, 1988.

———. "On the Nursery Floor." In Turner, *A Pursuit of Miracles*. North Adelaide, South Australia: Aphelion Publications, 1990, 95–128. Story first published in 1985.

Tushnet, Leonard. "Aunt Jennie's Tonic." In Donald A. Wollheim, editor, *The 1972 Annual World's Best SF*. New York: DAW, 1972, 207–225. Story first published in 1971.

Verne, Jules. "Doctor Ox's Experiment." In Verne, *Dr. Ox's Experiment and Other Stories Translated from the French of Jules Verne*, editor and translator unidentified. Boston: James R. Osgood & Co., 1875, 1–102. Story first published in 1872.

———. "Frritt-Flacc." In Verne, *Yesterday and Tomorrow*. Translated by I. O. Evans. New York: Ace, 1965, 124–132. Story first published in 1888.

Viehl, S. L. *Endurance: A StarDoc Novel*. New York: New American Library, 2001. StarDoc #3.

———. *Shockball*. New York: New American Library, 2001. StarDoc #4.

———. *StarDoc: A Novel*. New York: New American Library, 2000. StarDoc #1.

———. *StarDoc II: Beyond Vallaran: A Novel*. New York: New American Library, 2000. StarDoc #2.

Vonnegut, Kurt, Jr. "Fortitude." In Byron Preiss, David Kellor, Megan Miller, and John Gregory Betancourt, editors, *The Ultimate Frankenstein*. New York: Dell, 1991, 59–88. Short play first published in 1968.

Webb, Sharon. *The Adventures of Terra Tarkington*. New York: Bantam, 1985.

———. *Earthchild*. 1982. New York: Bantam, 1983. Earth Song #1.

———. *Earth Song*. New York: Atheneum, 1983. Earth Song #2.

———. *Ram Song*. New York: Atheneum, 1984. Earth Song #3.

Weinbaum, Stanley G. "The Adaptive Ultimate." In Weinbaum, *A Martian Odyssey, and Other Science Fiction Tales*. Westport, CT: Hyperion Press, 1974, 54–78. Story first published in 1935.

———. "Proteus Island." In Weinbaum, *A Martian Odyssey, and Other Science Fiction Tales*, 342–375.

Wellen, Edward. "Origins of Galactic Medicine." In Martin Greenberg, editor, *All about the Future*. New York: Gnome Press, 1955, 365–374. Story first published in 1953.

Wells, H. G. *The Food of the Gods*. 1904. New York: Berkley, 1967.

———. *The Island of Dr. Moreau*. 1896. New York: Berkley, 1964.

———. "A Slip under the Microscope." In Wells, *The Complete Short Stories of H. G. Wells*. New York: St. Martin's Press, 1927, 529–548. Story first published in 1897.

———. "The Stolen Bacillus." In Wells, *The Complete Short Stories of H. G. Wells*, 195–202. Story first published in 1895.

———. *The Time Machine*. 1895. New York: Bantam, 1968.

———. "Under the Knife." In Wells, *The Complete Short Stories of H. G. Wells*. New York: St. Martin's Press, 1927, 403–417. Story first published in 1897.

White, James. *Ambulance Ship*. New York: Del Rey/Ballantine, 1979. Sector General #4.

———. *Code Blue: Emergency*. New York: Del Rey/Ballantine, 1987. Sector General #7.

———. "Countercharm." In White, *The Aliens among Us*. 1969. New York: Del Rey/Ballantine, 1981, 1–21. Story first published in 1960.

———. *Double Contact*. New York: Tor, 1999. Sector General #12.

———. *Final Diagnosis*. New York: Tor, 1997. Sector General #10.

———. *The Galactic Gourmet*. New York: Tor, 1994. Sector General #9.

———. *The Genocidal Healer*. 1991. New York: Del Rey/Ballantine, 1992. Sector General #8.

———. *Hospital Station*. 1962. In White, *Beginning Operations: A Sector General Omnibus*. New York: Tor, 2001, 17–199. Sector General #1.

———. *Major Operation*. 1971. In White, *Beginning Operations: A Sector General Omnibus*. New York: Tor, 2001, 365–511. Sector General #3.

———. *Mind Changer*. 1998. New York: Tor, 1999. Sector General #10.

———. *Underkill*. London: Corgi, 1979.

———. *Sector General*. New York: Del Rey/Ballantine, 1983. Sector General #5.

———. "Spacebird." In White, *Futures Past*. New York: Del Rey/Ballantine, 1982, 1–23.

———. *Star Healer*. New York: Del Rey/Ballantine, 1984. Sector General #6.

———. *Star Surgeon*. 1963. In White, *Beginning Operations: A Sector General Omnibus*. New York: Tor, 2001, 201–363. Sector General #2.

———. "To Kill or Cure." In White, *The Aliens among Us*. New York: Del Rey/Ballantine, 1981, 22–52.

———. *The White Papers*. Edited by Mark Olson and Bruce Pelz. Boston: NESFA Press, 1996.

Wilhelm, Kate. *The Clewiston Test*. New York: Farrar, Straus & Giroux, 1976.

———. "The Planners." In Poul Anderson, editor, *Nebula Award Stories Four*. 1969. New York: Pocket Books, 1971, 53–67. Story first published in 1968.

———. *Welcome, Chaos*. 1983. Boston: Houghton Mifflin, 1983.

Wiliams, Walter Jon. "Wall, Stone, Craft." In Williams, *Frankensteins and Foreign Devils*. Framingham, MA: NESFA Press, 1998, 311–378. Novella first published in 1993.

Willis, Connie. *The Doomsday Book*. New York: Bantam, 1992.

Wilson, F. Paul, editor. *Diagnosis: Terminal*. New York: Tor, 1996.

Winter, Joseph A. "Expedition Mercy." *Astounding Science Fiction*, 42 (November, 1948),

7–27. Also in *Great Science Fiction about Doctors.*

———. "Expedition Polychrome." In Andre Norton, editor, *Space Service.* Cleveland: World Publishing Co., 1953, 207–228. Story first published in 1949.

Wolfe, Bernard. *Limbo.* New York: Random House, 1952.

Wright, S. Fowler. "Brain." In Wright, *S. Fowler Wright's Short Stories.* Ludlow, England: FWB, 1996, 50–74. Story first published in 1932.

———. "The Rat." In Wright, *S. Fowler Wright's Short Stories,* 133–152. Story first published in 1929.

Wyndham, John. *Trouble with Lichen.* New York: Ballantine, 1960.

Yarbro, Chelsea Quinn. *Time of the Fourth Horseman.* Garden City, NY: Doubleday, 1976.

Yount, Rena. "Pursuit of Excellence." In Damon Knight, editor, *The Clarion Awards.* Garden City, NY: Doubleday, 1984, 155–175.

Zamiatin, Yevgeny. *We.* 1924. Translated by Gregory Zilboorg. New York: E. P. Dutton & Co., 1959.

II. Films and Television Programs

Alien. Twentieth-Century Fox, 1979.

Alien Resurrection. Twentieth-Century Fox, 1997.

Aliens. Twentieth-Century Fox, 1986.

Alien3. Twentieth-Century Fox, 1992.

Altered States. Warner Brothers, 1980.

Anatomy. Deutsche Columbia, 2000.

The Andromeda Strain. Universal/Robert Wise Productions, 1970.

"Aqua Vita." Episode of *Twilight Zone.* New York: CBS-TV, October 4, 1986.

The Astro-Zombies. A. Ram Ltd./T. V. Mikels Production, 1968.

The Awful Dr. Orloff. Hispamer, 1962.

"Babalao." Episode of *The Incredible Hulk.* New York: CBS-TV, December 14, 1979.

"The Beholder." Episode of *The Outer Limits.* New York: Showtime, February 25, 2000.

The Bionic Woman. Television series. New York: ABC-TV, 1976–1977. New York: NBC-TV, 1977–1978.

Blade Runner. Ladd Co., 1982.

The Blob. Tonylyn Productions/Paramount, 1958.

"Blood Brothers." Episode of *The Outer Limits.* New York: Showtime, April 7, 1995.

Body Snatchers. Warner Brothers, 1993.

The Boys from Brazil. Producer Circle, 1978.

Brain Candy. Paramount, 1996.

"The Brain of Colonel Barham." Episode of *The Outer Limits.* New York: ABC-TV, January 2, 1965.

The Brain That Wouldn't Die. Sterling Productions/Carlton, 1959.

Brainstorm. JF Metro-Goldwyn-Mayer/United Artists, 1983.

"Breakdown." Episode of *Blake's Seven.* London: BBC-TV, March 6, 1978.

The Bride. Columbia/Delphi Productions, 1985.

The Bride of Frankenstein. Universal, 1935.

The Brood. Mutual Productions/Elgin International, 1979.

"Cause of Death." Episode of *Doomwatch.* London: BBC-TV, 1972.

Change of Mind. Sagittarius, 1969.

Charly. Selmur/Robinson Associates, 1968.

"Children of Auron." Episode of *Blake's Seven*. London: BBC-TV, February 19, 1980.
Close Encounters of the Third Kind. Columbia/EMI, 1977.
Cold Lazarus. Television series. London: BBC-TV, 1996.
Coma. Metro-Goldwyn-Mayer, 1978.
The Crawling Hand. Joseph F. Robertson, 1963.
Creature. Universal/Kings Road Productions, 1985.
Creature with the Atom Brain. Clover Films, 1955.
Crimes of the Future. Cronenberg, 1970.
"The Cure." Episode of *Planet of the Apes*. New York: CBS-TV, November 29, 1974.
The Curious Dr. Humpp. Productores Argentinos Associados, 1967.
The Curse of Frankenstein. Hammer, 1957.
The Damned. Hammer/Swallow, 1961.
The Dark Eyes of London. Rialto Films, 1961.
"Dark Outpost." Episode of *The Invaders*. New York: ABC-TV, 1967.
The Day the Earth Stood Still. Twentieth-Century Fox, 1951.
"The Dead Man." Episode of *Night Gallery*. New York: NBC-TV, December 16, 1970.
Death Watch. Selta Film/Little Bear/Sara Film/Gaumont/Antenne 2/TV 15, 1979.
"Deliveries in the Rear." Episode of *Night Gallery*. New York: NBC-TV, February 9, 1972.
Dr. Black and Mr. Hyde. Charles Walker-Manfred Bernhard Productions, 1976.
Dr. Cook's Garden. Paramount, 1971.
Dr. Jekyll and Mr. Hyde. Paramount, 1931.
Dr. Jekyll and Mr. Hyde. Metro-Goldwyn-Mayer, 1941.
Doctor Renault's Secret. Twentieth-Century Fox, 1942.
Doctor X. First National Pictures, 1932.
"Donor." Episode of *The Outer Limits*. New York: Showtime, January 29, 1999.
Donovan's Brain. Dowling Productions, 1953.
Doomwatch. Tigon British, 1971.
Embryo. Sandy Howard Productions, 1976.
"The Enemy." Episode of *The Invaders*. New York: ABC-TV, 1967.
Enterprise. Television series. New York: UPN-TV, 2001–present.
"Essence of Life." Episode of *The Outer Limits*. New York: Showtime, July 23, 1999.
E.T.: The Extraterrestrial. Universal, 1982.
"Expanding Human." Episode of *The Outer Limits*. New York: ABC-TV, October 10, 1964.
"The Eye of the Beholder." Episode of *The Twilight Zone*. New York: CBS-TV, November 11, 1960.
Eyes without a Face. [*The Horror Chamber of Dr. Faustus*] Champs Elysees/Lux Film, 1959.
Face of Terror. Documento Films, 1962.
Fantastic Voyage. Twentieth-Century Fox, 1966.
Forbidden Planet. Metro-Goldwyn-Mayer, 1956.
"The Fosters." Episode of *Out of the Unknown*. London: BBC-TV, March 11, 1969.
Frankenstein. Universal, 1931.
Frankenstein. Dan Curtis Productions, 1973.
"Frankenstein." Episode of *Tales of Tomorrow*. New York: ABC-TV, 1952.
Frankenstein Meets the Wolf Man. Universal, 1943.
Frankenstein 1970. Allied Artists, 1958.
Frankenstein: The True Story. Universal, 1973.
"Friday's Child." Episode of *Doomwatch*. London: BBC-TV, 1970.
The Frozen Dead. Goldstar Productions/Seven Arts, 1966.

Gattaca. Columbia, 1997.

Ghost of Frankenstein. Universal, 1942.

Goldengirl. Backstage Productions, 1979.

The Groundstar Conspiracy. Universal/Hal Roach International, 1971.

"The Hand of Borgus Weems." Episode of *Night Gallery.* New York: NBC-TV, September 18, 1971.

Hauser's Memory. Universal, 1970.

Horror Hospital. Noteworthy Films, 1973.

House of Dracula. Universal, 1945.

House of Frankenstein. Universal, 1944.

House of the Living Dead. Associated Film Producers, 1973.

I Married a Monster from Outer Space. Paramount, 1958.

I, Monster. Amicus, 1970.

The Immortal. Paramount, 1969.

The Immortal. Television series. New York: ABC-TV, 1970.

"In the Dark." Episode of *Doomwatch.* London: BBC-TV, 1971.

The Incredible Shrinking Man. Universal, 1957.

The Incredible Two-Headed Transplant. Mutual General Corporation/Trident Enterprises, 1970.

Innerspace. Warner Brothers, 1987.

Invaders from Mars. National Pictures Corp., 1953.

Invasion of the Body Snatchers. Walter Wanger Productions, 1956.

Invasion of the Body Snatchers. MGM/United Artists, 1978.

"The Iron Doctor." Episode of *Doomwatch.* London: BBC-TV, 1971.

The Island of Dr. Moreau. Cinema 77/American International, 1977.

The Island of Dr. Moreau. New Line Cinema, 1996.

Island of Lost Souls. Paramount, 1932.

It Lives Again. Larco/Warner Brothers, 1978.

It's Alive. Larco, 1973.

La Jetée. Argos Films, 1963.

Johnny Mnemonic. Alliance Communications Corporation/Cinevision/ Tristar Pictures, 1995.

The Lady and the Monster. Republic, 1944.

Lady Frankenstein. Condor International, 1971.

The Lawnmover Man. Allied Vision Lane Pringle Productions/Fuji Eight Co., 1993.

Lifeforce. London Cannon Films, 1985.

The Lifeforce Experiment. Filmline International/Screen Partners Ltd., 1994.

"The Little Black Bag." Episode of *Night Gallery.* New York: NBC-TV, December 23, 1970.

"The Little Black Bag." Episode of *Out of the Unknown.* London: BBC-TV, February 25, 1969.

"Living Hell." Episode of *The Outer Limits.* New York: Showtime, May 12, 1995.

Looker. Ladd Co., 1981.

The Lost Face. Svabik-Prochazka, 1966.

Mad Love. Metro-Goldwyn-Mayer, 1935.

Man Facing Southeast. FilmDallas Pictures, 1994.

The Man They Could Not Hang. Columbia, 1939.

The Man Who Changed His Mind. Gainsborough, 1936.

The Man with the Transplanted Brain. Parc Film/Mag Bodard/Marianne Productions/

UGC/Mars Produzione/Paramount Orion Film, 1971.

The Man with Two Brains. Aspen Film Society, 1983.

Mansion of the Doomed. Charles Band, 1975.

"Many, Many Monkeys." Episode of *Twilight Zone.* Syndicated, 1988.

Mars Needs Women. Azalea, 1966.

Mary Shelley's Frankenstein. American Zoetrope, 1994.

Max Headroom. Television series. New York: ABC-TV, 1987–1989.

"Medicine Show." Episode of *Out of This World.* London: ITV-TV, August 4, 1962.

Mercy Point. Television series. New York: UPN-TV, 1998–1999.

The Mind of Mr. Soames. Amicus, 1969.

"The Mind of Simon Foster." Episode of *Twilight Zone.* Syndicated, 1988.

"The Miracle of Dr. Dove." Episode of *Science Fiction Theatre.* Syndicated, August 31, 1956.

Monkey Business. Twentieth-Century Fox, 1952.

1984. Holiday Films Productions, 1956.

Nineteen Eighty-Four. Umbrella-Rosenblum Virgin Films, 1984.

"No Room for Error." Episode of *Doomwatch.* London: BBC-TV, 1971.

"Number Twelve Looks Just Like You." Episode of *The Twilight Zone.* New York: CBS-TV, January 27, 1964.

The Nutty Professor. Jerry Lewis Productions, 1963.

The Nutty Professor. Imagine Entertainment/Universal, 1996.

The Nutty Professor II: The Klumps. Imagine Entertainment, 2000.

Osmosis Jones. Warner Brothers, 2001.

Outbreak. Warner Brothers, 1995.

Outland. Ladd Co., 1981.

"Paradise." Episode of *The Outer Limits.* New York: Showtime, June 16, 1996.

The Parasite Murders. [*They Came from Within; Shivers*] Cinepix/Canadian Film Development Corp., 1974.

Percy. Anglo-EMI/Welbeck, 1971.

Percy's Progress. Betty E. Box/Ralph Thomas Productions, 1974.

Phenomenon. Touchstone Pictures, 1996.

The President's Analyst. Panpiper/Paramount, 1967.

Rabid. Cinepix/Dibar Sundicate/Canadian Film Development Corp./Famous Players, 1976.

"Re-Generation." Episode of *The Outer Limits.* New York: Showtime, January 24, 1997.

The Resurrection of Zachary Wheeler. Gold Key Entertainment/ Vidtronics Company/Madison Productions/New Mexico Film Industry Commission, 1971.

The Return of Doctor X. First National Pictures, 1939.

The Rocky Horror Picture Show. Twentieth-Century Fox, 1975.

The Satan Bug. Mirisch/Kappa, 1965.

Scanners. Filmplan International, 1980.

"Second Thoughts." Episode of *The Outer Limits.* New York: Showtime, January 19, 1997.

Seconds. Paramount/Joel Gibralter, 1966.

She Devil. Regal Films, 1957.

The Six Million Dollar Man. Television series. New York: ABC-TV, 1973–1978.

"The Sixth Finger." Episode of *The Outer Limits.* New York: ABC-TV, October 14, 1963.

Sleeper. Jack Rollins and Charles Joffe Productions, 1973.

Solaris. Mosfilm, 1971.

"Some Lapse of Time." Episode of *Out of the Unknown.* London: BBC-TV, December 6, 1965.

Son of Frankenstein. Universal, 1939.
Spacevets. Television series. London: BBC-TV, 1992–1994.
Star Trek. Television series. New York: NBC-TV, 1966–1969.
Star Trek: Deep Space Nine. Television series. Syndicated: 1993–1999.
Star Trek: First Contact. Paramount, 1996.
Star Trek V: The Final Frontier. Paramount, 1989.
Star Trek IV: The Voyage Home. Paramount, 1986.
Star Trek: Generations. Paramount, 1994.
Star Trek: Insurrection. Paramount, 1998.
Star Trek VI: The Undiscovered Country. Paramount, 1992.
Star Trek: The Motion Picture. Paramount, 1979.
Star Trek: The Next Generation. Television series. Syndicated, 1987–1994.
Star Trek III: The Search for Spock. Paramount/Cinema Group Venture, 1984.
Star Trek II: The Wrath of Khan. Paramount, 1982.
Star Trek: Voyager. Television series. New York: UPN-TV, 1995–2001.
Star Wars. Lucasfilm/Fox, 1977.
Star Wars: The Empire Strikes Back. Lucasfilm/Fox, 1980.
Star Wars, Episode One: The Phantom Menace. Lucasfilm, 1999.
Star Wars, Episode Two: Attack of the Clones. Lucasfilm, 2002.
Star Wars: Return of the Jedi. Lucasfilm, 1983.
Stereo. Emergent Films, 1969.
The Strange Case of Dr. Jekyll and Mr. Hyde. Dan Curtis Productions, 1974.
"The Surgeon." Episode of *Planet of the Apes.* New York: CBS-TV, October 25, 1974.
Tarantula. Universal, 1955.
The Terminal Man. Warner Brothers, 1974.
The Terminator. Cinema 84/Pacific Western Productions, 1984.
Terminator 2: Judgment Day. Carolco Pictures/Lightstorm Entertainment/Pacific Western
    Productions, 1991.
The Thing with Two Heads. Saber, 1971.
This Island Earth. Universal, 1955.
Threshold. Paragon, 1981.
"Tooth and Consequences." Episode of *Twilight Zone.* New York: CBS-TV, February 7,
    1986.
"The Trade-Ins." Episode of *The Twilight Zone.* New York: CBS-TV, April 20, 1962.
12 Monkeys. Universal Pictures, 1995.
2001: A Space Odyssey. Metro-Goldwyn-Mayer, 1968.
"Unnatural Selection." Episode of *The Outer Limits.* New York: Showtime, January 19,
    1996.
"Vaccine." Episode of *The Outer Limits.* New York: Showtime, April 3, 1998.
Vengeance. [*The Brain*] CCC/Governor Productions, 1962.
Videodrome. Filmplan International, 1982.
"Walk's End." Episode of *Out of the Unknown.* London: BBC-TV, December 22, 1966.
War of the Worlds. Television series. Syndicated, 1988–1990.
"Where the Dead Are." Segment of television movie *The Twilight Zone: Rod Serling's Lost
    Classics.* New York: CBS-TV, May 26, 1994.
Who? Lion International/Hemisphere Productions, 1974.
X—The Man with X-Ray Eyes. Alta Vista, 1963.
"You Killed Toby Wren." Episode of *Doomwatch.* London: BBC-TV, 1970.
Young Frankenstein. Gruskoff/Venture Films/Crossbow Productions, 1974.

III. Nonfiction and Critical Studies

Aldridge, Susan. "Medical Mystery Tour: Robin Cook's Medical Thrillers Are Discussed by Science Journalist." *Interzone*, No. 51 (September, 1991), 35–37.

Anderson, Charles. "Literature and Medicine: Why Should the Physician Read . . . or Write?" In Stuart Peterfreund, editor, *Literature and Science: Theory and Practice*. Boston: Northeastern University Press, 1990, 59–90.

Baldick, Chris. *In Frankenstein's Shadow: Myth, Monstrosity, and Nineteenth-Century Writing*. New York: Oxford University Press, 1987.

Balsamo, Anne. *Technologies of the Gendered Body: Reading Cyborg Women*. Durham, NC: Duke University Press, 1996.

Bann, Stephen. *Frankenstein, Creation, and Monstrosity*. London: Reaktion, 1994.

Baxter, John. "The Doctor Will See You Now." In Baxter, *Science Fiction in the Cinema*. New York: Paperback Library, 1970, 39–52.

Berenbaum, May R., and Richard J. Leskosky. "Life History Strategies and Population Biology in Science Fiction Films." *Bulletin of the Ecological Society of America*, 73 (December, 1992), 236–240.

Brown, James. "Cyborgs and Symbionts: Technology, Politics and Identity." In Edward James and Farah Mendlesohn, editors, *The Parliament of Dreams: Conferring on Babylon 5*. Reading, UK: Science Fiction Foundation, 1998, 110–129.

Brunner, John. "In Our Pharmaceutical Future, the Cure May Be Worse Than the Disease." *Science Fiction Age*, 3 (November, 1994), 34–40.

Campbell, John W., Jr. "Louis Pasteur, Medical Quack." In Campbell, *Collected Editorials from Analog*, selected by Harry Harrison. Garden City, NY: Doubleday, 1966, 109–122. Article first published in 1964.

Casimir, Viviane. "Data and Dick's Deckard: Cyborg as Problematic Signifier." *Extrapolation*, 38 (Winter, 1997), 278–291.

Caulfield, Deborah. "Two Real-Life Doctors Cure Sci-Fi Movies' Ills." *Los Angeles Times*, July 9, 1982, Section 6, 11.

Clarke, Arthur C. "Brain and Body." In Clarke, *Profiles of the Future: An Inquiry into the Limits of the Possible*. 1962. New York: Warner, 1985, 235–252.

———. "Life Meets Death and Twists Its Tail." In Clarke, *July 20, 2019: Life in the Twenty-First Century*. New York: Macmillan Publishing Company, 1986, 229–247.

Collins, Michael J. "Medicine, Lust, Surrealism, and Death: Three Early Films of David Cronenberg." *Post Script*, 15 (Winter/Spring, 1996), 62–69.

Cooke, Brett. "Sociobiology, Science Fiction and the Future." *Foundation: The Review of Science Fiction*, No. 60 (Spring, 1994), 42–51.

Cooke, Brett, and Frederick Turner, editors. *Biopoetics: Evolutionary Explorations in the Arts*. Lexington, KY: Paragon House/International Conference on the Unity of the Sciences, 1999.

Crawford, T. Hugh. "Visual Knowledge in Medicine and Popular Film." *Literature and Medicine*, 17 (Spring, 1998), 24–44.

Davis-Floyd, Robbie, and Joseph Dumit, editors. *Cyborg Babies: From Techno-Sex to Techno-Tots*. New York: Routledge, 1998.

Desmarets, Hubert. *Création Littéraire et Créatures Artificielles: l'"Eve Future," "Frankenstein," le "Marchand de Sable" ou le Je(u) du Miroir*. Paris: Ed. du Temps, 1999.

Dionne, Mark J. Reinventing Gender: The Figure of the Artificial Human in American Science Fiction. Master's Thesis, University of Connecticut, 1996.

Donaldson, Thomas M. "24th Century Medicine." *Analog Science Fiction/Science Fact*, 108 (September, 1988), 64–80.

Fergus, George. "Sex Roles, Biology, and Science Fiction, or There's No Vinism like Chau-Vinism." *Mythologies*, 11 (February, 1977), 16–35.

Florescu, Radu. *In Search of Frankenstein.* New York: Warner, 1975.

Forry, Steven Earl. *Hideous Progenies: Dramatizations of Frankenstein from Mary Shelley to the Present.* Philadelphia: University of Pennsylvania Press, 1990.

Francavilla, Joseph. "The Android as Doppelgänger." In Judith B. Kernan, editor, *Retrofitting Blade Runner*, Second Edition. Bowling Green, OH: Bowling Green State University Popular Press, 1997, 4–15.

Franklin, H. Bruce. " 'Doctor' Frankenstein and 'Scientific' Medicine." In Anne Hunsaker Hawkins and Marilyn Chandler McEntyre, editors, *Teaching Literature and Medicine*. New York: Modern Language Association, 2000, 218–225.

Franklin, Sarah. "Postmodern Mutant Cyborg Cinema." *New Scientist*, 128 (December 22/29, 1990), 70–71.

Gaitonde, Vishwas R. "Leper Kings, Witch Doctors and Stricken Artists: Leprosy in Burroughs and Maugham." *Burroughs Bulletin*, No. 46 (Spring, 2001), 6–14.

Glassy, Mark C. *The Biology of Science Fiction Cinema*. Jefferson, NC: McFarland, 2001.

Goodson, A. C. "Frankenstein in the Age of Prozac." *Literature and Medicine*, 15 (1996), 16–32.

Gordon, Andrew. "*Indiana Jones and the Temple of Doom*: Bad Medicine." In Gary Westfahl, George Slusser, and Eric S. Rabkin, editors, *Foods of the Gods: Eating and the Eaten in Fantasy and Science Fiction*. Athens: University of Georgia Press, 1996, 76–85.

Gray, Chris Hables. *Cyborg Citizen: Politics in the Posthuman Age.* New York: Routledge, 2001.

Gray, Chris Hables, editor. *The Cyborg Handbook*. New York: Routledge, 1995.

Hantke, Steffen. "Surgical Strikes and Prosthetic Warriors: The Soldier's Body in Contemporary Science Fiction." *Science-Fiction Studies*, 25 (November, 1998), 495–509.

Haraway, Donna. "A Manifesto for Cyborgs: Science, Technology, and Socialist Feminism in the 1980s." *Socialist Review*, 15 (March/April, 1985), 65–107.

Hayles, N. Katherine. *How We Became Posthuman: Virtual Bodies in Cybernetics, Literature, and Informatics.* Chicago: University of Chicago Press, 1999.

Holden, Rebecca J. "The High Costs of Cyborg Survival: Octavia Butler's Xenogenesis Trilogy." *Foundation: The International Review of Science Fiction*, No. 72 (Spring, 1998), 49–56.

Holland, Samantha. "Descartes Goes to Hollywood: Mind, Body and Gender in Contemporary Cyborg Cinema." In Mike Featherstone and Roger Burrows, editors, *Cyberspace/Cyberbodies/Cyberpunk: Cultures of Technological Embodiment*. London: Sage Publications, 1995, 157–174.

Hughes, James J., and John Lantos. "Medical Ethics Through the *Star Trek* Lens." *Literature and Medicine*, 20 (Spring, 2001), 26–38.

Indick, Ben P. " 'Come Out Here and Take Your Medicine!': King and Drugs." In Don Herron, editor, *Reign of Fear*. Los Angeles: Underwood-Miller, 1988, 149–175.

Isaacs, Leonard. *Darwin to Double Helix: The Biological Theme in Science Fiction*. London and Boston: Butterworth, 1977.

James, Edward F. "Life in Sector General." *Zenith Science Fiction*, 5 (July/July, 1964), 9–13.

Jones, A. H. "Feminist Science Fiction and Medical Ethics: Piercy's *Woman on the Edge of Time*." In R. E. Myers, editor, *The Intersection of Science Fiction and Philosophy*. Westport, CT: Greenwood Press, 1983, 171–183.

Kerrod, Robin. "Health and Medicine." In Kerrod, *The World of Tomorrow*. London: Galley Press, 1980, 24–27.

Ketterer, David. *Frankenstein's Creation: The Book, The Monster, and Human Reality*. British Columbia: University of Victoria, 1979.

Kirkup, Gill, Linda Janes, Kathryn Woodward, and Fiona Hovenden, editors. *The Gendered Cyborg: A Reader*. London: Routledge, 2000.

Kitei, Mindy. "Prescription for the Future." In Anthea Disney, editor, *Star Trek: Four Generations*. New York: New America Publications, 1995, 34–39.

Klugman, Craig M. "From Cyborg Fiction to Medical Reality." *Literature and Medicine*, 20 (Spring, 2001), 39–54.

Kopp, James J. "Cosimo Noto's *The Ideal City* (1903): New Orleans as Medical Utopia." *Utopian Studies*, 1 (1990), 115–122.

Krasner, James. "Arthur Conan Doyle as Doctor and Writer." *Mosaic*, 33 (December, 2000), 19–34.

Kuryllo, Helen A. "Cyborgs, Sorcery, and the Struggle for Utopia." *Utopian Studies*, 5 (1994), 50–55.

Lederer, Susan E. "Repellent Subjects: Hollywood Censorship and Surgical Images in the 1903s." *Literature and Medicine*, 17 (Spring, 1998), 91–113.

Levine, George, and U. C. Knoepflmacher, editors. *The Endurance of Frankenstein: Essays on Mary Shelley's Novel*. Berkeley: University of California Press, 1979.

Liggins, Emma. "The Medical Gaze and the Female Corpse: Looking in Bodies in Mary Shelley's *Frankenstein*." *Studies in the Novel*, 32 (Summer, 2000), 129–146.

Lovett-Graff, Bennett. "Shadows over Lovecraft: Reactionary Fantasy and Immigrant Eugenics." *Extrapolation*, 38 (Fall, 1997), 175–192.

Lykee, Nina, and Rosi Braidotti, editors. *Between Monsters, Goddesses and Cyborgs: Feminist Confrontations with Science, Medicine and Cyberspace*. London: Zed, 1996.

Lynch, Lisa " 'Not a Virus, But an Upgrade': The Ethics of Epidemic Evolution in Greg Bear's *Darwin's Radio*." *Literature and Medicine*, 20 (Spring, 2001), 71–93.

Mank, Gregory William. *It's Alive: The Classic Cinema Saga of Frankenstein*. San Diego, CA: A. S. Barnes, 1981.

Marks, G. H. "Teaching Biology with Science Fiction." *American Biology Teacher*, 40 (May, 1978), 275–279.

Marshall, Tim. *Murdering to Dissect: Grave-Robbing, Frankenstein and the Anatomy Literature*. Manchester: Manchester University Press, 1995.

Miksanek, Tony. "Microscopic Doctors and Molecular Black Bags: Science Fiction's Prescription for Nanotechnology and Medicine." *Literature and Medicine*, 20 (Spring, 2001), 55–70.

Miller, Joseph D. "Sex, Superman, and Sociobiology." In George Slusser and Eric S. Rabkin, editors, *Aliens: The Anthropology of Science Fiction*. Carbondale: Southern Illinois University Press, 1987, 78–87.

Moody, Nickianne. "Medicine, Morality and Faith." In Edward James and Farah Mendlesohn, editors, *The Parliament of Dreams: Conferring on Babylon 5*. Reading: Science Fiction Foundation, 1998, 145–152.

Mulvey-Roberts, Marie. "Dracula and the Doctors: Bad Blood, Menstrual Taboo, and the New Woman." In William Hughes and Andrew Smith, editors, *Bram Stoker: History, Psychoanalysis and the Gothic*. New York: St. Martin's Press, 1998. 78–95.

Nicholls, Peter, David Langford, and Brian Stableford. "Men and Supermen." In Nicholls, Langford, and Stableford, *The Science in Science Fiction*. 1982. New York: Alfred A. Knopf, 1983, 136–155.

Nordley, G. David, and H. G. Stratmann. "Biological Hazards and Medical Care in Space." *Analog Science Fiction/Science Fact*, 118 (April, 1998), 60–75, (May, 1998), 55–69.

Nourse, Alan E. "One Foot in the Grave: Medicine in Future Warfare." In Reginald Bretnor, editor, *The Future at War, Volume 1: Thor's Hammer*. New York: Ace, 1979, 297–317.

Parker, Helen N. *Biological Themes in Modern Science Fiction*. Ann Arbor, MI: UMI Research Press, 1984.

Picart, Caroline Joan, Frank Smoot, and Jayne Blodgett. *The Frankenstein Film Sourcebook*. Westport, CT: Greenwood Press, 2001.

Pyle, Forest. "Making Cyborgs, Making Humans: Of Terminators and Blade Runners." In Jim Collins, Hilary Radner, and Ava Preacher Collins, editors, *Film Theory Goes to the Movies*. New York: Routledge, 1993, 227–241.

Raben, Hans-Jürgen. *Der Frankenstein Komplex: Science-Fiction-Kurzgeschichten*. Berlin: Frieling, 1995.

Rabkin, Eric S. "The Medical Lessons of Science Fiction." *Literature and Medicine*, 20 (Spring, 2001), 13–25.

Rushing, Janice, and Thomas S. Frenz. *Projecting the Shadow: The Cyborg Hero in American Film*. Chicago: University of Chicago Press, 1995.

Sammon, Paul M. *Future Noir: The Making of Blade Runner*. New York: Harper Prism, 1996.

Semmler, Iliana A. "Ebola Goes Pop: The Filovirus from Literature into Film." *Literature and Medicine*, 17 (Spring, 1998), 149–174.

Shapiro, Jerome F. "Atomic Bomb Cinema: Illness, Suffering, and the Apocalyptic Narrative." *Literature and Medicine*, 17 (1998), 126–148.

Shaw, Debra Benita. *Women, Science, and Fiction: The Frankenstein Inheritance*. New York: Palgrave, 2000.

Shelton, Robert. "Images of Health and Disease: Pathology and Ideology in *Looking Backward*." In Lisa Leibacher-Ouvrard and Nicholas D. Smith, editors, *Utopian Studies IV*. Lanham, NY: University Press of America, 1991, 17–21.

———. "The Social Text as Body: Images of Health and Disease in Three Recent Feminist Utopias." *Literature and Medicine*, 12:2 (Fall, 1993), 161–177.

Slusser, George. "Souls on Ice: Cryonics and the Bodily Utopia." In Slusser, Paul Alkon, Roger Gaillard, and Danièle Chatelain, editors, *Transformations of Utopia: Changing Views of the Perfect Society*. New York: AMS Press, 1999, 139–152.

Slusser, George, Gary Westfahl, and Eric S. Rabkin, editors. *Immortal Engines: Life Extension and Immortality in Science Fiction and Fantasy*. Athens: University of Georgia Press, 1996.

Small, Christopher. *Mary Shelley's "Frankenstein": Tracing the Myth*. Pittsburgh: University of Pittsburgh Press, 1973.

Stableford, Brian. "Introduction to the First Sector General Omnibus." In James White, *Beginning Operations: A Sector General Omnibus*. New York: Tor, 2001, 7–12.

Stableford, Brian, and John Scarborough. "Medicine." In John Clute and Peter Nicholls, editors, *The Encyclopedia of Science Fiction*. New York: St. Martin's Press, 1993, 794–795.

Stoker, John. *The Illustrated Frankenstein*. New York: Sterling Publishing Co., 1980.

Stookey, Lorena Laura. *Robin Cook: A Critical Companion*. Westport, CT: Greenwood Press, 1996.

Thompson, Linda W. The Image of Nursing in Science Fiction Literature. Thesis (D.S.N.), University of Alabama at Birmingham School of Nursing, 1993.

Tullock, Joyce. " 'Just' a Simple Country Doctor?" In Walter Irwin and G. B. Love, editors, *The Best of the Best of Trek*. New York: Roc, 1990, 36–42.

Van Dommelen, Erica. "Biology in Science Fiction." *Bioscience*, 39 (November, 1989), 729–731.

Van Hise, James. "Exobiology: Space Medicine at the Time of *Star Trek*." In James Van Hise, editor, *Trek Celebration Two*. Las Vegas, NV: Pioneer, 1994, 102–110.

Vasbinder, Samuel Holmes. *Scientific Attitudes in Mary Shelley's Frankenstein*. Ann Arbor, MI: UMI Research Press, 1984.

Veeder, William R. *Mary Shelley and Frankenstein: The Fate of Androgyny*. Chicago: University of Chicago Press, 1986.

Weiss, Allan. "Beyond Human: Fading Boundaries Between Human and Machine in Canadian Science Fiction." *Foundation: The International Review of Science Fiction*, No. 81 (Spring, 2001), 68–75.

Westfahl, Gary. "For Tomorrow We Dine: The Sad Gourmet in the Scienticafé." In Westfahl, George Slusser, and Eric S. Rabkin, editors, *Foods of the Gods: Eating and the Eaten in Fantasy and Science Fiction*. Athens: University of Georgia Press, 1996, 213–223.

———. "Sector General: The Next Generation?" *Interzone*, No. 179 (May, 2002), 52–54.

White, D. E. "Medical Morals and Narrative Necessity." In R. E. Myers, editor, *The Intersection of Science Fiction and Philosophy*. Westport, CT: Greenwood Press, 1983, 185–194.

Wolf, Leonard, editor. *The Annotated Frankenstein: "Frankenstein" by Mary Shelley*. New York: Clarkson N. Potter, 1977.

Wolmark, Jenny, editor. *Cybersexualities: A Reader on Feminist Theory Cyborgs and Cyberspace*. Edinburgh: Edinburgh University Press, 1999.

Wood, Brent D. Cyborgs and Soft Machines: Control and Chaos in Technological Evolution. Master's Thesis, Trent University, 1995.

Wyatt, Garry. "Medical Science Fiction." *Sirius*, No. 8 (March, 1994), 4–10.

Yoke, Carl B., and Donald M. Hassler, editors. *Death and the Serpent: Immortality in Science Fiction and Fantasy*. Westport, CT: Greenwood Press, 1985.

Index

About the Contributors

GREG BEAR is the Hugo and Nebula Award-winning author of twenty-seven books of science fiction and fantasy, including *Blood Music, Eon, Queen of Angels*, and *Darwin's Radio*.

DAVID K. DANOW, Professor of Comparative Literature at the University of California, Riverside, is the author of *The Thought of Mikhail Bakhtin: From Word to Culture, The Spirit of Carnival Magical Realism and the Grotesque*, and *The Dialogic Sign: Essays on the Major Novels of Dostojefsky*.

H. BRUCE FRANKLIN, John Cotton Dana Professor of English and American Studies at Rutgers University, is the author of several critical studies, including *Future Perfect: 19th Century American Science Fiction, War Stars: The Superweapon and the American Imagination, Vietnam and Other American Fantasies*, and *Robert A. Heinlein: America as Science Fiction*.

SUSAN A. GEORGE, who teaches at the University of California, Davis, has published a chapter in the volume *Space and Beyond: The Frontier Theme in Science Fiction* along with other articles and reviews involving science fiction films.

KIRK HAMPTON is the author of *The Moonhare*, a "Wakean science fantasy," as well as the forthcoming novel *Lisho* and several conference papers co-authored with Carol MacKay.

HOWARD V. HENDRIX is the author of the novels *Lightpaths, Standing Wave, Better Angels*, and *Deserted Cities of the Heart*, as well as the critical study *The Ecstasy of Catastrophe* and numerous stories, articles, and reviews. He is also a university professor and academic administrator.

DAVID HINCKLEY teaches at the University of Redlands. He has presented several conference papers, contributed entries to *McGill's Guide to Science Fiction and Fantasy Literature*, and wrote a chapter of *Unearthly Visions: Approaches to Science Fiction and Fantasy Art*.

CAROL MACKAY is Associate Professor of English at the University of Texas at Austin. She is the author of *Soliloquy in Nineteenth-Century Fiction* and editor of *The Two Thackerays* and *Dramatic Dickens*.

FRANK MCCONNELL, late Professor of English at the University of California, Santa Barbara, was the author of several books on literature, numerous essays and reviews in critical anthologies and magazines, and five detective novels. He also served on the Pulitzer Prize committee for fiction, twice as its chair.

JOSEPH D. MILLER is a neurophysiologist and neuropharmacologist now part of the faculty of the University of Southern California. He is also an ex-Project Director for the Space Shuttle program and a long-time science fiction critic.

MARY PHARR, Professor of English at Florida Southern College, has written numerous articles and conference papers, was co-editor with Leonard Heldreth of *The Blood Is the Life: Vampires in Literature*, and is editor of the forthcoming *Fantastic Odysseys*.

GEORGE SLUSSER, Professor of Comparative Literature at the University of California at Riverside, has written several books about science fiction authors and co-edited numerous critical anthologies. In 1986, he received the Pilgrim Award for his lifetime contributions to science fiction scholarship.

ROBERT VAN CLEAVE, now completing graduate work at the University of California, Irvine, has presented several papers at university conferences.

GARY WESTFAHL, who teaches at the University of California at Riverside, is the author, editor, or co-editor of twelve books about science fiction and fantasy and writes a bimonthly column for the science fiction magazine *Interzone*.